Praise for *Compassionate Counterterrorism*

"This book brings a refreshing alternative to the .... long-term solution to terrorism. A thoughtful, personal, and impressive analysis of why a broader approach to the challenge may yield more effective long-term outcomes."

—**Sir Hugh Orde, OBE, QPM, former Chief Constable, Police Service of Northern Ireland**

"A brilliant and fresh analysis of one of the most misunderstood global problems of our age. If you read one book on terrorism, choose this one."

—**Lisa Schirch, PhD, editor of *The Ecology of Violent Extremism* and Senior Policy Advisor, Human Security, Alliance for Peacebuilding**

"An honest, comprehensive, and thoughtful critique highlighting and challenging stereotypes and assumptions about terrorism and violent extremism. A must-read for anyone involved in peace building and conflict resolution."

—**Eva Grosman, CEO, Centre for Democracy and Peace Building, and Director for Public Affairs, Centre for the Resolution of Intractable Conflict, University of Oxford**

"A provocative and concise examination of why we cannot bomb our way to ending terrorism. While the author is careful not to advocate for the absence of a hard security approach, she does a masterful job at highlighting many innovations that have proven effective in reducing and transforming political violence in various parts of the world and challenges the world to do much better and to have higher aspirations."

—**Craig Zelizer, PhD, founder and CEO, Peace and Collaborative Development Network; former Associate Director, Conflict Resolution Program, Georgetown University; and cofounder of Alliance for Conflict Transformation**

"Intelligent and intrepid work. Leena's effort to unearth a critical societal fault line is the first step toward building a postfundamentalist future for our next generation."

—**Tariq Cheema, founder of World Congress of Muslim Philanthropists**

"In a refreshing and candid style that goes far beyond conventional analyses and commonly suggested solutions, Al Olaimy delivers a powerful counterargument on how to deal with terrorism. Insightful and persuasive, her book should be required reading for those in policy circles who routinely deal with strategies to combat terrorism."

—**Dirk Vandewalle, Associate Professor of Government, Dartmouth College**

"As we face a global crisis of increased intolerance and exclusion, Leena makes a compelling case for a radical nonviolent approach to defeating terrorism that transforms our current oppressive measures into opportunities for greater peacefulness. Full of unorthodox approaches like invoking the use of religion as an antidote for violent extremism; exploring untapped collaboration between civil society, business, and the military; and even using love to demobilize a terrorist group—this is an important contribution and fascinating read that defies disciplines!"

—**Kavita N. Ramdas, Director, Women's Rights Program, Open Society Foundations; Strategy Advisor, MADRE; cofounder of KNR Sisters; and former Strategic Advisor to the President, Ford Foundation**

"This is an insightful book. Compassion is not a word generally associated with terrorism, but the message needs to be heard. Bravo, Leena!"

—**John Marks, coeditor of *Common Ground on Terrorism* and founder and former President, Search for Common Ground**

"It could easily be argued that compassion is the number one leadership skill. Leena's suggestion of leading with compassion provides possibility for bringing opposing forces together. It is more than time for the world to recognize our shared humanity and Leena inspires us to do just that!"

—**J'Lein Liese, PhD, Managing Partner, Equanimity Leadership Solutions, and President, Foundation for Global Leadership, Inc.**

COMPASSIONATE COUNTER TERRORISM

The Power of Inclusion in Fighting Fundamentalism

LEENA AL OLAIMY

BK

Berrett–Koehler Publishers, Inc.

Berrett-Koehler Publishers, Inc.
1333 Broadway, Suite 1000
Oakland, CA 94612-1921
Tel: (510) 817-2277
Fax: (510) 817-2278
www.bkconnection.com

ORDERING INFORMATION

Quantity sales. Special discounts are available on quantity purchases by corporations, associations, and others. For details, contact the "Special Sales Department" at the Berrett-Koehler address above.

Individual sales. Berrett-Koehler publications are available through most bookstores. They can also be ordered directly from Berrett-Koehler: Tel: (800) 929-2929; Fax: (802) 864-7626; www.bkconnection.com.

Orders for college textbook / course adoption use. Please contact Berrett-Koehler: Tel: (800) 929-2929; Fax: (802) 864-7626.

Distributed to the U.S. trade and internationally by Penguin Random House Publisher Services.

Berrett-Koehler and the BK logo are registered trademarks of Berrett-Koehler Publishers, Inc.

Printed in Canada

Berrett-Koehler books are printed on long-lasting acid-free paper. When it is available, we choose paper that has been manufactured by environmentally responsible processes. These may include using trees grown in sustainable forests, incorporating recycled paper, minimizing chlorine in bleaching, or recycling the energy produced at the paper mill.

Library of Congress Cataloging-in-Publication Data
    Names: Al Olaimy, Leena, author.
    Title: Compassionate counterterrorism : the power of inclusion in fighting
        fundamentalism / Leena Al Olaimy.
    Description: First edition. | Oakland, CA : Berrett-Koehler Publishers, Inc.,
        [2019] | Includes bibliographical references.
    Identifiers: LCCN 2018048907 | ISBN 9781523098576 (paperpack)
    Subjects: LCSH: Terrorism—Prevention. | Terrorism--Religious aspects—Islam.
        | Violence—Religious aspects—Islam. | Social integration.
    Classification: LCC HV6431 .A4295 2019 | DDC 363.325/16—dc23
    LC record available at https://lccn.loc.gov/2018048907

First Edition

25 24 23 22 21 20 19 18 17   Friesens   10 9 8 7 6 5 4 3 2 1

Book producer and text designer: Maureen Forys, Happenstance Type-O-Rama
Cover designer: Tariq Al Olaimy and Luma Shihabeldin

For all the

radical peace-builders,

change-makers, and

social entrepreneurs

seeding peace

CONTENTS

PART III

PREFACE

EIGHTEEN YEARS AGO, I was a senior at New York University volunteering at Ground Zero. After receiving my assigned volunteer station, I hesitated but opted to stay silent. *After spending months pulling human remains out of rubble, how would they react when I told them it was Ramadan and that I was Muslim and fasting?* As I served food and drinks to the rescue workers—who good-naturedly and relentlessly tried to persuade me to take a break and eat with them at various intervals—I wondered how long I would be able to defer. "I will! I will! Later!" I kept promising. Twelve hours into the day, my discernibly evasive excuses were categorically rejected. I felt afraid. Confused. Betrayed. Angered by what my religion had come to represent, and at those brandishing their perverted version of it. Finally, I timidly confessed my reasons for abstaining from food and water. A female Red Cross worker stared at me for a few seconds. Then she held my shoulders pulling me towards her. We hugged. It was a beautiful moment of shared humanity that was implicit in its power.

Back in my native Bahrain a few years later, in 2005, I befriended a group of US Navy SEALs. On June 28, three months into their deployment, they lost half of their platoon during an ambush in Afghanistan. Emotionally charged conversations ensued for months as the group grieved and tried to make sense of their loss. Only one member, Marcus Luttrell, managed to escape, and he went on to write the bestselling memoir *Lone Survivor*, which was turned into a Hollywood blockbuster. As I attempted, in both my personal and professional lives, to suture the growing lacerations between Islam and the West, I obsessively self-questioned: *How do I explain what compels individuals to such violent extremism, even—and especially—towards their own people, in the name of my religion? And, more importantly, how can we prevent them from doing so?* "Prevent" being the operative word.

It's easy for some people to dismiss the more liberal Muslims, such as myself, as "cultural Muslims," whereas the "real Muslims" are the fundamentalists insidiously trying to impose a global caliphate. I've debated as much with one of those US Navy SEALs, who has, over the years, expressed increasingly anti-Muslim sentiments—despite his personal affection for me as an individual. I later had the opportunity to dedicate two years to researching the question that had possessed me: What causes violent radicalization, and could nonmilitary interventions serve as a more powerful first line of defense? During this period at Dartmouth College, which I spent as an international Fulbright scholar, I was surprised to uncover patterns of unbelievable contradictions among so-called Muslim terrorist martyrs, operatives, and, in some cases, even leaders. In an academic setting, however, one is typically steered towards being research oriented rather than solutions oriented. More than a decade later, this book attempts to satiate the need to contribute to a more sustainable prevention of violent extremism.

——INTRODUCTION——

The three freedoms which all human beings crave—
freedom from want, freedom from war or large-scale
violence, and freedom from arbitrary or degrading
treatment—are closely interconnected. There is no
long-term security without development. There is
no development without security.

—KOFI ANNAN, former UN Secretary General[1]

IF WE LOOK to the data on how terrorist groups end, the Global Terrorism Index (GTI), an analysis of 586 terrorist groups that operated between 1970 and 2007, found that repressive counterterrorism measures enforced by military and security agents achieved the least success with religious terrorist organizations—contributing to the demise of only 12 percent.[2] However, this book is less concerned with defeating terrorist organizations. Rather, it seeks to pinpoint what makes those organizations so appealing to recruits in the first place.

Assuming that our goal is to defeat terrorism and ensure greater universal human security, the central thesis of this book is that a long-term sustainable solution to counterterrorism necessitates a pivotal emphasis on social, political, and economic inclusion. Why? Simply because humanizing counterterrorism forces us to confront the underlying conditions that lead to violent extremism and terror-prone environments—the disease, rather than the symptoms. What are these conditions, and how do we transform them to create greater peacefulness? These are the questions *Compassionate Counterterrorism* attempts to answer.

In writing this book, I wanted to make terrorism accessible to a wider audience, in the way that books like *Freakonomics* and *Nudge* enticed us into the fascinating field of behavioral economics. The intellectually curious reader and concerned global citizen will find that this book curates a rich collection of diversely sourced data and materials and is peppered with insightful anecdotes, personal reflections, and narratives that bring the data to life. In a way, it mirrors my own multidisciplinary background; it traverses politics, business, development, and spirituality. My hope is that beyond the academic community, its appeal embraces a mainstream audience, including entrepreneurs, businesses, development agencies, and policymakers. And mostly—despite the limitations of finite time—I hope that it is an enabler in making our individual investments in collective human security somewhat more accessible.

The book is divided into three parts. Although some academics and other experts may be familiar with the history of Islam and the Middle East in Part I, and others may be well-acquainted with the commonly cited drivers of terrorism in Part II, the distillation and interwoven information and narratives provided are important in framing Part III of this book; therefore, I recommend reading the chapters sequentially. Moreover, in disassociating the "Islamic State" from religion, I refer to them using the Arabic acronym Daesh throughout this book.

CHAPTER BREAKDOWN

An Islamic militant walks into a bar and hires a stripper. One week later, he blows himself up. Does his act count as terrorism? According to a West Point Combating Terrorism Center (CTC) study, over 85 percent of the "Islamic" militants in their dataset had no formal religious education.[3] Half of the foreign-trained fighters (FTFs) traveling from other countries to join Daesh in Iraq and Syria did not even known how to pray, according to a United Nations (UN) Counter-Terrorism Centre study, while only 16 percent even believed in the idea of establishing an Islamic State or caliphate in the Levant.[4] How do we reconcile contradictions between why someone says they do something and their real motivations? Moreover, if terrorism is a form of psychological fear and intimidation, should the very same actions be held to different standards when perpetrated by a "legitimate" actor versus an "illegitimate" actor? **Chapter 1** frames the controversies around our definitions of terrorism and covers a brief historical overview of the major turning points for terrorism, which lead us to present day.

Understanding contemporary violent Islamism necessitates a historical understanding of the *Game-of-Thrones*-like barbarism the advent of seventh-century Islam sought to remedy and reform in the first place. **Chapter 2** covers this history in brief, introduces the spiritual godfathers of fundamentalism, and explains why the reinstatement of a modern-day caliphate represents a nostalgia for the Islamic Empire's Golden Age of ascendancy. Following this is **Chapter 3**, which contextualizes the post-colonial baggage, as it were, and the failures of Arab nationalism to remedy it—providing the perfect confluence of circumstances for Islam to be transformed from a religion into a political method of sustaining un-Islamic regimes.

Although the leaders of terrorist organizations may be ideologically driven, **Chapters 4–6** focus specifically on the nonideological drivers of violent extremism—"the why," if you will. It is largely accepted based on diverse sources of multilateral, military, and academic research and data that these drivers exist. Therefore, it is in our self-interest to acknowledge them if we are to be active participants in ensuring our own security. **Chapter 4** focuses on the spiritual incongruence between the nonobservant behaviors of so-called "Muslim" suicide attackers and their self-proclaimed religious motivations. **Chapter 5** captures the role of economic exclusion and inequality—rather than poverty in isolation—and how current military interventions exacerbate the systemic and deeply entrenched conditions that we seek to overcome. Similarly, **Chapter 6** provides evidence of the potency of social exclusion in violent radicalization, and why, rather than drive them out, we need to reintegrate the extremists into the folds of society. Acknowledging that many marginalized groups have not turned to terrorism, this chapter also reflects on other influencing factors like empathy and social injustice.

Chapter 7 may be emotionally difficult to read for some; it is both a factual and spiritual reflection on ethics, compassion, absolutism, and moral humility. In failing to recognize the perils of dehumanization and the justification of pursuing what we believe to be a noble outcome using immoral means, have we inadvertently embodied what we are fighting? Is counterterrorism simply terrorism by another name? Prior to being rendered stateless for his vocal political dissent in Saudi Arabia, Osama Bin Laden was described as a mild-mannered conflict arbitrator and incompetent idealist. What triggered Bin Laden's transformation into one of the world's most nefarious and destructive terrorists?

In seeking practical solutions, **Chapter 8** looks at the data and evidence around the counterproductiveness of current counterterrorism strategies so we can better design policies that don't manifest like a hydra—multiplying problems and grievances that take us one step forwards and hurl us three steps back. **Chapter 9** displaces the common rhetoric of Islam as the fountainhead of fundamentalism—reframing it instead as a solution. Examples of peace practitioners and former extremists who have used the Quran to successfully deradicalize the likes of the chief imam of Boko Haram are highlighted, and this chapter cautions against the pitfalls of counternarrative campaigns.

Chapters 10–12 look to social entrepreneurship, public sector innovation, business solutions, and community interventions that have used the power of political, social, and economic inclusion to prevent violent extremism, making the case for these interventions and the need to support them with a greater mobilization of resources.

If terrorism is largely defined as the achievement of political objectives through using violence and intimidation, then we may consider how political accommodation and inclusion can inhibit or even end support for terrorist organizations. **Chapter 10** looks at how countries like Indonesia—where the world's largest Muslim population resides, numbering around 225 million people—massively decreased terrorism while paradoxically becoming more overtly religious, and how the Moroccan model of religious education has ranked it among the countries suffering "no impact from terrorism," while Moroccan immigrants in Europe are among those most susceptible to violent radicalization.[5] And with youth "forming the backbone of many paramilitary and terrorist organizations," this chapter also shares examples of youth engagement through political and civic participation.[6]

Chapter 11 uncovers community-wide inclusive policies that have made cities like Mechelen resilient to radicalization—despite having the largest Muslim population in Belgium. Other examples capture the power of love and compassion in demobilizing terrorists whatever end of the spectrum they fall on: from Neo-Nazis to Black Septemberists (a ruthless terrorist group responsible for the infamous 1972 Munich Olympics massacre).

Chapter 12 explores the untapped role of business and entrepreneurship and highlights examples of development-based interventions that have successfully deterred terrorist recruitment—including some of the pitfalls of poor implementation. **Chapter 13** concludes with the economics of peace and proposes a reframing and reinvention of our current approach to counterterrorism—challenging us to abandon self-imposed limitations and preconceived notions on what counterterrorism solutions should and could look like. Central to this refreshed approach to counterterrorism is the importance of collaborative, synchronized efforts between unlikely bedfellows—which leverages the social capital and human expertise of the peace-building community and pairs it with the military's resources and aptitude for innovation and the strategic and financial muscle of mission-driven business approaches.

This book is my humble contribution to addressing one of our most urgent global threats. And although, at times, I may be critical of policies, it is to advance progress on an issue I am deeply passionate about, rather than to simply criticize or alienate politicians. I also wish to highlight the distinction between peoples, races, and religions and the actions of the governments that represent them.

And finally, in referring to the Prophet Muhammad and other prophets named in the book, it is customary in Islamic tradition to invoke blessings upon them by saying "Peace be upon him" or (pbuh) after their name. In this book, I consider this implicit and for the reader to utter as appropriate. Also, recall that in disassociating the "Islamic State" from religion, I refer to them using the Arabic acronym Daesh throughout this book.

PART I

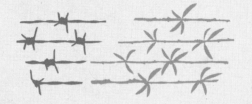

1

WHO IS THE
TERRORIST?

IN HIS 2010 TED talk "Superheroes Inspired by Islam," a fellow Arab, Muslim social entrepreneur, and psychologist, Dr. Naif Al-Mutawa, recalls a lecture he gave in Kuwait on the biological basis of behavior. His students were handed two articles: one from the *New York Times* and the other from *New York* magazine. He took out the names of the writers and other details, leaving only the facts. The first article was about a group called "The Party of God" that wanted to ban Valentine's Day—red was outlawed and any boys and girls caught flirting were to be married off immediately. The second article described a woman's complaints against six bearded men who pulled up in three minivans to interrogate her for talking to a man who wasn't related to her. Dr. Naif's students were asked to identify the locations of the two incidents.[1] Can you guess where they took place?

In unanimous agreement, the class determined the first incident was definitely in Saudi Arabia. The second, they debated, was either in Saudi Arabia or Afghanistan. Astonishingly, they learned that the first was actually in India—the party of a Hindu god—whereas the second took place in upstate New York in an orthodox Jewish community.[2] Not only has the media perpetuated an unconscious bias towards identifying extremism as intrinsically and distinctly Islamic, but this unconscious bias has sadly become a self-identification for Muslims. I recall running a corporate diversity and inclusion workshop in my native Bahrain where a Muslim female participant admitted that while traveling on a bus in London, she was embarrassed to observe her unease and suspicion as a long-bearded man a few aisles down irately spoke on his phone in Urdu.

Every time there is a highly publicized shooting or attack, we—the Muslim community—bait our breath, hoping he is not "one of ours." I imagine African Americans feel similar sentiments. Following the British Royal Wedding of Prince Harry and biracial American actress Meghan Markle, *The Daily Show* comedian Trevor Noah made a joke loaded with political truth. It had emerged that Markle's father had conspired with paparazzi to stage positive photos of himself. "I'm not gonna lie, I was glad it was the white side of the family!" Noah—who is also biracial—quipped.[3] No matter how many Caucasian or Christian dysfunctional individuals, school shooters, or terrorists there are, those individuals are not held accountable as representatives of an entire race or religion. Nor am I suggesting that they should be— yet many other races and religions are subjected to entirely different standards.

At the time of Dr. Naif's TED talk—which was pre–San Bernardino and Orlando nightclub shootings—right-wing terrorist attacks in the US had killed almost twice as many Americans as Islamist attacks since 9/11.[4] And according to Europol, the majority of terrorist attacks in the EU had been perpetrated by separatist movements such as Basque separatist terrorism in Spain and France, and Corsican terrorism in France.[5] These numbers have shifted more recently in the US, and Europol reported that 2016 was the first year in which Islamist terror attacks outpaced separatist terrorism. Yet the number of white nationalists and self-identified Nazi sympathizers on Twitter continues to multiply—outperforming the so-called Islamic State (Daesh)—increasing by more than 600 percent between 2012 and 2016, according to a study.[6]

And although Muslims have made tremendous contributions to civilization, terrorism was not one such invention. Despite the fact that this lethal tactic predates the 1,400-year-old religion of Islam, at the time of this writing, if one typed "Did terrorism exist before . . ." into Google, the query is completed with "9/11," implying the Islamic and contemporary nature of the beast. Further complicating the discourse around terrorism is the blurry lens through which different individuals and governments view and define it. The term *terrorism* has over 100 scholarly and diplomatic definitions. Given its deeply contested interpretation, even the UN has no internationally agreed-upon definition.

Unless we unanimously condemn all forms of violence, leaving no grounds for its justification, we are unlikely to agree on what terrorism is and isn't. For example, is the Palestinian armed struggle for liberation and self-determination against an occupying force considered terrorism? No, not according to Arabs. Was Nazi Germany an example of state-sponsored terrorism? In applying many modern-day definitions of terrorism, "legitimate" state-actors are specifically excluded from the definition of terrorism. Which prompts the question: Who is the legitimate state-actor? We may even find, over time, that a historical lens changes our global understanding of what constitutes terrorism versus a liberation struggle.

To be clear, terrorism and the murder of innocent lives is wrong, regardless of the motives and actors, and definitions are of little solace to the victims and their families. That said, depending on the reader's background, some of these not-so-hypothetical scenarios will be clear-cut, others murky, and some uncomfortable. Mental health is another factor in the mix, and one that often fails to cross our consciousness when the shooter is Muslim. Which also leads to the question of intention. A mentally ill or deranged individual lacking motivation is classified differently than a religiously or ideologically motivated shooter. So if the same act and consequences can be classified differently depending solely on the perpetrator's intention, does it matter if a so-called "soldier of Allah" drinks alcohol and eats pork? How do we reconcile contradictions between why someone says they commit violence and their real motivations?

Fundamentally speaking, the ancient, unadulterated wisdom forming the bedrock of all religions and spiritual teachings is kindness and compassion. All religions can be distorted and misused—even Buddhism, which is perhaps the religious tradition most associated with peace and enlightenment. Consider the ethnic cleansing of the Rohingya Muslims in Myanmar by Buddhist monks, whose leader, ironically, calls himself the "Burmese Bin Laden."[7] The common denominator is not religion but rather "violent extremism." So perhaps we should reconsider the stereotype that religion itself is the problem. Our own absolutism and lack of moral humility could potentially surreptitiously metamorphose from extremist thought into extremist action—no matter how noble, and *especially* the more noble we believe our objectives to be. Everyone believes him- or herself to be defending some form of "virtue" against some form of "malice." But before deep-diving into morality, let us take a brief journey to explore the origins of terrorism.

A TIMELINE

The term *terrorism* was first used in a political context accusing dissidents like Maximilien Robespierre—a frontrunner of the French Revolution—for using violence in the name of the state, aka the Reign of Terror. Robespierre notoriously sent thousands to execution under the guillotine—including the infamous Queen Marie Antoinette, to whom the outrageous quote "Let them eat cake" has been attributed, in obliviousness to the poor's inability to buy bread.

However, by the late nineteenth century, Russian and French anarchists started using the word *terrorism* to describe their own violent uprisings against the state.[8]

The origins of terrorism as a phenomenon, however, far predate the French Revolution. In Byzantine Rome, the state used violence and executions as a form of intimidation to win elections. Jewish uprisings against the Romans in 66 CE, and against the Greeks in 115 CE and 134 CE, represent some of the earliest examples of non-state actors engaged in a national liberation struggle.[9] Terrorism reached its zenith towards the end of the nineteenth century; the major active terrorist groups during this period included the Irish rebels fighting against British rule, the Russian Socialist Revolutionaries—who succeeded in killing Tsar Alexander II—and other anarchists in North America and Europe.[10]

After World War I, terrorism emerged in what became Nazi Germany and the Balkans—perpetuated in large part by both Fascists and Communists. Cold-blooded Kremlin dictator Joseph Stalin terrorized tens of millions of citizens—assassinating political opponents, imprisoning suspected dissenters in Gulags (forced labor camps), and engineering the worst man-made famine in history.[11] Even Stalin's first son, Yakov, allegedly tried to kill himself because of his father's harshness towards him. As Yakov lay in a pool of blood—ultimately failing to fatally shoot himself—Stalin reportedly berated his son, saying, "He can't even shoot straight."[12]

One of the most prominent terrorist attacks of the twentieth century was the 1946 King David Hotel bombing on British administrative headquarters for Palestine, carried out by the Irgun, a right-wing Zionist group. Following World War II, however, there was very little terrorism, which explains why it seemed so unprecedented when it resurfaced some twenty-five years later.[13] And when it did reemerge, it made a strong comeback. Replete with controversial classifications depending on which "side" you were on, this unparalleled era for terrorism included the Irish Republican Army (IRA), the Italian militant group the Red Brigades, antiwar militants (note the oxymoron), ethnic and nationalist terrorist groups, revolutionary groups like the Black Panthers in the US, and the highly publicized Palestinian-led kidnapping and massacre of Israeli athletes at the 1972 Munich Olympics.

Airline hijackings and bombings were far more frequent then than they are today—occurring at an astounding monthly rate.[14] In fact, US plane hijackings diverted to Cuba were so frequent in the late '60s that the Cubans had a holding lounge for unexpected American visitors, where, upon arrival, they were served Cuban sandwiches (for which the Cubans then charged the US government $35 apiece!). Pilots even kept maps of Jose Marti airport on hand in the cockpit. Despite all this, there was no airport security, no metal detectors, and no luggage screening until 1973.[15]

Less than a decade later, suicide bombings were made popular by the secular Sri Lankan Tamil Tiger rebels. In their fight for an independent Tamil state, the rebels were known for pioneering the suicide vest—although they did not invent it.[16] Between 1980 and 2003 the Tamil Tigers carried out more suicide attacks than any Islamist terrorist groups had up until 2009.[17] Suicide killing as a tactic, however, first surfaced in nineteenth-century Southeast Asia as Muslims retaliated against colonialism and conversion attempts by Christian missionaries. A knife-wielding attacker would set out to fight any Christian or European ally and would continue killing as many as he could before he himself was killed.[18] Suicide missions were also executed to destroy warships during World War II. Japanese kamikaze pilots held the largest record of suicide missions in history, numbering over 3,000 between 1943 and 1945, and leading to an estimated 5,000 US naval deaths.[19]

Four years in particular marked major turning points for modern-day terrorism: 1968, 1979, 1983, and 2001. Palestinians began to use terrorism as a publicity stunt following the 1967 six-day war, and in 1968, Latin American insurgents launched their urban guerrilla strategy. In 1979, radical Shiite Muslims emerged victorious during the Iranian revolution and directly influenced Lebanon's Hezbollah, as well as indirectly influencing radical Sunni Islamists such as Hamas and Al Qaeda. Hezbollah's suicide bombings against American and French occupying forces in Lebanon forced troop withdrawals and a partial Israeli withdrawal in 1985; this was perhaps the greatest example of victory for Islamists. And finally, the attacks of September 11, 2001, provoked the most significant counterterrorism operation ever undertaken: the US-led "War on Terror."[20]

[TER-ER-IST]: ONE WHO TERRORIZES

Residents of Austin, Texas, were terrorized for weeks in 2018 by Mark Anthony Conditt, a white Christian serial bomber. Conditt was characterized as a "troubled young man"—which one assumes goes without saying for any individual committing such acts, irrespective of their self-declared motivations, political agenda, or lack thereof.[21] Stephen Paddock, who committed the worst mass shooting in modern American history—killing 58 people at the Mandalay Bay Resort and Casino in Las Vegas in 2017—was also "troubled."[22] I suspect that had he been a Muslim, he would have been labeled a terrorist, even without explicitly declaring a political agenda.

According to the US State Department, *terrorism* is "premeditated, politically motivated violence perpetrated against noncombatant targets by sub-national groups or clandestine agents, usually intended to influence an audience."[23] While it may be true that many terrorist attacks perpetrated by Muslims are politically motivated, it is worth considering the upside. While a lack of motive may render us powerless with seemingly "senseless" shooters, at least politically motivated violence has a more tangible antidote—the fulfillment of those political objectives. I will come back to the psychology and drivers of suicide attackers in Chapter 4 and the misappropriation of religion as a moral veil to achieve personal objectives. But fundamentally, the circumstances that drive an individual to utilize terrorism as a tactic are both race- and religion-agnostic. In fact, I would argue that provoked with sufficient moral outrage, and a particular confluence of circumstances, any one of us could selflessly become a "terrorist," simply because terrorists perceive themselves as supremely dedicated to a higher cause. But, again, I'm jumping ahead of a deeper dive in Chapter 7.

The US State Department definition also overlooks the classification of a country as a terrorist state. Terrorism is defined as a political act committed specifically by *non-state actors* to achieve objectives such as policy changes, changes in leadership, changes in government, and even changes in a nation's territorial boundaries. So while it may be definitionally disputed, I personally would unquestionably categorize Nazi Germany as a terrorist state, whereas, given America's use of violence and Israeli aggression against the Palestinians, many Arabs and Muslims would classify the United States and Israel as terrorist states.

A Congressional report by international security specialist Richard F. Grimmett, entitled *Instances of Use of U.S. Armed Forces Abroad 1798–2008*, cites well over 300 instances in which the United States has utilized military forces abroad in both overt and covert operations.[24] Conversely, the US was attacked three times during that same period: by the British during the war of 1812, the Japanese attack on Pearl Harbor in 1941, and the September 11th attacks in 2001. And although 9/11 killed 2,996 people, conservative estimates number the innocent civilian body count from the US War on Terror at 1.3 million in Iraq, Afghanistan, and Pakistan, according to a report by Physicians for Social Responsibility, Physicians for Global Survival, and the Nobel Prize–winning International Physicians for the Prevention of Nuclear War.[25]

Accountability for civilian deaths is shared across America's main two-party system. Micah Zenko, at the Council on Foreign Relations, concluded that in 2016 alone, the Obama administration dropped at least 26,171 bombs in just seven countries (Pakistan, Yemen, Somalia, Libya, Syria, Iraq, and Afghanistan).[26] That's an average of three bombs every hour, terrorizing innocent people. "Crowd killings," which target group events like weddings and funerals, introduce the reality that either the happiest or the most traumatic days of one's life could also end in fatality. When people floated the idea of Michelle Obama as a presidential candidate, I often wondered if her reluctance to make these lethal decisions partially contributed to her reasons not to run.

Death-by-drone civilian casualties between 2009 and 2015 ranged from 380 to 801 in Pakistan, Yemen, Somalia, and Libya, according to the Bureau of Investigative Journalism, whereas the US Government claims killing six times fewer. In wondering how such an extreme discrepancy in numbers can exist, we learn that the Administration categorizes all military-age males as combatants, unless explicit evidence of their innocence is found posthumously.[27] So in essence, the universal human right of being innocent until proven guilty fails to apply to citizens whose crime was simply being born in one of these targeted countries.

One may argue for the "greater good" in the context of a hypothetically higher death toll of local civilians and international citizens at the hands of terrorists. But for human beings subjected to the psychological torture of omnipresent danger, and the anxiety of being caught in the crossfire as collateral damage en route to accessing an education or celebrating a union of love, this cruel form of intimidation is as much terrorism as an untimely death. Such morbid prospects make pre-wedding "cold feet" and "not wanting to go to school today" perfectly reasonable objections. But on a more somber note, doesn't this self-appointed benevolent stewardship—the conviction of knowing what's right and just—leave us morally vulnerable to the subjective definitions of the "greater good" and an ethically dubious valuation of human life?

LEGITIMATE FREEDOM FIGHTERS

Bruce Hoffman, who has been studying terrorism for nearly 40 years, elaborates on the fear-inducing, psychological nature of terrorism, saying: "Terrorism is ineluctably political in aims and motives, violent—or, equally important, threatens violence, designed to have far-reaching psychological repercussions beyond the immediate victim or target. . . ."[28] However, Hoffman's definition also excludes state-actors. Part of why this is problematic lies in the controversy surrounding which party is a "legitimate" government and which party is a non-state entity.

For example, during World War II, the German occupation forces in France labeled members of the French Resistance terrorists. During South Africa's Apartheid era, the African National Congress (ANC) led by Nelson Mandela, was labeled a terrorist organization. In fact, Tata Madiba, as Mandela was known—who won the Nobel Peace Prize in 1993 in addition to winning the affections and admiration of many around the world for his wisdom and compassion—remained on the US terrorism watch list until 2008! Condoleezza Rice, former US Secretary of State, was admittedly "embarrassed" by having to waive Mandela's travel restrictions for an official stateside visit.[29]

So whereas the United States and Israel would classify organizations leading the Palestinian liberation struggle as "terrorist groups," the Arab Terrorism Convention and the Terrorism Convention of the Organization of the Islamic Conference (OIC) exclude an armed struggle for liberation and self-determination from their definition. According to the OIC, Palestinian attacks against Israeli forces fall within the realm of a justified liberation struggle against occupying forces.[30]

Ultimately, there are no easy answers or unilateral agreement around the complications and controversies surrounding *who* a terrorist is when the same actions perpetrated by a party deemed to be "illegitimate" are held to different standards than the same ones committed by a "legitimate" actor. This raises questions around the prejudiced standards we apply. Through our actions, we are effectively saying that some lives are worth less and can be acceptably terrorized. Imagine the international outrage if 1.3 million innocent civilians were killed in California, Texas, and Florida, compared with Iraq, Pakistan, and Afghanistan. Or if we discriminately stripped the human rights of New Yorkers and rescinded their innocence until proven guilty based on factors they were unable to change, like their gender (male), age (military appropriate), and where they were born.

TERRORISM TODAY

From 1970 to 2017, the Global Terrorism Index (GTI) has codified more than 180,000 terrorist incidents. Their annual reports, which are produced by the Institute for Economics and Peace, are based on data from the Global Terrorism Database, which is collected and collated by the National Consortium for the Study of Terrorism and Responses to Terrorism (START)—a Department of Homeland Security Center of Excellence—led by the University of Maryland.[31]

For the second consecutive year, deaths from terrorism declined globally to 25,673 people, which is a 22 percent improvement compared to the peak of terror activity in 2014. The deadliest groups are Daesh, Al Qaeda, Boko Haram, and the Taliban. Terrorism deaths have fallen most significantly in Syria, Pakistan, Afghanistan, and Nigeria. However, Daesh defied this positive trend, killing 50 percent *more* people—with over 9,000 deaths, primarily in Iraq.[32]

And while the number of deaths in Nigeria showed the most significant improvement, falling by 80 percent, this has coincided with the splintering of Boko Haram into three separate groups. In fact, in 2016, attacks in Nigeria were executed by thirteen separate groups, including attacks in the Niger Delta and by Fulani extremists in the Middle Belt.[33]

Nigeria, Syria, Pakistan, Afghanistan, and Iraq also represent the "Big Five" most affected by terrorism. Disproportionate media coverage and public attention surrounding terrorism incidents in Western countries may distort the fact that since 2000, an overwhelming

99 percent of deaths have occurred in countries with high levels of political terror (defined as extrajudicial killings, torture, and imprisonment without trial) or that are engaged in some form of internal or international conflict. In 2016, 94 percent of all terrorist deaths were located in the Middle East and North Africa, sub-Saharan Africa, and South Asia. By contrast, Organisation for Co-operation and Development (OECD) countries experienced only 265 deaths in 2016.[34]

A little less than half (42 percent) of attackers had a clear operational connection to an established jihadist group—which was Daesh in most cases. Over the past decade, "lone-actor" terror attacks in OECD countries have increased from just one in 2008, to fifty-six in 2016. The greatest number occurred in the United States.[35] Since 2006, 98 percent of all deaths from terrorism in the US were perpetrated by lone actors, leading to 156 deaths.[36] This is a consequence of both technology enabling the decentralization of attacks and the systems-level impact of successful military interventions abroad, which can often cause domestic problems to emerge.

Border security does little to protect from lone actors, as 73 percent of these attacks were perpetrated by "homegrown" citizens of the country in which they committed the attack, according to *Fear Thy Neighbor: Radicalization and Jihadist Attacks in the West*.[37] The study, conducted by The George Washington University Program on Extremism, the Italian Institute for International Political Studies (ISPI), and the International Centre for Counter-Terrorism–The Hague (ICCT), also found that only 5 percent were refugees or asylum seekers at the time of attack. According to the same report, France suffered the highest number of attacks overall (17), followed by the United States (16). During this period only eight countries in Europe and North America were targeted. The other six include Germany (6), the UK (4), Belgium (3), Canada (3), Denmark (1) and Sweden (1).[38]

Incidents of domestic terrorism across Europe and North America, however, were dwarfed by the alarming numbers of foreign fighters who were flocking to the so-called Islamic State in Iraq and Syria circa 2014. Based on its own investigations, a study by The Soufan Group, a security intelligence consulting firm, calculated that between 27,000 and 31,000 people had traveled to Syria and Iraq to join Daesh and other violent extremist groups.[39] Putting these numbers in perspective, Peter Neumann, director of the International Centre for the Study of Radicalisation and Political Violence (ICSR), underscores that this surpasses the 20,000 foreign fighters who fought in Afghanistan during the ten-year Afghan-Soviet war.[40] Numbers in The Soufan Group's study—which are based on information directly provided by government officials, academic studies, and other research and reports by the United Nations and other bodies—corresponds with US intelligence estimates.

Daesh fighters, the majority of whom came from Arab states, represented eighty-six countries. Tunisia topped the list with 6,000, followed by Saudi Arabia, Russia, Turkey and Jordan, which each had between 2,000 and 2,500 fighters. France led the European Union with 1,700 recruits, followed by 760 fighters from the United Kingdom, another 760 from Germany, and 470 from Belgium, as of October 2015. Daesh's more recent loss of control over its "state" and economic resources has correlated with a decline of in-flows and an exodus of foreign fighters—many of whom were drawn by both economic prosperity and an apocalyptic promise of victory. Given that the average rate of returnees to Western countries is now at around 20 to 30 percent, this presents a significant challenge to security and law enforcement agencies that must assess the threat they pose.[41]

At this point, we may begin to ask: If terrorism is defined as a tactic that attempts to achieve a political objective, is it reasonable to hypothesize that being more politically inclusive and reconciling those objectives might be more effective in deescalating violence? Especially if, ultimately, we deem (at least some of) those political objectives to be reasonable? Or is violent repression more effective and more conducive to our safety and security in the long run, even if it leaves grievances unresolved (at best) and exacerbates them (at worst)?

As you will find in later chapters, I argue that a long-term sustainable solution to counterterrorism necessitates a "less is more" military approach that is strongly reinforced with soft power and, more specifically, a pivotal emphasis on social, political, and economic inclusion. Assuming that the goal is to defeat terrorism and ensure greater human security, we may consider that true power is efficacy and the achievement of objectives using as little force as possible.

2

MAKE THE *UMMA* GREAT AGAIN

VISUALIZING LIFE IN a Daesh-dominated global caliphate would likely conjure up images of women concealed under amorphous cloaks and tyrannical rule—obviously devoid of any political and civil liberties and minority rights. In framing contemporary violent Islamism, it is crucial to provide a brief historical narrative on what the advent of Islam sought to remedy and reform in the first place. I also emphasize here the difference between the terms *Islam* and *Islamism*. *Islam* is the religion, the followers of which are known as Muslims. *Islamism*, on the other hand, is the political use of Islam. Therefore, an *Islamist* is someone who advances a political agenda through the application of Shariah or Islamic law—whether peaceful or violent. Out of the 1.8 billion Muslims, the percentage of violent Islamists is relatively marginal. According to Western European intelligence agency estimates, for instance, less than 1 percent of Muslims living within their borders are at risk of radicalization—moreover, not all of the 1 percent will radicalize and those that do are not necessarily violent.[1]

REFORM OF SAVAGERY

Typically, aspiring to reform governance despite the risks of mortality and *Game-of-Thrones*-like torture and execution methods originates from a vehement desire to dramatically improve the current state of affairs. Upon preaching Islam, and a more enlightened way of living, the Prophet Muhammad and his companions were horrifically persecuted. In fact, the savagery and barbarism they were subjected to at the hands of the Al Quraysh tribe in Mecca more closely mirrored modern-day Daesh practices. Inhumane tribal practices like burying newborn girls alive, as well as plunder, torture, lynching, and mutilation, were all standard. Pregnant women were pushed off camels without hesitation.[2] Muslim converts were dragged over burning sand and stones like animals, starved, and imprisoned.[3] The Prophet himself was hunted for assassination. His children were murdered, and his uncle Hamza's liver was cut out of his body, chewed, and spat out.[4] Hamza's body parts were turned into ornaments, setting a grotesque fashion trend among non-Muslim women, who followed suit by accessorizing themselves with other dead Muslim body parts.[5]

Recognizing—as all spiritually grounded and morally resolute leaders do—that there are no shortcuts to social transformation and that one must "be the change," the Prophet demonstrated remarkable patience, compassion, and fortitude. If Islam sought to enlighten this pre-Islamic state of ignorance, or *jahiliya* as it is called in Arabic, sustainable change could only be achieved by modeling exemplar values and ethics. Despite pleas by the Prophet's companions to retaliate, he responded that he had not been given permission to fight. Having faced unbearable persecution for nearly thirteen years, the Prophet and his companions still didn't fight. Instead, they fled Mecca, and traveled 280 miles on camel-back to Medina, where they formed a secular government.

JUSTICE, LIBERTY, AND EQUALITY

I fondly recall having a spirited debate about the incompatibility of Islam with democracy with one of my favorite graduate school professors. George Demko, God rest his soul, was a Marine Corps veteran who had served as Ronald Reagan's geographer and is most remembered by his students as having been a highly engaging educator and Russian vodka aficionado. Resolving to prove him wrong, I wrote a research paper on the topic, through which I learned information that surprised and challenged my unconscious biases towards my own religion. I knew that Islam was founded on democratic and egalitarian principles,[6] but I was unaware of the constitution of Medina (known as the Medina Charter), which predated the Magna Carta by 500–600 years.[7]

Similar to the US Constitution, the establishment of Medina represented the founding of a state that would ensure, "justice ... domestic tranquility, provide for the common defense, promote the general welfare, and secure the blessings of liberty."[8] The constitutional pact was signed by the Prophet and representatives of the citizens of Medina. These citizens comprised non-Muslim tribes made up of pagans and Christians, but mostly Jews.

Some of the articles in the Medina Charter—many of which are light-years ahead of their time and are far more progressive than early twentieth-century laws in the West—included equality in the eyes of the law, a bill of rights, voting rights (including those of women and minorities), freedom of speech, right to a free and fair trial, right to religious freedom, and a welfare system.[9] So the "evil and draconian" Shariah law—at least in its original form—is more akin to the justice, freedom, and egalitarianism of modern-day Western societies than it is to a Daesh-ite form of governance. And only when the barbarian Meccan extremists pursued to attack the burgeoning multi-religious Islamic state in Medina was the Prophet finally given permission to fight in defense of people of all faiths. I cannot over-stress how crucial this context is when evaluating the Quran's more bellicose verses.

Moreover, when the Prophet eventually returned to Mecca twenty years later, he neither forced the conversion of the Quraysh tribe nor sought retribution for the atrocities he and his followers had been subjected to. Instead, he offered forgiveness.[10] This is a demonstration of the *greater jihad* that the Prophet himself emphasized—an inner struggle to maintain compassion and morality in the face of adversity.

THE BREAKUP

Umma, which means "community" or "nation" in Arabic, represents a vital ideological element, and the word appears over sixty times in the Quran.[11] Pre-Islam, nomadic and isolated tribes dominated Arabia; Islam united them in the form of one religious community bound by faith, love, and loyalty towards one another. However, the unity was short-lived, and after the Prophet's death, a tumultuous and violent Shiite-Sunni schism over who should rightfully succeed the Prophet as *Imam*, or spiritual leader, led to enduring fragmentation—something the Quran specifically warns against (verse 6:159).

Essentially, one group of the Prophet's companions (later becoming today's Sunnis) believed that the Prophet's senior companion and father-in-law, Abu Bakr as-Siddiq, should be *caliph*—the spiritual leader of the Islamic community—while another group (modern-day Shiites) believed that Ali Ibn Abi Talib, the Prophet's son-in-law and cousin, was the rightful leader. Abu Bakr as-Siddiq's camp believed Ali Ibn Abi Talib's pacifism and form of anemic leadership made him unfit to serve and protect the umma.[12] We can begin to see the markers of this uncompromising DNA in contemporary Islamist movements that seek to impose unity and homogeneity on the umma.

Militancy was also reinforced—perhaps inadvertently—by three founding fathers of fundamentalist thought. Taqi ad-Din Ahmad Ibn Taymiyya, Muhammad Ibn Abd Al-Wahhab, and Sayyid Qutb have all provided a source of ideological inspiration for terrorist organizations, including Daesh and Al Qaeda. However, all three spiritual gurus ironically sought to limit violence, and one of them even berated the *ulama* (religious scholars) for their literal, rather than contextual, interpretation of the Quran. Ibn Taymiyya, however, was not an example of the latter.

IBN TAYMIYYA

Taqi ad-Din Ahmad Ibn Taymiyya was a fourteenth-century scholar and reformer who sought a return to the fundamentals of Islam by strictly relying on the supremacy of the Quran and the *sunnah* (the way of the Prophet). He encouraged a literal interpretation of religious scriptures and rejected theology and the metaphysical aspects of Sufism. He also attacked the great philosophers that had flourished under the aegis of Islamic civilization—arguing that their questioning could lead believers astray. His vocal protests and iconoclastic views made him deeply unpopular among the majority of religious scholars and also resulted in his numerous incarcerations. Given Ibn Taymiyya's influence over many contemporary Islamist thinkers and organizations—including Al Qaeda, Daesh, and Saudi Arabia's ultraconservative Wahhabi religious sect—he is regarded as a controversial and polarizing figure.[13]

An eloquent writer and fierce traditionalist, Ibn Taymiyya condemned what he believed to be deviations from Islam. He rejected the Shiite practices of venerating Muslim saints and imams, maintaining that religious shrines should be reserved only for God and his prophets. Consequently, in his view, such aberrant beliefs adulterated pure Islam.[14] Knowing this precedent somewhat demystifies Daesh's destruction of churches and even sacred and historic mosques in Mosul.[15]

Ibn Taymiyya believed the divided umma could only be reunited through a religious reboot of sorts, so he began promoting the *takfir* doctrine—a controversial practice where a Muslim declares another Muslim to be an infidel.[16] Now unleashed was the possibility—and perhaps even self-appointed duty—for self-righteous Muslims otherwise lacking social or religious clout to declare those who do not adhere with an austere interpretation of Islam as "apostates."

MUHAMMAD IBN ABD AL-WAHHAB

Muhammad Ibn Abd Al-Wahhab was born in what is modern-day Saudi Arabia. Similar to his predecessor (Ibn Taymiyya), the eighteenth-century preacher and scholar was also a religious purist who was deeply disconcerted by the deterioration of true Islamic beliefs and practices.[17] Wahabbis—as the followers of his doctrine later became known—earned a violent reputation for their practice of destroying tombs and shrines, the veneration of which, they felt, was too reminiscent of pre-Islamic idol worshipping. However, Abd Al-Wahhab believed in violence only when necessary—such as in cases of self-defense, for example—but he did not actually advocate aggression.[18] He called for engagement in missionary work, favoring nonviolent approaches such as dialogue, debate, and discussion over a combative approach. He glorified knowledge, emphasizing ongoing education, and called for treaties with the Christians and the Jews. In fact, Abd Al-Wahhab sought to limit violence, so much so that he discounted use of the death penalty, saying it produced fear, not faith. According to his vision, winning faith of the heart was not through offensive jihad or aggression.[19]

Interestingly, Abd Al-Wahhab berated the *ulama* for their literal, rather than contextual, interpretation of the Quran and warned them of the dangers of taking too literal an approach to Quranic verses such as "Kill the idolaters wherever you find them!" He argued that such verses belonged to a historical context in response to aggressions against early Muslims, rather than as an open invitation to go on a killing spree.[20] Moderate Muslims may find this fact surprising, as today's Muslim terrorists are literalism personified.

One can infer, then, that current radical Islamist ideologies are rooted in contemporary political issues rather than pure theology. Like astute politicians tapping into deep-seated populist frustrations, terrorist groups adeptly identify and exploit shared grievances across a broad spectrum of Muslims and manipulate religious texts and doctrines to justify the use of violence. Sayyid Qutb, the father of modern fundamentalism—often cited as Bin Laden's greatest inspiration—is one such contemporary.

SAYYID QUTB

Sayyid Qutb was an Egyptian intellectual, educator, and leading member of the Muslim Brotherhood, which was founded by Imam Hassan al-Banna in opposition to British rule.[21] Having studied at a teachers college in Colorado in the late 1940s, Qutb became intensely disapproving of US culture. His moral indictment extended to the "animalistic" mixing of the sexes in sanctified places of worship. The jazz standard "Baby, It's Cold Outside," which Qutb first heard in church, exemplified his disgust with American licentiousness.[22] In fairness, the song has been subject to debate for its predatory and sexually coercive innuendo, although it is unlikely that the disturbing "date-rape" undertones of the song are what vexed Qutb.

Besides his hatred for America, the fanatical Qutb also loathed those whom he believed to be false Muslims. In his view, Egyptian President Gamal Abdel Nasser—a poster-child for Arab nationalism—had made no serious attempt to implement Shariah law in government. Qutb was convinced that the West had corrupted Middle Eastern regimes in general, veering them off a morally austere path.[23] In his eyes, the modern world had become akin to the era of *jahiliya*, which frames the self-perceived heroism of modern-day terrorist groups to reinstate the caliphate.[24]

Qutb authored dozens of books; one of his most influential and seminal works was *Ma'alim fi'l-tareeq* (which translates to *Signposts on the Road*), which has been compared to Vladimir Lenin's *What Is to Be Done?* The latter is said to have fomented Russia's Bolshevik Revolution, along with Karl Marx and Friedrich Engels' *The Communist Manifesto*.[25] Like his predecessors, Qutb did not advocate indiscriminate violence—though he was eventually executed by hanging after being convicted of plotting the assassination of President Nasser. Consequently, Islamists have come to regard him as a martyr.

ISLAMISM AND ITS DISCONTENTS

Today's Islamist movements are reactions to political and economic dislocations, and they are particularly pronounced where there are mass inequalities in access to political power and economic opportunities. Islamist movements gain momentum when they are either ignored by the regime in power (like the Muslim Brotherhood) or alternatively, when they are supported by the state in opposition to secularist or progressive forces. For instance, in a secular 1970s Iran, the Shah's American advisors perceived Iranian pro-Soviet leftists to be a bigger threat to the regime than the religious clerics. Consequently, the Americans allied themselves with the Islamists against the communists, and the repercussions have endured for decades.[26]

Islamist movements are also borne out of discontent with an unjust status quo and policies linked with Westernization. Predictably, there is also a positive correlation between Islamist movements and a nation's level of conflict and violence. Islamism has thrived in conditions of civil strife, such as in Iraq, Bosnia, Egypt, Syria, and Sudan, or in countries affected by external violence like in Afghanistan and Chechnya.[27] It is also difficult to ignore the significance of humiliation in fanning the flames of fundamentalism. The once superior Islamic world has been repeatedly degraded through imperialism; economic exploitation of natural resources; lower levels of social, political, and economic development; and a bombardment of military interventions. Where nationalism failed, Islamism provided alternative hope and offered a restoration of wounded pride.

GOLDEN AGE OF ENLIGHTENMENT

Two weeks after the 9/11 attacks, Carly Fiorina, who was CEO of Hewlett-Packard at the time and more recently a 2016 GOP presidential hopeful, gave a daring speech at the corporation's worldwide manager meeting:

> *There was once a civilization that was the greatest in the world. It was able to create a continental super-state that stretched from ocean to ocean and from northern climes to tropics and deserts. Within its dominion lived hundreds of millions of people, of different creeds and ethnic origins . . . its military protection allowed a degree of peace and prosperity that had never been known . . . And this civilization was driven more than anything, by invention. Its architects designed buildings that defied gravity. Its mathematicians created the algebra and algorithms that would enable the building of computers, and the creation of encryption. When other nations were afraid of ideas, this civilization thrived on them, and kept them alive . . . I'm talking about . . . the Islamic world from the year 800 to 1600 . . . The technology industry would not exist without the contributions of Arab mathematicians.*[28]

Even 100 years after the Prophet's death, the Islamic Empire's greatness surpassed that of Rome at the zenith of its power.[29] Arabic texts on science, mathematics, and medicine were translated into Latin. Antecedent Greek scientific and methodological thought was furthered and enriched. The arts and sciences flourished. Germophobes, the "selfie"-obsessed, Rumi lovers, and anyone who has ever seen a shrink have the Islamic Empire's contributions to thank for good hygiene, cameras, mystical poetry, and psychotherapy—among a myriad of other indispensables. (Also note that when I use the term *Islamic* here, it is a civilizational adjective rather than a religious one; Islamic sciences did not contain a religious component.)

Unlike the siloed specialist roles many of us adopt today, great Muslim thinkers like Al-Kindi and Al-Farabi were commonly polymaths—much like Aristotle, Leonardo Da Vinci, and Elon Musk. Their expertise crossed disciplines, enabling complex insights, inventions, and discoveries.[30] Abu Ali Ibn Sina, for example, who is commonly known by his Latinized name Avicenna, was a physician, philosopher, astronomer, chemist, geologist, paleontologist, mathematician, logician, physicist, psychologist, scientist, teacher, musician, and poet.[31] Imagine what his résumé would look like today, or a job description in today's world that would accommodate such ingenuity.

From engineering dams to inventing algebra, cryptography, and code-breaking—although I am just grazing the depth of inventions and contributions—suffice to say that at one point in time, Islamic civilization represented the greatest power on earth. It was at the forefront of trade, intellectually advanced, and militarily and economically superior.[32] In many respects, the reinstatement of a modern-day caliphate, or Islamic Empire, is a nostalgia for this era of ascendancy.

THE DECLINE

Many have attributed the waning Islamic civilization to an upsurge of religious thought, based on the paradigm that religion and science fundamentally conflict. Piety was believed to have come at the expense of scientific thought and innovation. This is only partially true. Many of the great Muslim scientists and philosophers were also religious men, holding official religious positions. In fact, some were more renowned for their Islamic jurisprudence than for their scientific contributions. Their multidisciplinary influence, however, may have simultaneously exalted and condemned them.

By the twelfth and thirteenth centuries, Arab philosophers began to attack others whose arguments could potentially lead Muslim believers astray. Consequently, allegorical interpretation of the Quran became permissible only for a select number of Muslims, rather than something that was achievable through knowledge, logic, and rational thinking. Ibn Taymiyya was one such adversary of philosophers and logicians.[33] Since the inquisitive nature of philosophy potentially conflicted with the all-knowing and powerful Creator, reasoning and religious innovation became synonymous with heresy.[34] Predictably, the fear of being branded an apostate led to a fear of discovery and diminished the quest for knowledge that Islam had not only encouraged but once demanded of the faithful.

As Europe entered an era of exceptional scientific revolution between 1500 and 1700, economic and political conditions in the Islamic world deteriorated. Notably, for the first time, the umma's fractures deepened in a massive three-way split of political power between the Shiite Safavids (1502–1736) in what is modern-day Iran, the Sunni Mughal Central Asian Empire (1526–1857), and the Sunni Ottoman Empire (1453–1920).[35] Religious sectarian competitiveness should not be overlooked, as it continues to color the Middle East's political climate—be it through sectarian civil conflicts, like in Iraq, or proxy wars like the Saudi-Iran pursuit of regional hegemony.

THE KNOWLEDGE GAP

In the sixth century, Imam Ali Ibn Abi Taleb wrote, "If God were to humiliate a human being, he would deny him knowledge."[36] Although Arabs today spend a higher percentage of GDP on education than the world average, a significant knowledge gap leaves the region lagging behind. A deeply ingrained fear of *fawda* (chaos) and *fitna* (schism) dominates much of the Arab and Islamic teaching paradigms. In some cases this is both religiously motivated and politically incentivized so that citizens do not question the authority of state-power in nondemocratic countries. Creative pursuits are also neglected, with generations of Arabs who have neither learned to play a musical instrument nor read literary works—reinforcing binary black and white thinking. Faint traces of the great Muslim thinkers are found not in classrooms, but occasionally as namesakes for hospitals and other buildings.

Innovation is largely a shadow of what it once was in the enterprising Islamic civilization. In the 2018 Global Innovation Index Rankings, only three Muslim countries—Malaysia, the United Arab Emirates, and Turkey—are among the top fifty.[37] When the United Nations (UN) published the Arab Human Development Report in 2002, it revealed Arab countries had produced a meager 171 international patents between 1980 and 1999, whereas South Korea alone had produced 16,328 patents in that same period.[38] Furthermore, the total GDP of the Arab world at this time (US$531 billion) was less than Spain's.[39] For Bin Laden, the UN report hit a raw nerve, summing up feelings of humiliation. In a taped message to Al Jazeera on January 4, 2004, he denounced Arab nations, saying this:

> It is enough to know that the economy of all the Arab countries is weaker than the economy of one country that had been part of our [Islamic] world when we used to truly adhere to Islam. That country is the lost Andalusia. Spain is an infidel country, but its economy is stronger than our economy because the ruler there is accountable. In our countries there is no accountability or punishment, but there is only obedience to the rulers and prayers of long life for them.[40]

Today, some fifteen years later, Bin Laden's native Saudi Arabia has made impressive advances in innovation, registering 664 Saudi patents in 2017 and outranking the world's most prestigious universities, like Harvard and the California Institute of Technology, according to the United States Patent and Trademark Office (USPTO).[41] Nevertheless, Bin Laden's statement reveals two widely held beliefs among Islamists.

The first is that the decline of the formerly ascendant Islamic world is due to a religious digression; a course correct necessitates a return to fundamentals. This is where the spiritual gurus mentioned earlier played a pivotal role in reinforcing the belief that an Islamic utopia could only be achieved through dogmatic and unyielding ideologies and practices. The second belief is that this regression is also a consequence of autocratic and corrupt rule—inferring that personal economic gain has outranked fidelity to Islam and to the umma.

By the time Bin Laden made his 2004 statement, Muslim humiliation was globally resounding as degrading images of hooded naked prisoners at Abu Ghraib prison and horrific tales of torture from Guantanamo Bay (Gitmo) were exposed. Iraqi insurgents who kidnapped and beheaded Americans did not coincidentally dress them in orange jumpsuits like the ones used for Gitmo prisoners; they were reciprocating the humiliation with headless corpses.[42] With all its virtues, the curse of the Internet is that it amplifies the "collective suffering" of Muslims worldwide.[43]

Similarly, shared victory when the "enemy" is humiliated becomes a potent restoration of annihilated pride. In addition to psychological intimidation and fear mongering, one now gains a deeper understanding of the purpose of hallmark theatrical and graphic videos showing beheadings, executions, and caged prisoners being burnt alive or submerged in water and drowned. Sadly, in their quest for Islamic ascendancy, violent extremists have paradoxically regressed us into a deeper state of *jahiliya*, which is what Islam sought to remedy in the first place. Irony would also have it that Daesh is perpetuating the demeaning Muslim and Arab stereotypes created by—what they would regard as—the Jewish-controlled Hollywood studios.

If there is a silver lining, one can take solace in the fact that, fortunately, this humiliation has not produced millions of extremists in the making. On the contrary, according to the more recent 2016 UN Arab Human Development Report, Arab youth perceived Daesh as the biggest obstacle facing the Middle East, followed by the general threat of terrorism and, thirdly, by unemployment.[44]

Humiliation alone is inadequate to drive violent extremism, but these pervasive sentiments felt across the Muslim community are a potent force when intermixed with other factors. So much so that one of the Saudi-born 9/11 hijackers, Ahmed Al-Haznawi, wrote this in his will:"The time of humiliation and slavery is over, and the time has come to kill Americans in their home and among their children and in front of their military forces and intelligence services. . . ."[45] Al-Haznawi's final words reflect deeply entrenched and widely shared political grievances against a Western world that has a legacy of duplicity and callousness with Muslim lives. This post-colonial baggage, as it were, and the failures of Arab nationalism to remedy it, provided the perfect constellation of circumstances for Islamists and violent extremisms to enter the sociopolitical void.

3

POST-COLONIAL
HANGOVER

OTHER BOOKS DETAIL Orientalist and non-Orientalist perspectives on where the Middle East "went wrong." For the purposes of this one, my objective is to demonstrate the significance of political memory and the region's most significant sociopolitical baggage and its enduring post-colonial hangover. Doing so permits a deeper appreciation for the origins of moral outrage that violent radical Islam exploits. And an understanding of this context enables us to create less favorable conditions under which terrorism can "sell."

Although the majority of the world's Muslims are in the Asia-Pacific region (almost one billion people), the radical Islamist identity was birthed in the Middle East. So, to start with the basics, the term *Middle East* itself is somewhat charged because of its imperialistic connotation. It was supposedly popularized in the 1850s by the British India Office—from which the British government held dominion over several Asian territories. Controversy springs from the typically imperial practice of classifying culturally heterogeneous

Arab and non-Arab states (Iran, Israel, and Turkey) together in one region. Moreover, for Islamists, these territorial boundaries confine the expanse of, and identification with, a global umma that transcends borders.

Nomadic and isolated tribes dominated Arabia before they transitioned to become a unified Islamic community and later became part of an Islamic empire in the sixteenth century. Therefore, the concept of a nation-state was somewhat obscure. Consequently, the dissolution of the Ottoman Empire in 1922 left much of the population disoriented. This unprecedented window of opportunity also gave the Allies (Britain and France) an entitled opportunity to serve their own geopolitical interests. Since the Arabs had been ruled for so long, they were considered "subject races" rather than "governing races."[1]

The Allies' decisions on how they carved up the Middle East were made according to their respective strategic objectives, thus creating artificial state boundaries that bore no consideration to the desires of the indigenous peoples of the region. In *Jihad vs. McWorld*, Benjamin Barber notes that the colonizers drew " ... arbitrary lines across maps they could not read with consequences still being endured throughout the ex-colonial world, above all in Africa and the Middle East. Jihad is then a rabid response to colonialism and imperialism and their economic children, capitalism and modernity . . . ."[2] Although this oversimplifies the reasons for waging holy war, many of the ethnic tensions and conflicts that taint Middle Eastern politics today are partially attributed to these legacy issues.

When they bulldozed the earth at the Syrian-Iraqi border in 2014, Daesh tweeted the destruction and symbolic erasure of the 1916 Sykes-Picot agreement. Named after the British and French diplomats Sir Mark Sykes and Francois Georges-Picot, the agreement symbolized a series of broken promises where the Allies sought to dismember and apportion the Arab provinces of the Ottoman Empire into various spheres of influence, while making duplicitous land jurisdictional promises that would later become impossible to honor.[3]

Syria was to be partitioned into the two French mandates of Lebanon and Syria. Britain agreed to give Amir Abdulla, son of the ousted former Amir of Mecca, jurisdiction over Transjordan—contingent on the French relinquishing Syria. However, France remained unyielding and Transjordan was eventually incorporated with the West Bank following the first Arab-Israeli War (1948–49), thus forming the Hashemite Kingdom of Jordan. France also expanded Lebanon's territory at Syria's expense. Consequently, the Christian Maronites in Lebanon came to view France as a protector, while Syria became a focal point for Arab nationalism.[4]

THE CASE OF PALESTINE

When the British established their League of Nations mandate in Palestine, which lasted from 1919 to 1948, Foreign Secretary Arthur Balfour conflictingly made a commitment to establish a Jewish homeland in Palestine while also promising the Palestinians their right to self-determination.[5] According to the official mandate of the League of Nations, Britain was supposed to assist the Palestinians in their transition to self-government. However, in the post–World War II period, pressure for a Jewish homeland in Palestine mounted and the rising influx of Jewish immigrants caused grievances and tensions between the two communities. The United Nations decided to partition Palestine between the Jews and the Arabs and place Jerusalem under international authority. This was rejected by the Arab world at large since it ignored the legitimate rights of the Palestinians to their land and was viewed as reparation for European guilt over the Holocaust.[6]

Decades of war, territorial losses, and stalled negotiations later, today, the United Nations Relief and Works Agency for Palestinian Refugees in the Near East (UNRWA) is responsible for over five million Palestinian refugees. Families in over 400 towns and cities either have been expelled so their land can be repopulated with Jews or have witnessed the systematic demolition of their homes.[7] Unfazed by the ire of the international community, settlement expansion continues. The number of Israeli settlers exceeds half a million, and their settlements now cover around 42 percent of the West Bank and parts of East Jerusalem.[8]

Western leaders sometimes underestimate the significance of the plight of the Palestinians, which is easily considered by Arabs to be the most consequential residuum of colonialism. For Islamists, it remains a highly exploitable symbol of Western hypocrisy, oppression, and injustice. Jewish-American intellectual Noam Chomsky recalls a statement made by a former Israeli intelligence head recognizing that "To offer an honorable solution to the Palestinians respecting their right to self-determination: that is the solution of the problem of terrorism. . .When the swamp disappears, there will be no more mosquitoes."[9]

US MEDDLING?

In an excerpt from the 2004 book *Deliver Us from Evil: Defeating Terrorism, Despotism, and Liberalism,* Sean Hannity comments,

> *More than 225 years after that Declaration [of Independence], America would become without rival the world's most beneficent nation. Ronald Reagan was fond of reminding his Society counterparts, we have the power to conquer any nation, but we don't. We have the power to enslave any people, but we don't. We have the power to loot any nation of its natural resources, but we don't. Instead America sends her young men and women to war to defend the weak. She sends her resources to help feed the poor. And she offers a hand to any nation that seeks friendship and peace.*[10]

I sincerely believe that this is what Hannity and many Americans—certainly my US military friends who sacrifice their lives—genuinely perceive as truth. Most of us are far from villains in the moral arc of the narratives we construct. Upon mindful contemplation, however, it shouldn't be a stretch to discern how the following events of conquering and looting might reframe one's perception from an Arab point of view.

Declining British and French influence in the Middle East in the post–World War II era marked a more assertive Soviet policy in the region. Faced with the threat of communism, the previously isolationist United States began to employ a more proactive foreign policy.[11] Disconcerted by the rise of Pan-Arab nationalism and the overthrow of the pro-Western, yet undemocratic, Iraqi Hashemite monarchy in 1958, President Eisenhower wanted to guarantee the election of the pro-Western Maronite Christian Camille Chamoun in Lebanon.

To influence the Lebanese election outcome, the US provided covert financial assistance to pro-Chamoun candidates and sponsored other activities.[12] Riots broke out as many alienated Muslims demonstrated against President Chamoun's relations with Western countries that had been hostile to Arab neighbors. As Lebanon's political climate deteriorated and destabilized, the US quickly intervened by deploying 14,000 American troops.[13] Consider the impact of alleged Russian interference in the 2016 US elections. Irrespective of one's political affiliation, most Americans would regard this as an egregious breach of sovereignty—even one instance of which would cement considerable distrust for generations to come.

By 1982, political winds in Washington shifted, however, and the support America had once provided to, and received from, the pro-Western Lebanese was abandoned in favor of arming and backing Israel's incursions into Lebanon. Even though it is well-acknowledged that other factors paved a path for the formation of Hezbollah three years later in 1985, these incursions legitimized the necessity of establishing an opposing force to protect Lebanon from America and Israel and to safeguard the interests of marginalized Shiites. At the end of the conflict, almost 17,500 mostly civilian people were killed—which is the equivalent of six 9/11 attacks.[14] Bin Laden later referenced this tragic loss of life as having planted the seeds of demolition in his mind, which eventually led to the destruction of the Twin Towers almost twenty years later.

Further east, the US also intervened in Iran—urging Reza Shah to help the Allies "stop Hitler's ambition of a world conquest" during World War II.[15] The Shah appealed for neutrality; however, Soviet and British troops simultaneously invaded Iran from the north and south in order to allow Britain to supply arms to the Soviets in their fight against Germany, and the Shah was overthrown. His son Mohammed Reza Pahlavi was installed to power.[16]

In 1951, under Mohammed Reza Pahlavi's rulership, Iran's democratically elected secular prime minister Mohammad Mosaddegh nationalized the Anglo-Persian Oil company, asserting Iran's ownership over its natural resources. In retaliation, Britain ordered a blockade of the Persian Gulf to prevent Iran from exporting oil, and the US joined in the boycott.[17] To further undermine Iran's newfound assertiveness, the CIA created a misinformation campaign to incite political instability and cause split factions between Islamic nationalists and secular democrats. Mosaddegh—who was named *TIME*'s Man of the Year in 1951—was arrested in a coup d'état in 1953 that was supported and funded by the US and British governments.[18] The United States even trained and armed Iran's brutal security police, SAVAK, under the custody of which thousands of Iranians were tortured—often to death. (It was within this context that US embassy personnel were taken hostage in Tehran later in 1979.[19]) In 1954, oil was denationalized—serving Western economic interests[20]—and the formerly Anglo-Persian Oil company was renamed British Petroleum (BP).[21]

Besides sowing the seeds of ethnic and religious tensions, another major legacy of Western colonialism is that it stunted much of the Muslim world's economic and political development. Since the realization of modern nation state governance was delayed for so long, Islam consequently became a tool to legitimize monarchies and theocracies. Essentially, it was transformed from a religion into a political method—used by both Muslim and Western governments—to sustain or support certain regimes. For instance, Norman Bailey, a US National Security Council staffer who monitored global terrorism by tracking movements of US money, discovered that during the Soviet-Afghan War, Washington funneled some US$2 billion to fund Bin Laden's mujahedeen.[22]

Given these historical precedents, 9/11 conspiracy theories alleging the involvement of the Israeli Intelligence agency, Mossad (to vilify Muslims worldwide), and the CIA (to justify invading Iraq and securing Iraqi oil resources), are a little less baffling. Before becoming George W. Bush's vice president in 2002, Dick Cheney, CEO of Halliburton, posed this question: "By 2010 we will need on the order of an additional fifty million barrels a day. So where is the oil going to come from? . . . While many regions of the world offer great oil opportunities, the Middle East, with two-thirds of the world's oil and the lowest cost, is still where the prize ultimately lies."[23] Cheney viewed war—by his own admission—as a growth opportunity. Production sharing agreements (PSAs) between the Iraqis and the International Tax and Investment Center (ITIC) led to hundreds of billions of dollars in lost revenues for Iraq, while funneling massive profits to foreign companies via offshore bank accounts, all under false pretenses of implementing "best practices" and providing necessary expertise.[24]

According to one study, the Bush administration publicly made 935 false statements about the security risk posed by Iraq in the two years following September 11, 2001—a fact later acknowledged by the White House.[25] US economic interests, which are often shrouded in a façade of justifications such as "spreading democracy" and "protection from WMDs," represent a very strong point of contention for Islamists, and for Arabs in general. And we continue to see how this legacy has unfurled post-2003 invasion of Iraq, with the emergence of Al Qaeda in Iraq, and its resurrected offshoot, Daesh.

So, in short, a common Arab narrative is as follows. The West colonized Arab lands and then drew arbitrary state boundaries serving their own political interests with a blatant disregard for the indigenous people. "Divide and conquer" legacies have persisted, given that these divisions mire intraregional conflicts in the Arab world today. The US spouts its democracy rhetoric while hypocritically supporting authoritarian regimes based on economic interests (oil and weapons sales); arming rebels when its suits its interests, then demonizing those same rebels it armed and trained; and toppling and replacing leaders like a game of chess. And after contributing to the quagmire of Iraq, the US is rejecting the refugees fleeing from the radical Islamists that America helped create.

However, these problems cannot be blamed solely on colonialism. Imperial powers may have delayed the formation of political identity and stunted economic growth, however, in many countries, they also laid the foundations and infrastructure for future autonomous development.

Since achieving sovereignty, many political Arab and Muslim elites have largely failed to offer coherent solutions to address economic dependencies and political stagnation.[26] The failures of nationalism and socialism, combined with the Muslim world's social, political, and economic ills, left many disillusioned and desperate for a new ideology. This especially intensified with the Arab world's repeated defeats by Israel.[27] Although most Muslims do not support or endorse the violence of terrorism, after centuries of decline, humiliation, and exploitation, some Muslims began to view terrorists like Bin Laden as having brought back a semblance of hope and dignity. In short: Islamism appealed to Muslim pride.[28]

Can the Arab world blame all of its failures on century-old borders? No. But if we consider that a 200-year-old country like America is still honing its democracy, the comparatively fledgling Arab states have been repeatedly denied the opportunity to mature their political institutions. Given that US military and economic assistance bolstered Islamist forces against the communist threat, in Arab countries, this synchronously amplified the threat that Islamist groups could potentially win democratic elections. Therefore, this potent pitfall became a tool—and sometimes an imperative—for more secular regimes to sustain nondemocratic governance as a buffer against a potentially violent extremist "Islamic" state that is similar to the one its Western counterparts fear.

PART II

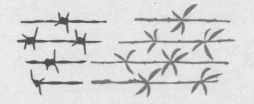

4

ISLAM MADE
ME DO IT

America has suffered repeated barbaric attacks—from the atrocities of September 11th to the devastation of the Boston Bombing, to the horrible killings in San Bernardino and Orlando . . . But, in sheer numbers, the deadliest toll has been exacted on the innocent people of Arab, Muslim, and Middle Eastern nations. They have borne the brunt of the killings and the worst of the destruction in this wave of fanatical violence. . . . This region should not be a place from which refugees flee, but to which newcomers flock. . . .

—US President Donald Trump[1]

"WHAT'S THE DIFFERENCE between a Muslim doll and an American doll?" a Navy SEAL asked me. We were at a summer barbecue in Juffair, Bahrain, minutes from the US Naval Base headquarters responsible for the Fifth Fleet in the Arabian Gulf, Red Sea, and Persian Gulf. I looked at him, raising my eyebrows in expectation of his politically incorrect punch-line. "A Muslim doll blows itself up!" he smirked. This was certainly not the first time a comment or incident had prompted me to scrutinize my religion and its interpretation.

However, discovering the spiritual incongruence between the non-observant behaviors of so-called "Muslim" suicide attackers and their self-proclaimed religious motivations gave me pause to interrogate their true motives. Acknowledging that there is never a straightforward and definitive "why," the following chapters sketch the nonideological drivers of terrorism. Understanding these drivers serves to frame the shortcomings and counterproductiveness of military interventions and, more importantly, supports the potential efficacy of alternative approaches to countering violent extremism, which are later presented.

Without absolving the responsibility of an individual, or exonerating a terrorist's behavior, one must recognize that violence simply does not occur in a vacuum. Ignoring the existence of externalities—particularly ones over which we have agency—is to our detriment. Thích Nhất Hạnh, the 92-year-old Vietnamese Buddhist monk and Zen Master—most renowned for his peace activism and mindfulness retreat center, Plum Village—captures this best when he writes,

> *When you plant lettuce, if it does not grow well, you don't blame the lettuce. You look for reasons it is not doing well. It may need fertilizer, or more water, or less sun. You never blame the lettuce. Yet if we have problems with our friends or family, we blame the other person. But if we know how to take care of them, they will grow well, like the lettuce. Blaming has no positive effect at all, nor does trying to persuade using reason and argument.[2]*

Scholarly consensus and spiritual wisdom have more or less converged on this concept. Unlike earlier decades where academics traced the roots of terrorism to personal pathology and affliction, today, it is generally agreed upon by military institutions, terrorism experts, intelligence officers, think-tanks, and multilaterals that the drivers of terrorism consist of a more complex confluence of conditions. And one discovers that despite the nuances, one common thread is entangled throughout the narratives of terrorists who vary in degrees of piety, and differ in race, gender, education, and socioeconomic background. In some shape or form, they have all suffered from personally significant social, economic, or political exclusion.

Indeed, many others have also been disenfranchised or suffered from poverty, and yet they have not been compelled towards a path of mutual destruction. As noted in a 2017 United Nations (UN) counterterrorism report entitled *Enhancing the Understanding of the Foreign Terrorist Fighters Phenomenon in Syria*, "there is inevitably a 'personal' factor that persuades one individual to become a FTF [Foreign Trained Fighter] while his neighbour, or even his sibling, although exposed to exactly the same environment and subject to the same conditions conducive to radicalisation and extremism chooses to remain at home."[3] A more profound examination of these exclusionary factors is provided in subsequent chapters, but first, this chapter unearths the "religious" roots of terrorism.

TERRORIST HALL OF SHAME

Picturing a "Muslim" terrorist is likely to conjure images of a long-bearded, AK-toting, religiously austere fanatic. One who apostatizes everything from the ungodly sight of an uncovered woman to the depravity of Western culture and devotes every waking moment not spent in prayer to plotting against infidels and establishing the reign of a caliphate. Now imagine this Islamic militant's social media feed. It features comments like "This night deserves Hennessy a bad bitch and an o [ounce] of weed the holy trinity." Probably not what one expects. This counterintuitive blasphemy of alcohol, drugs, sex, and thuggery may initially render disbelief, and eventually be reconciled as an anomaly. But is it an anomaly?

Before blowing himself up at Manchester Arena in 2017, Salman Ramadan Abedi was a pothead and vodka drinker who partied regularly.[4] Maybe this was to cope with his cultural displacement as a disconnected second-generation European immigrant—not feeling Libyan enough, nor British enough. But also, because Abedi came from an extremely religious family, it is likely that his escape into drinking and drugs temporarily pacified, and later amplified, his feelings of shame.

After shooting a police officer and careening down the motorway in a vehicle stolen at gunpoint, Ziyed Ben Belgacem, a French-born citizen, made a phone call to his father. "Dad, please forgive me. I've screwed up," Belgacem pleaded. He proceeded to Orly Airport in Paris where he put a gun to a soldier's head, declaring: "I am here to die in the name of Allah ...There will be deaths."[5] Belgacem's aggregate criminal history included drug dealing, armed robbery, theft, and receiving stolen goods. Postmortem toxicology tests revealed the presence of alcohol, cannabis, and cocaine in his blood. Hardly Allah-approved, one would argue. And Belgacem was probably both acutely aware of and deeply uncomfortable with this caustic moral incongruity.

In the summer of 2016, Mohamed Lahouaiej-Bouhlel "answered ISIS calls" by bulldozing through a Bastille Day parade in Nice, killing eighty-six people. Was he a devoted Muslim who dutifully performed his obligatory daily prayers? On the contrary, he ate pork and had an unbridled penchant for alcohol, drugs, and wild sex—allegedly with men and women.[6] Similarly, an imam implicated in the 2017 Barcelona attacks on La Rambla held a record of drug offenses.[7]

Marginally different were the Belgian-born Abdeslam brothers. Salah, the younger of the two, was involved in the gruesome Bataclan theatre shooting in Paris, whereas the older brother, Brahim, self-detonated outside the Comptoir Voltaire cafe in Brussels—killing no one but himself. The Abdeslam brothers didn't need to go to bars; they owned one. This is the ultimate Islamic sin because by extension, one is responsible for any lives detracted or destructed by intoxication. Repentantly, the brothers sold Les Beguines bar—which also served hallucinogenics—six weeks before the attacks.[8] In a spectacle of revolting hypocrisy, the Bataclan gunmen's first order of business was to shoot everyone standing at the theatre bar. They proceeded to subject victims to horrific torture like castration and gouging out their eyes, according to witnesses. As irony would have it, the Abdeslam surname refers to one of God's ninety-nine qualities and translates into "servant of peace."

These characterizations are not unique to Europe. Abu Musab al-Zarqawi, the deceased Jordanian, tattooed, one-legged mac daddy of Al Qaeda in Iraq, was a notorious pimp, thug, heavy drinker, and junkie. With thirty-seven criminal cases against him, he "returned to Islam" after a missionary group convinced him that it was time to cleanse himself of his salacious lifestyle.[9]

And despite differences in the integration of immigrants in Europe and the US—the latter being more assimilated into Western society—spiritual incongruities are also discernible across the Atlantic. Major Nidal Hasan, who killed thirteen people at Fort Hood, Texas, in 2009, was a non-observant Muslim who reinvented himself as a "Soldier of Allah," according to his business cards.[10] Computer science major Faisal Shahzad, who was sentenced to life in prison for an attempted Times Square car bombing in New York, spent his weekends like a typical college student: drinking at nightclubs and hitting on women.[11] Jahar Tsarnaev, the younger of the Boston marathon bomber brothers, was also a typical American college student. His partygoing lifestyle, sleeping in late, girls, sex, alcohol, and marijuana were unabashedly plastered on Facebook and Twitter. Yes—including the tweet "This night deserves Hennessy a bad bitch and an o of weed the holy trinity."[12]

Hardly a case of bottom-up perversion, "the fish rots from the head down" adage applies to the Boston brothers and many others—including the 2005 London bombers, and three of the 9/11 hijackers, who were influenced by American Muslim cleric and Al Qaeda leader Anwar al-Awlaki. The deceased-by-drone infamous spiritual guide is said to have inspired many violent extremists, even from the grave. It is unclear whether or not al-Awlaki drank, but this supposed exemplar of faith did engage in other "extracurricular" activities.

In 1996 and 1997 al-Awlaki was arrested in San Diego for soliciting prostitutes. When the news of his arrest later became public, the married and "respected" al-Awlaki claimed he had been set up by the government. Still, old habits die hard, and in the months following 9/11, he continued to visit high-end Washington DC escorts to relieve his stress—paying upwards of three hundred dollars a session for sexual services.[13] Perhaps he over-compensated for his sexual debauchery with religious fanaticism. Or perhaps he justified antecedently rewarding himself for what he believed were his paradise-worthy achievements. We will never know for sure.

SPIRITUAL REDEMPTION

Whether explicitly referenced or implicitly demonstrated by spiritually incongruent behavior, evidently, these accounts demonstrate an emblematic undulation between self-disgust and radical piety. My intention is not to voice judgement over the non-Islamic activities these individuals engaged in; rather, I am highlighting the fundamental absence of moderation in their actions and the inner struggle such a conflicted identity inevitably creates. My own view of extreme religious piety became much more nuanced as my awareness of deeply embedded cultural and religious contradictions grew. At some point it stopped surprising me to discover that those who were fanatically pious in public had "impure" pasts and occasionally "impure" presents. And those who had outwardly rejected and abandoned their past were significantly more self-righteous than those who delicately tried to balance their see-sawing identity.

For instance, as a twenty-something, I recounted an incident of an Islamist Parliamentarian's outlandishly inappropriate behavior, ogling me at a work function. Naively, I was puzzled by how someone with such religiosity could behave in such a manner—publicly, no less. An older family member of mine snickered with contempt as she raised her eyebrows. "But of course!" she exclaimed. "Everyone knows he used to be a playboy before growing his beard and shortening his thobe!" This was the first—but would not be the last—time I would encounter outwardly extremist men (and women) who were once a version of what they now loathed. Predictably; the ones who carried the most shame were the loudest and most self-righteous in their *takfir* (apostasy) of others.

Even the 9/11 hijackers epitomized this polarity by embodying two extremes as they were confronted with overt Western sexuality. In a lame attempt to shield their lustful wandering eyes, they draped towels over pictures of semi-nude women hanging on the walls of their seedy Florida motel room. Instead, they satiated their desires by devouring pay-per-view pornographic movies. They scraped the frosting off American muffins in case they contained pork fat yet indulged in gambling, boozing, and lap dances.[14] And, in complete dissonance with the pervasive generosity characteristic of Muslims, they weren't even good tippers, according to one of the dancers at the strip club they visited.[15] Suggesting a sort of displaced aggression and self-hatred, one of the hijackers, Mohammed Atta, reportedly beat the prostitute whom he regularly hired when he lived in Hamburg, Germany.[16]

A confused identity can carry considerable weight in the decision to seek an avenue of militancy and terror and should not be overlooked. Most sexually frustrated males, for instance, channel their feelings into religious or moral defense, rather than directing them towards countering socioeconomic injustice.[17] This diverges from the hypothesis that sexually frustrated males become radicalized to achieve the promise of sexual fulfillment and any number of virgins in paradise. Fatima Mernissi, a social psychologist who was regarded as the founder of Islamic feminism, long observed that as Islamists internalize the discomfort experienced by Western seduction, those feelings become compounded by an obsession with sexual purity.[18]

Particularly for such conflicted individuals, the most compelling message of martyrdom is the promise of purification, redemption, and atonement. A promise that is consecrated into rites and rituals— like the ceremonial script discovered in the baggage of one of the 9/11 hijackers. Detailing their final preparations, the document instructed them to purify their souls from all unclean things and to bless their bodies by rubbing verses of holy scripture on their clothes, passport, and even their luggage. Unlike the ghastlier Daesh-inspired attackers—gouging out eyes and burning people alive—the Al Qaeda-led 9/11 hijackers were directed to ensure their knife blades were sharp to avoid discomforting their sacrifice, in line with the *halal* Islamic practice of humane animal slaughter.[19]

Scholars like the French political scientist and terrorism expert Olivier Roy have postulated that many seeking martyrdom simply have a death wish, and I would agree. "The large majority of Al-Qaida and Islamic State jihadis, including the Manchester attacker Abedi, commit suicide attacks not because it makes sense strategically from a military perspective or because it's consistent with the Salafi creed. . .These attacks don't weaken the enemy significantly, and Islam condemns self-immolation as interference with God's will. These kids seek death as an end-goal in itself," says Roy.[20] Similarly, as Daniel Benjamin, a former State Department coordinator for counterterrorism and Dartmouth College professor, observes ". . .the Islamic State and jihadism has become a kind of refuge for some unstable people who are at the end of their rope and decide they can redeem their screwed-up lives."[21]

Substantiating this hypothesis are explicit examples like Major Nidal Hasan, who, months after the Fort Hood attack, told a psychiatric panel he had wished to die during the assault. Expressing his hopes for execution, Major Hasan reasoned that "If I died by lethal injection, I would still be a martyr." Similarly, in 2017, Amor Ftouhi, the attacker who stabbed airport police in Michigan, seeking retribution for America's killing of people in Syria, Iraq, and Afghanistan, later asked an officer who subdued him why he did not kill him.[22] I should also point out that this doesn't only apply to Muslims. Darren Osborne, the Londoner who drove a van into Muslim worshipers near Finsbury Park Mosque in June 2017, had attempted suicide a few weeks earlier, according to his sister—a life and aspirational death made less ordinary through a "heroic" gesture of moral outrage and a decisive stance to "do his bit" to kill all Muslims.[23]

Like human traffickers preying on those seeking a better life, extremist rhetoric sequins martyrdom with the promise of a better afterlife—a pass to paradise bestowing purification, redemption, and atonement, while also pacifying unbearable shame and self-disgust. Presented with the options of glory, or being written off as an irrelevant and unnoticed suicide statistic or sinner, attackers are seduced with the prospects of atonement and self-validation. Suddenly, a miserable or conflicted existence is cosmetically reconstructed into a more meaningful martyr's badge of honor. Daesh media frequently, and intentionally, post smiling dead jihadists with their right-hand index finger pointing heavenward.[24]

NON-OBSERVANT HUMAN BEINGS

Replete with spiritual contradictions, these examples should, at the very least, give one pause to challenge the motivations of suicide attackers proclaiming holy war. A conflicted sense of identity, compounded with insufferable shame, seems to be a greater instigator of the decision to seek militant self-sacrifice. Paradoxically, while drugs and alcohol serve as more palatable indicators of Islamic insubordination, the most compelling giveaway should really go without saying: murdering innocent people.

These are actions not only of non-observant Muslims, but rather of non-observant human beings. Notably, Islamic terrorist attacks affect more Muslims than non-Muslims and eight of the top ten countries with the biggest terrorism threats are Muslim majority nations.[25] Even in Saudi Arabia, authorities thwarted a suicide attack on the Grand Mosque in Mecca during Islam's holiest month of Ramadan in 2017; the mosque is considered Islam's godliest site and fifteen million pilgrims congregate there annually.[26] Imagine a "Catholic" terrorist attempting to blow up the Vatican on Good Friday.

As His Holiness the Dalai Lama quite fittingly asserts: there is no "Muslim terrorist" or "Buddhist terrorist"; terrorists have renounced religion.[27] President Trump has also echoed this sentiment, saying, "Every time a terrorist murders an innocent person, and falsely invokes the name of God, it should be an insult to every person of faith. Terrorists do not worship God, they worship death."[28]

Essentially, just because someone claims to have done something in the name of religion, that doesn't make it true. Wars have been fought over the same claims for millennia. Religion is a façade. For instance, following the rise of Daesh, a battle between Taliban and former Taliban-turned-Daesh-loyalists in Nangarhar Province ensued over the control of illicit trade and money laundering channels. In particular, this battle was over the heroin that passes through from Peshawar in Pakistan to the Nangarhar provincial capital, Jalalabad, making its way to Western Europe.[29] Criminal mafias in Pakistan misappropriate religious doctrines to weaken state legitimacy and security enforcement capabilities to sustain an environment conducive for lucrative and illicit activities like the drug trade, smuggling of weapons, tax and duties evasion, and so on. It's no secret that these activities are categorically un-Islamic.

ISLAM FOR DUMMIES

In corroborating the aforementioned contradictions, a leaked MI5 report found that those involved in terrorism lacked religious literacy, that some consumed drugs and alcohol and visited prostitutes, and that there was evidence that a secure religious identity actually *protects* from violent radicalization.[30] Likewise, after interviewing hundreds of people convicted of terrorism at Guantanamo and other prisons since 9/11, forensic psychiatrists—including one who worked for the CIA— concluded that "Islam had nothing to do with it."[31] Renowned historian Karen Armstrong shares this fact during an interview on her book *Fields of Blood: Religion and the History of Violence.* According to Armstrong, the problem is not Islam at all, but rather the ignorance of it:

> *Had they had a proper Muslim education they wouldn't be doing this. Only 20% of them has had a regular Muslim upbringing. The rest are either new converts—like the gunmen who recently attacked the Canadian Parliament; or non-observant, which means they don't go to the mosque—like the bombers in the Boston marathon; or self-taught. Two young men who left Britain to join the Jihad in Syria ordered from Amazon a book called* Islam for Dummies. *That says it, you see.*[32]

Since Islam does not require an intermediary to connect with God, not going to the mosque is not necessarily synonymous with not being observant, although one would reasonably expect a person with the religious zeal to join an Islamic militant group to at least congregate in the mosque for Friday prayers. Nevertheless, prayer at home is perfectly acceptable. Yet despite this prerequisite of the faithful, over half of foreign-trained fighters (FTFs) who traveled to Syria and Iraq to join Daesh did not even know how to pray, according to a study by the UN Counter-Terrorism Centre (UNOCT).[33]

Similarly, for many Boko Haram militants in Nigeria, their first encounter with a Quran is during a prison deradicalization program.[34] An analysis of 500 former members of various extremist organizations in Africa found that while over half of respondents said they were motivated to join because they perceived their religion to be under attack, 57 percent admitted to having a limited understanding of religious texts in the first place.[35] I suspect that, in reality, this number is actually much higher.

Likewise, interviewees in the UN Counter-Terrorism Centre study defended their knowledge of the specific conditions and stipulations of jihad, responding with vague statements like "We know jihad by intuition. Every Muslim knows it by intuition. You don't need to study it." In any case, only 35 percent of the sample even deemed the role of *jihad* as "extremely important" in their decision, and even fewer (16 percent) believed in the idea of establishing an Islamic state or caliphate in the Levant.[36]

Those skeptical of the UN and even Armstrong—a former British nun, interfaith advocate, and TED Prize winner who called for the creation of a global Compassion Charter—will find that these views are also shared with US military researchers. After analyzing leaked Daesh documents, a study conducted by West Point's Combating Terrorism Center (CTC) found that the vast majority of militants in the dataset (over 85 percent) had no formal religious education. Most (around 70 percent) had not adhered to Islam for their entire lives; and 32 percent were identified as converts to Islam. Depth of religious knowledge also appeared to influence the roles chosen by fighters. Those who had more advanced knowledge of Islam and Shariah law were far less likely to choose a suicide role over their less knowledgeable peers.[37]

Given the contradictory martyr narratives described, this should come as no surprise. Most of the foreign fighters appeared to be more isolated from both local figures and from their communities at large, according to the report.[38] Predictably, militant groups have a recruiting preference for the religiously uneducated since they are incapable of critically scrutinizing the violent jihadi narrative and ideology and tend to have less exposure to contrasting schools of Islamic jurisprudence.

Nonetheless, for some new recruits the superficial two-week religious indoctrination courses taught in Daesh territories marked a critical juncture. One said: "I began to think about leaving Syria as soon as I arrived. I started to think, could the armed group, with its reputation and might, provide a kind of teaching and teachers as simple as that? I started immediately to question the reputation of the armed group altogether: its purpose; its teachers; its philosophy; everything."[39] While Daesh's public brand identity and media apparatus rivals that of a Fortune 500 company, its internal culture and operations are a shell of its grandiose claims. When it failed to make good on its promises, these were the main reasons FTFs renounced their allegiance to the militant group:

- The perception that "IS is more interested in fighting fellow (Sunni) Muslims than the [Government of Syria]."

- The perception that "IS is involved in brutality and atrocities against (Sunni) Muslims."

- The perception that "IS is corrupt and un-Islamic," with the "corruption narrative cover[ing] a range of behaviours that defectors considered unjust, selfish, and contrary to the group's ideals and standards of conduct."

- The perception that "life under IS" is "harsh and disappointing."[40]

Moreover, young Islamists don't see their faith in terms of piety and spirituality. Rather, they view it in terms of justice and injustice, according to the previously mentioned UN Counter-Terrorism Centre study entitled *Enhancing the Understanding of the Foreign Terrorist Fighters Phenomenon in Syria*. Most FTFs interviewed were driven by a sense of injustice and a duty to defend their "in-group" in Syria rather than by religion.[41] As the female war reporter Souad Mekhennet notes, when speaking to European-born members of both Daesh and Al Qaeda about their motivations for joining, "most of them talk about politics and social issues, not faith. It is not the religion that has radicalized them, they have radicalized the religion."[42]

5

POVERTY OF HOPE

Poverty doesn't cause terrorism. . . . Yet persistent pov-
erty and oppression can lead to hopelessness and despair.
And when governments fail to meet the most basic needs
of their people, these failed states can become havens for
terror. . . . Development provides the resources to build
hope and prosperity, and security.

—PRESIDENT George W. Bush[1]

IN THE TERRORIST playbook *The Management of Savagery,* which
was written by a chief Al Qaeda strategist going by the pseudonym
Abu Bakr Naji, he outlines his game plan to lure the rank-and-file
with financial rewards. Although he admits money is a superficial
goal, Naji recognizes that desperation is the gateway to manipulation,
because dubious hope is more palpable than a current reality. With
many recruits coming from economically impoverished backgrounds
and the lower echelons of society, economic prosperity simply serves

as bait, while commingling with other extremists will supposedly solidify the faith of new recruits.[2]

To get a sense of the levels of destitution, in Afghanistan—which was so poor that the World Bank didn't even estimate its gross domestic product between 1981 and 2001—Bin Laden's purchasing power could buy an army of 15,000 soldiers for a meagre US$35,000 a month.[3] That's US$2.33 a person *per month*, which is egregiously lower than the commonly denoted extreme poverty line of "a dollar a day."

More than 70 percent of Afghan youth said unemployment was their biggest challenge, and with declining private investment, the formal labor market struggles to absorb the 400,000 Afghans who join the workforce each year.[4] For these individuals, drivers such as poverty are far from eliminated or sustainably addressed through military interventions. On the contrary, warfare and other commonly utilized methods of force compound the problem, which is the scarcity of legitimate and viable economic opportunities.

Nigeria, which is among the top five countries most severely impacted by terrorism as measured by the Global Terrorism Index (GTI), shares parallels with Afghanistan's economic landscape. ORB International conducted a face-to-face survey of 3,910 people between December 2016 and January 2017 in the northeastern parts of the country that have been regularly attacked by Boko Haram militants. Unemployment was deemed the most critical problem, followed by the interrelated issues of rising prices and corruption. Joblessness ranges between an astounding 42 and 74 percent in the three states surveyed.[5]

Reassuringly, the researchers found over 83 percent of Nigerian Muslims to be unsupportive of extremist groups, and an overwhelming 97 percent indicated that they had a negative view of violent extremists.[6] So how does one explain the discrepancy between the survey responses and Boko Haram's appeal? Whereas religion was less of a determinant, unemployed respondents were more than twice as likely to sympathize with extremists than their employed counter-parts—regardless of their level of education. One is hardly puzzled by the fact that 58 percent of survey respondents cited income and employment as the number one reason people join Boko Haram.[7]

Given the international community's preoccupation with defeating terrorist organizations, the systemic issues motivating individuals to join them tend to be overlooked. Mindful of this relative neglect, the UN conducted a study on the motivation of foreign-trained fighters (FTFs) traveling to join Daesh in Syria. Disappointingly, only seven UN Member States chose to cooperate by facilitating access to the FTF returnees. Nevertheless, between August 2015 and November 2016, the United Nations Centre for Counter-Terrorism (UNCCT) managed to interview forty-three individuals representing twelve nationalities.[8]

While the study acknowledges the small sample, the research suggests that the vulnerabilities created by marginalization facilitate recruitment by transnational terrorist organizations who brandish an effortlessly attainable vision of a new life. It is difficult to comprehend the extent of delusion that would lead any reasonable person to believe that employment in the world's most dangerous war-zone would be effortless. Who are these fighters, and what are their profiles?

Most FTFs interviewed in the study were young males lacking an advanced education—46 percent had not even finished high school. They were mostly farmers and small business owners, operating on the fringes of society and relatively isolated from mainstream economic, social, and political activity. Half of them earned less than US$500 a month. Only one of them—a criminal gang leader—made more than US$4,000 a month. According to the report, these were the five main motivations for joining Daesh:

- Material and personal interests, such as cash payments in the form of a salary, food, accommodation, furniture, and other rewards given to fighters for "good work."

- Ideological and faith motivation. *Faith* and *ideology* here refer to the desire to learn and study the Shariah and join religious classes run by Daesh for its members because "they had been largely denied religious education under the [Government of Syria]."

- Daesh's ability to bring security, reduce crime, and achieve equality in the areas under its control through the embrace of a strict Islamic code.

- Purification and cleansing, especially of past sins, and;

- Fear of a worse alternative.[9]

So, to summarize, the FTFs were driven by the fulfillment of basic needs like food, shelter, and income, the desire to receive a religious education—which they had been denied—human security and protection, a purification of sins, and the fear of remaining in a deteriorating environment. Corroborating the UN study findings were researchers at the Combating Terrorism Center (CTC) at West Point, who found that approximately 65 percent of Daesh foreign fighters did not have an education beyond high school, and almost 90 percent were either unemployed or engaged in low-skilled work.[10]

In Jordan, a report entitled "Trapped Between Destructive Choices: Radicalization Drivers Affecting Youth in Jordan" by the West Asia North Africa Institute (WANA) found that young people perceive their viable earning options to be limited to "either *jihad* or drugs." Ostensibly, jihad is the nobler of the two. The data is based on findings from focus group discussions with fifty-two youth (thirty-three males and nineteen females), including sixteen Syrian refugees. For the young Syrians in the focus groups, the key drivers appeared to be idleness and unemployment, with one participant sarcastically asking "Where would anyone who finished high school go? To university [in tone implying that this is not an option for Syrian refugees in Jordan]?! A Syrian refugee cannot work here, so what would he do?!"[11]

Richard Branson didn't go to university either, but one can only imagine what the business opportunities and investment landscape must be like in refugee camps and conflict zones. It reminds me of a bad joke where a US Navy personnel member, recounting his deployment to Afghanistan, facetiously describes the nightlife in Kabul as "explosive." What are the rates of startup success when one must incorporate bombings and power disruptions into one's business plan? Risk and uncertainty are taken to another level. Talent retention takes on a whole new meaning. If anything, these obstacles make entrepreneurs more resilient and innovative, but how eager are investors to funnel their funds into high-risk areas and avert the far greater global risk posed by the lack of jobs and economic opportunities?

Gender dynamics also dictate pressure. Men who are either unable to marry or unable to meet their family's needs are encouraged by their wives and mothers to join militant groups. This has been true for Iraq, Nigeria, and other societies in which men are expected to be providers and feel emasculated by their socioeconomic impotence.[12] One can easily empathize with the frustration of youth burdened with the shame of being unemployed or unemployable and the inability to become a family provider or to get married.

ENTER: DAESH

Amid a scarcity of legitimate economic opportunities for disenfranchised and displaced persons who are unable to escape an abyss of despair, along comes Daesh, parading its utopia as an equal opportunity employer. Having amassed more than US$2 billion in wealth at one point, it is not hard to see how, or why, Daesh attracted so many to its informal and superficially lucrative labor market, particularly during its 2015 heyday, when it was winning territories and the social media war.[13] Fighters were promised free cars, homes, municipal services like waste collection, water and electricity, food and groceries, healthcare, matrimonial matchmaking services, and a competitive tax-free salary.

They were also beguiled with greater freedom—no home mortgages, kill whoever you want, and have sex with an assortment of sex slaves. It's the dichotomous appeal of an ungoverned space that continues to fulfill the patriarchal social contract being rewritten in many Arab countries that face fiscal deficits and difficulties in meeting their population's socioeconomic needs. Daesh even offers a form of life insurance—promising to pay benefits to families of martyrs and soldiers killed in battle.

Regrettably for the recruits, much like the infamous "Nigerian prince" emails that prey on the financially desperate, Daesh is selling a scam. Returning FTFs lament the lack of material possessions and freedoms promised to them—including steady jobs and salaries, furnished houses, and even wives. For six of the interviewees in a UNCCT study, it was precisely this failure to deliver on its promises that contributed to their decision to leave Syria.[14] Had the FTFs conferred with other former violent extremists, they would have discovered that disillusionment with this endemic corruption, and the opportunistic nature of terrorist organizations, far precedes the Daesh era.

Jessica Stern, who spent four years interviewing multireligious extremists in prisons, refugee camps, and madrassas for her 2003 book *Terror in the Name of God: Why Religious Militants Kill,* exposes the moral justifications used by terrorist groups—such as those that accumulate riches through so-called jihad but serve the rank and file bad food and operate in dirty offices to feign their financial deficits. One of her interviewees says that, initially, he thought his leaders were serving a religious cause:

> . . . now I feel they are running a business. They are . . . suppliers of human beings. They use poor and illiterate boys for their own private cause and call it jihad. . . . The . . . real methods for raising funds is smuggling of goods through Afghanistan, Iran and India.

This includes drug trafficking. . . . . The mujahideen bring with them
many smuggled items such as cosmetics and . . . electronic goods
from Afghanistan and Pakistan to raise funds.[15]

Another disaffected member says, "Initially I was of the view that
they were doing jihad, but now I believe that it is a business and people are earning wealth through it. . . . I thought [the leaders] were
true Muslims, but now I believe that they are fraud, they are selling
Islam as a product. . . . First I was there for jihad, now I am there for
my financial reasons."[16]

WEAK STATES AND SOCIAL SERVICES

Oversimplifying the "poverty equals terrorism" argument would be
misleading. However, unstable governments, chaos, and lawlessness
are precisely the fertile ground in which mass mobilized terrorism can
thrive. Excessive military force only serves to further weaken fragile
and failed states, setting in motion a reinforcing cycle of violence and
economic abyss. By comparison, economic development expands a
new middle class. In this scenario, communities that may have previously supported terrorist organizations experience the first-hand
benefits of maintaining peace and naturally inhibit local support for
terrorists by refusing them the space in which to operate.

Prior to the US invasion of Iraq in 2003, for example, there was
no Al Qaeda presence. Daesh would have had neither the license to
operate nor the social capital to recruit local fighters in a more stable environment that was economically more inclusive of Sunnis.
Social capital is a pivotal enabler for radical organizations to build
their support base by fulfilling the socioeconomic needs of vulnerable
and marginalized groups. In Palestine, for instance, Hamas secured a
wide support base for a variety of reasons, including the provision of
social welfare. Hezbollah's support in Lebanon is similarly attributed,
in large part, to its role as being a more reliable social welfare provider

than the state. In addition to providing orphanages, social assistance programs, micro-credit lending, and broadcast news, this paramilitary group provides free healthcare, education, agricultural assistance, and at times, even municipal services like garbage collection and water.[17]

When a weak state cannot, or does not, provide for its people, other organizations may emerge as ad hoc social welfare providers. While nonprofits also emerge in response, organizations with the financial means to effectively fill this void are typically terrorist and resistance groups. Providing womb-to-tomb services increases their political legitimacy and represents an implicit form of coercion and silencing dissent, as the local population is so reliant on the ad hoc welfare provider.

Impoverished families in Pakistan, for example, don't have the luxury of opposing the hand that literally feeds them. Confronted with the impossible choices of perpetuating an intergenerational cycle of poverty as their emaciated and malnourished children grow into uneducated adults, devoid of dignity and even proper clothing, or "jihad," many parents choose Option B. In other words, they choose the possibility that they *might* improve their children's prospects for a better life. Unfortunately for them, opportunity cannot be untangled from militancy and the indoctrination of the notorious madrassas. But parents can seek solace in the religious blessings to be bestowed upon their offspring.

ECONOMIC EXCLUSION

One interesting finding that emerged in a World Bank study—contrasting with conventional perceptions and definitions of poverty—was that unemployment among the educated leads to a greater probability of radicalization.[18] Therefore, the researchers hypothesize that it is not poverty that is a driver of violent extremism, but rather economic exclusion or inequality. This phenomenon is particularly pronounced in Western European countries that have one or two dominant immigrant groups such as Algerians in France, or Moroccans and Turks in the Netherlands. In 2013, France's national statistical agency found that the unemployment rate for all immigrants was almost double the nonimmigrant rate. Similarly, a Stanford University study concluded that a Christian citizen in France is 2.5 times more likely than a Muslim citizen with the same qualifications to get called for a job interview.[19] In Nigeria, Boko Haram also prospered amidst the socioeconomic (and other) inequalities between the underdeveloped and mostly Muslim North and the relatively better-off and predominantly Christian South.[20] In such a context, reestablishing an Islamic caliphate becomes a wonderland where all the grievances of the disenfranchised related to perceived inequality will melt away.

Underemployment is another form of relative deprivation that receives considerably less attention. In Tunisia—which exported the highest number of FTFs to Daesh territories—out of an estimated 700,000 job seekers, 200,000 were university graduates competing to fill just 79,000 low-skill vacancies.[21] While similar parallels can be found in other countries like Argentina, where many qualified MDs work as taxi drivers, it is important to note that no singular variable can be isolated from a more complex system of interrelated factors conducive to terrorism. For Tunisia in particular, this is elaborated in Chapter 8.

Nonetheless, epitomizing relative deprivation due to inequality is the textbook tale of a young man in Kyrgyzstan who completed a computer science degree with distinction only to find himself employed as a village school teacher.[22] Noble as the role of an educator may be, imagine the mismatch between one's hopes and expectations of working at, say, Google, which are then torpedoed by the reality of nepotism and labor market discrimination.

In other words, when one ticks all the boxes of what society expects, is competent, and sees opportunities that are available, it is far worse when those opportunities are specifically unavailable *to you*. Daesh then presented a far more exciting job prospect for this young man, which instantly elevated his self-esteem and actualized his potential. Up to this point, I had been optimistic that there would be a silver lining and that the peace-building organization that I spoke with who recounted this story had managed to reclaim this computer science graduate, but I have been told that after he left for "ISIS territories," no one knows what happened to him.

The interplay between these economic conditions and extremism is not unique to Islam; it is univerally human. Throughout history and the present, we have witnessed the consequences and manifestations of displaced frustration with economic deprivation or exclusion—whether perceived or real, absolute or relative. For instance, Nazis scapegoated the Jews following Germany's humiliating World War I defeat. While more recently, the term *alt-right* incidentally first emerged in November 2008, which was also the year of the worst global financial crisis since the Great Depression of the 1930s. When the filmmaker of the documentary *White Right: Meeting the Enemy* asked the National Socialist Movement (NSM, an American Neo-Nazi political party) why they moved to Detroit, this was their response: "It's the perfect time to recruit for NSM because of the economic decline."[23] And as Europe navigates the fourth industrial revolution with mass automation of jobs, an aging population requiring greater public expenditure, and reduced economic productivity, we have seen the rise of xenophobic groups, and even Brexit, where many Britons voted to leave the European Union, signaling both economic protectionism and a disposition for monoculturalism.

Ultimately, although terrorism and violent extremism are more than just economics, neglecting these systemic grievances and failing to account for their consequences—sometimes even exacerbating them—will present us with recurring and more ominous permutations of the problems we are attempting to annihilate. According to Hriar Cabayan, who runs the Pentagon's Strategic Multilayer Assessment (SMA) program—including a counterterrorism unit that taps the expertise of 300 scientists from academia, industry, intelligence agencies, and military universities—the US counterterrorism strategy of decapitating insurgency leadership and bombing terrorist strongholds is fundamentally counterproductive.[24]

Based on Cabayan's analysis, if Iraq's economic and social infrastructure continues to deteriorate, a global war on terror that has, to date, cost US$4 trillion will continue, and "The Sunnis in Iraq have a genuine grudge ... They were left out of the Shia-dominated government that we set up; they are under attack, nobody is protecting them. We can and should provide off-ramps for defeated ISIS members—safety, jobs, civil rights. If not, after the fall of Mosul, we will be facing ISIS 2.0."[25]

BORN A TERRORIST

No one is born evil or a terrorist—and it is in our self-interest to examine the circumstances that can drive people to such extremes. It saddens me to reflect on the potency of desperation—particularly when it is entirely unavoidable, given our ability to reallocate the resources to meet those very reasonable and basic human rights and needs through legitimate means. The individual is certainly responsible for their actions, but aren't we collectively responsible for providing alternatives?

Unlike the suicide attackers mentioned in the previous chapter who are seeking otherworldly riches, many terrorist recruits appear to be far more practical. And we are failing them. Terrorism may be a tactic, but the conditions driving terrorists are systemic and deeply entrenched. Alarmingly, employing brute force aggravates these influences as opposed to containing them. These observations warrant a more weighty consideration of socioeconomic factors when designing preventative measures. But first we must accept the existence and legitimacy of these nonideological elements, and adopt a systems-thinking approach by incorporating them into our military and policy decision-making. By recognizing that Daesh and other terrorist groups often fail to provide what they falsely advertise, we are well-positioned to provide an alternative that is more conducive to human security—that of the prospective terrorist's, and that of our own.

6

DIS-INTEGRATED

A rising mass movement attracts and holds a following not by its doctrine and promises but by the refuge it offers from the anxieties, barrenness and meaninglessness of an individual existence.

—ERIC Hoffer, *The True Believer*[1]

IN AN ONLINE forum, Umar Farouk Abdulmutallab wrote, "I do not have a friend, I have no one to speak to, no one to consult, no one to support me, and I feel depressed and lonely. I do not know what to do."[2] These were not the words of a societal outcast or an only child. As the son of the First Bank of Nigeria's former chairman, Abdulmutallab grew up in a large and affluent household with sixteen siblings. He may have been surrounded by people, but evidently, he did not feel "seen."

The nineteen-year-old found both the fraternity he was lacking and the answers he was seeking in an internet chat room. There, a series of exchanges led him on an adventure to an Al Qaeda training camp in Yemen. Then, under the direction of US-born Muslim cleric Anwar al-Awlaki—who, it appears, is perpetually preoccupied with what is in one's underpants—Abdulmutallab, aka the "underwear bomber," attempted to detonate a bomb aboard a Detroit-bound flight from Amsterdam on Christmas day. Unfortunately for Abdulmutallab, his inventive flair for an otherwise more traditional airline bombing method backfired.

The underwear bomber's affliction of loneliness is one example US Army Colonel and psychologist John M. Venhaus cites in a 2010 United States Institute of Peace (USIP) Special Report.[3] Like me, Colonel Venhaus was preoccupied with understanding who seeks to join terrorist groups like Al Qaeda, and why, rather than how to defeat terrorist organizations. After extensively studying the interviews and personal histories of 2,032 foreign fighters, he came to the following conclusion: "Potential recruits have an unfulfilled need to define themselves. Al Qaeda's ability to turn them to violence is rooted in what each seeks: Revenge seekers need an outlet for their frustration, status seekers need recognition, identity seekers need a group to join, and thrill seekers need adventure."[4] The four archetypes Venhaus identifies are applicable not only to Al Qaeda or Daesh, but also to gangs and other criminal groups operating at the fringe of society.

If one were to hazard a guess as to which of these types was the most prevalent among the fighters flocking to join terrorist groups, revenge and adventure seekers would perhaps be the most logical assumptions. That assumption would be incorrect. Status seekers, on the other hand, represented more than 25 percent of the sample. Venhaus continues, pointing out that mounting prejudice and mistrust of Middle Easterners (and Muslims) only exacerbates their humiliation, as well as their fervent need for validation. But as it turns out, status seekers were also not the most common archetype in the sample.

Most prevalent were those in pursuit of an identity—the need to define oneself as part of a group. The same need for brotherhood and belonging that drives those joining a club, or a platoon, is what compels identity seekers joining terrorist groups. Like social animals forming packs and prides, many isolated individuals have been drawn to extremist groups for the amplified feeling of power through belonging to something larger than they are. Adding to that is the enticing prospect of "finding oneself" in adventure: *What if I am an undiscovered superhero? All my life I have gone unnoticed and undervalued, but here is a group giving me the opportunity to reinvent myself.* And what could be more epic than the nobility of a holy warrior bringing about Armageddon?

Preventing radicalization, the USIP report suggested, could be addressed through the provision of groups for the identity seekers to join, like sports leagues, model governments, student societies, community service programs, and adventure groups.[5] One might posit that such groups and clubs are readily available options—if not in Iraq and Syria, then at the very least in Western countries. So why have the latter still exported significant numbers of foreign fighters?

As the examples in this chapter will depict—both empirically and anecdotally—perpetual marginalization steers many into the wicked embrace of violent extremism. That is neither to justify nor displace the responsibility of the individual over their decisions. We can debate free will, and cast moral judgment, but ultimately, what I intend to reflect is "what is," so we can be more active participants in the peacefulness of our communities.

CONNECTING THE DOTS

On Maslow's hierarchy of needs, the importance of belonging ranks directly after safety and physiological needs like food and water. Social connection is a fundamental part of human nature. It's why many men I have known to leave the US Navy reenlist shortly thereafter—for the brotherhood and to belong to an honorable group of men with whom they lead and serve. It is somewhat ironic that the US military excels at fostering camaraderie—potentially powerful ammunition against terrorist recruitment—yet fails to utilize this powerful knowledge in its fight against terrorism.

Meanwhile, juxtaposed with images of brutality, Daesh positions itself as an idealistic, emotionally fulfilling place of familial belonging. Propaganda videos feature a motley crew of foreign fighters waving their guns against the setting sun in a postcard-like screenshot, subtitled "Wish you were here." An evolving Islamic street slang on social media draws in the white millennials through a "Jihadi Cool."[6] Instagrammers depict fighters playing with kittens and women bemoaning the lack of acceptable fashionwear.[7] Cue here the controversial BBC *Revolting* skit "The Real Housewives of ISIS": "Does this suicide vest make me look fat?"[8]

In reality, many of those chasing pipe dreams of an Islamic utopia are sorely disappointed. In the previously mentioned UN report that interviewed returning foreign-trained fighters (FTFs), many returnees spoke of the rejection they felt—particularly if they were not referred or sponsored by someone well-known in the group. In seeking to escape prejudice, the freshmen quickly learned that Daesh territories were no more welcoming. The grass is not greener on the other side, it is greener where you water it, and the so-called Islamic State was an infertile haven for the inclusivity and diversity it masqueraded. At least half of the FTFs in the study departed for these reasons.

One of the most eminent terrorism experts, psychologist and former CIA officer Marc Sageman, thoroughly investigates the phenomenon of isolation in his 500-page book *Turning to Political Violence: The Emergence of Terrorism*.[9] Using news reports and court trial transcripts, Sageman constructed biographies and profiles for 172 Al Qaeda operatives to expose "the human behind the militant," as it were. From his data set, patterns began to emerge. Most of the men had a mainstream religious upbringing in middle- to upper-class families. Most had been radicalized in the West. And, the most counterintuitive of conclusions—even for Sageman—the initial drivers of enlistment were neither religious ideology nor political grievances.

During a debriefing on his research to the September 11th Commission, Sageman posited his *"halal* theory of terrorism." That is, socially and emotionally alienated individuals find belonging in places of congregation and community, like mosques, and begin to build friendships over halal meals and activities. One-upmanship likely played a role in the increasing radicalization of men trying to outdo one another.[10] Since "lone wolf" terrorism in the West poses a greater risk than foreign-perpetrated attacks, one should consider the conditions likely to escalate this phenomenon.

REMARKABLY UNREMARKABLE

A report prepared by the NYPD Intelligence Division, *Radicalization in the West: The Homegrown Threat*, describes America's "lone wolves" as mediocre: "The majority of these individuals began as 'unremarkable'—they had 'unremarkable' jobs, had lived 'unremarkable' lives and had little, if any criminal history."[11] Namely, the NYPD findings were as follows:

- *It is a phenomenon that occurs because the individual is looking for an identity and a cause and unfortunately, often finds them in the extremist Islam.*

- *There is no useful profile to assist law enforcement or intelligence to predict who will follow this trajectory of radicalization. Rather, the individuals who take this course begin as "unremarkable" from various walks of life.*[12]

Peter Bergen delightfully chronicles the stories and profiles of some of America's unremarkable and self-radicalized lone wolves in his book *United States of Jihad*. In kaleidoscopic detail, Bergen describes US Army Major Nidal Hasan's mediocre and unnoticed existence, saying he "passed through high school like a ghost, making few friends or lasting impressions."[13] After graduating from Virginia Tech with a degree in biochemistry, Nidal entered a US Army officer-training program in Texas with the intention of heroically serving his country. His lackluster—and often very contentious—performance at work was offset by his stellar performance in religion. Bergen's book recounts a local real estate agent seeing Hasan at the 4:30 a.m. dawn prayer service: "[He] used to score all the points in Islam: He did the prayers. He read the Koran. He listened to lectures. He was one of those perfect guys who did everything right."[14]

In 2009, at Fort Hood, Texas, Major Nidal Hasan committed the deadliest mass shooting to ever take place on an American military base. Some years later, in an HBO documentary, *Homegrown: The Counter-Terror Dilemma*, Nidal's cousin, Nader Hasan, reflects on the precipitating event, which he believes to have been the prospect of Nidal's imminent deployment to Afghanistan and Nidal's feelings of conflictedness.[15] In Nader's view, Nidal had a death wish; Islam, could exonerate him as a sinner, and exalt him as a winner.

Put another way, according to Bergen's analysis: "He was about to turn forty, with no prospects of marriage and no children. His parents were both dead; he had few, if any, real friends; and he was about to be sent to a war zone where Americans were killing Muslims. Suicide was against his religion, but what if he went out in a blaze of glory as a martyr for his religion ...?"[16] Illustrating these delusions of grandeur are the business cards Major Hasan printed appointing himself as "Soldier of Allah."[17]

Another example is Tamerlan Tsarnaev, an alienated Chechen American who could neither relate to Americans, nor had a single American friend. With the dream of becoming an Olympic boxer, Tamerlan had become the Golden Gloves heavyweight champion of New England and one of the top amateur boxers in Massachusetts.

But a rule change that began prohibiting non-US citizens from competing in the national championships shattered his dreams and knocked out his purpose. Tamerlan's photo essay entitled *Will Box for Passport* gives some indication of his desires for self-actualization through representing America.[18] Feeling denied of the opportunity to do so, he retaliated with a counterpunch against the country that had rejected him by masterminding the Boston Marathon attack in 2013.

An extensive five-month investigation by the *Boston Globe* revealed other dysfunctionalities as well, like the stigma of mental illness that led Tamerlan's parents to downplay his schizophrenia.[19] Social exclusion was not the only contributing factor here—nor in Major Hasan's case—and in general, there is never one isolated factor, but a confluence of many. Yet patterns are discernible. Moreover, as these narratives illustrate, the perpetrators were not initially observant Muslims. As they became more "devout," they appear to have found mainstream Islam to be insufficiently "remarkable," or extreme enough to satiate the depth of their emptiness and fulfill their lofty needs for validation.

And perplexing as it may be that women have also been drawn to extremist groups—particularly Daesh—the appeal is, somewhat oxymoronically, the desire for greater agency over one's life and an outlet for self-expression. Extremist groups offer women a renaissance from marginalized victims, to fighters and lionesses raising the cubs of the caliphate. Guns and weapons give women the illusion of power. And much like the men seeking camaraderie, the women seek sisterhood. One Jordanian woman noted, "for us, it is either joining 'jihad' or committing suicide."[20] As of 2015, around 250 Americans have attempted to join violent jihadists in Syria; according to government estimates, one in six are women.[21]

And while homegrown attackers tend to be of immigrant descent, there are also several puzzling cases of white American violent extremists, such as Colleen LaRose, aka Jihad Jane; Californian-born Adam Gadahn, who was a senior Al Qaeda operative; and the Catholic-baptized "American Taliban," John Walker Lindh. Aside from their skin color, they share a commonality with a large number of politically violent people throughout history who have acted on behalf of a larger societal segment—whether "jihadis," "anarchists," "liberators," "defenders of the constitution," or "defenders of unborn babies." They were loners.[22]

VIOLENCE STARTS WITH DISCONNECTION

Cultivating empathy is among the most critical skills for a future-fit society. And it is challenging to ascertain exactly why some of us who were bullied at school become more emotionally intelligent and adept leaders and human beings, whereas others go on a school-shooting rampage. Scanning headlines of tragic school shooters, we often see things like "Shooter was depressed loner," "Mass shooter was bullied teen loner," "School shooter was quiet loner," and "School shooter described as angry loner."

There are, of course, anomalies, and as with terrorism, the reasons are complex and cannot be oversimplified. Similar to the nuances between relative and absolute poverty, seemingly socially integrated shooters and terrorists exist as well. Before becoming an al-Shabaab leader (a Somali Al Qaeda affiliate), Omar Hammami was popular enough to become class president and date one of the prettiest girls in school. White American Zachary Chesser, who was convicted for aiding al-Shabaab, was also one of the cool kids; a US Homeland Security report attributed his wrongdoings to his upbringing, and the fact that he was an attention-seeker who lacked direction in life.[23] Jaelyn Young, an African American from Mississippi who was intercepted upon trying to join Daesh, was a fun-loving cheerleader and a singer; she was also on homecoming court and part of the robotics club.

But one of Jaelyn's robotics teammates made a revealing observation. Despite being surrounded by people, "A lot of times, she seemed almost lonely."[24] Jaelyn's mother had noticed her daughter's self-mutilated legs; razor scars signaling self-harm and suicidal thoughts. Often those surrounded by many people can feel the loneliest and most disconnected, just as people in empty marriages and relationships can feel lonelier than those who are single. Loneliness and isolation—like poverty—are not necessarily an externality, but often an inner reality—which is much more difficult for an outsider to ascertain. It's why many veterans have such an impossibly difficult time reintegrating into society and often express feeling alone in a crowd.

Recognizing that all violence begins with disconnection, ever since the tragic Columbine High School Massacre in 1999, one teacher (who teaches the son of bestselling author, Momastery blogger, and activist Glennon Doyle Melton) preemptively monitors loneliness. Disconnection can be external and emotional. So during her weekly ritual, the teacher conducts a ballot in which students privately write down the names of four other children they'd like to sit next to the following week and one exceptional "classroom citizen" student who they believe should be honored. Week on week, the teacher analyzes the names, looking for the children who are being overlooked. The ones who have suddenly been socially ostracized and have fallen from peer favor. The ones continuing to drift to the fringes of isolation. The ones who give no names at all; the ones most at risk.[25]

ISLAM(OPHOBIA) DRIVES TERRORISM

According to the 2016 Global Terrorism Index (GTI), the primary drivers prompting 31,000 people from all around the world to converge in Iraq and Syria to join extremist groups are a strong sense of isolation and difficulty assimilating into Western culture.[26] In considering the military research conducted by West Point's Combating Terrorism Center (CTC) study, we also learn that 70 percent of the foreign fighters who left their countries to fight in Daesh territories are immigrants coming from specific subculture communities in the West. Moreover, 41 percent of homegrown jihadists in the West also come from these subcultural enclaves.[27] These numbers are very telling.

Based on the data, and the anecdotes, one may deduce that this is a problem of immigrants. It's not. As the CTC study itself highlights, this is a problem of communities. It is the multigenerational diaspora enclaves with limited connections and integration within mainstream society. Whether the isolation is self-imposed by the immigrants or whether the diasporas are indeed societal outcasts is irrelevant. As the researchers pointedly remark: "Placing blame for this lack of connection is unproductive. It exists and, based on our data, appears to play a role in the radicalization and mobilization of foreign fighters. Solutions need to take these dynamics into account if governments are to effectively confront the foreign fighter problem now and in the future."[28]

If Islam—and the ignorance of it—has something to do with terrorism, then we would be equally remiss not to concede that Islamophobia is also intricately interlinked with terrorism. As it turns out, discriminating against people who are struggling to culturally assimilate can make them more susceptible to extremism. These were the findings of Stanford University social psychologist Sarah Lyons-Padilla, who conducted a study surveying approximately 400 Muslim immigrants living in the US and Germany. "We found that immigrants who identify with neither their heritage culture nor the culture they are living in feel marginalized and insignificant. . . . Experiences of discrimination make the situation worse."[29]

These findings reinforce previous studies, like the work of Arie Kruglanski, at Maryland University, who posited that people can be psychologically motivated to commit acts of terror to restore a sense of significance and a feeling that they matter—something extremist organizations are adept at promising them.[30] Therefore, making immigrants feel valued and desegregated—as opposed to making them feel like strangers in their homeland—is critical to neutralizing the appeal of militant groups.

Given the charged immigration issues in the US, it is absolutely imperative to highlight that although second-generation immigrants tend to have higher crime rates than first-generation immigrants, overall, numerous studies have found immigrant crime rates to be lower than that of the local born population in America.[31] Analysts have largely attributed this to the relative assimilation of immigrants in suburban multiethnic communities, compared with their European counterparts.

Though its cultural diversity may comparatively seem to be under threat, the US has historically been a country of immigrants. Consequently, there is a more mainstream multicultural American identity. In fact, just the Muslim population in America comes from seventy-five countries, according to a Pew Research Center study—meaning that Islam is not dominated by a single sect or ethnicity.[32] The American-Islamic blend of traditions breeds tolerance, not only within the community but also beyond. Fifteen percent of American Muslims who are married or living with someone have a spouse of a different faith.[33] Paramount to America's security is ensuring that this cultural fusion continues.

Cautioning against complacency, the NYPD report *Radicalization in the West: The Homegrown Threat* warns that "Muslims in the U.S. are more resistant, but not immune to the radical message."[34] According to a 2009 study, around half of a nationally representative sample of Mormons, Protestants, Catholics, Muslims, and Jews agreed that, in general, most Americans are prejudiced towards Muslim Americans—who are more than twice as likely to say they experienced discrimination.[35] A decade later, a higher proportion of Muslims (61 percent) than any other faith group (or nonaffiliated groups) reported experiencing some frequency of religious discrimination in the past year, according to the Islamophobia Index.[36]

Across the Atlantic, the circumstances for Muslim immigrants are bleaker. Around 60 percent of European Muslim violent extremists are second-generation immigrants who are displaced between their culture of origin—to which they don't fully belong—and the Western societies in which they live. Encouragingly, third generations tend to be better integrated and account for only 15 percent of homegrown violent extremists.[37]

A 2008 *Foreign Policy Association* article entitled "Analysis: Homegrown Terrorism in the U.S. and UK" analyzed the comparative assimilation in Britain and the US in correlation with the homegrown Muslim extremism.[38] In the UK, large numbers of disenfranchised youth living in lower-class homogenous and isolated ghettos viewed themselves as "other" than British. This otherness and isolation was found to make youth more susceptible to recruitment by militant groups that are able to fulfill a sense of belonging.[39] The NYPD report also underscores this dynamic:

> *Europe's failure to integrate the 2nd and 3rd generation of its immigrants into society, both economically and socially, has left many young Muslims torn between the secular West and their religious heritage. This inner conflict makes them especially vulnerable to extremism—the radical views, philosophy, and rhetoric that is highly advertised and becoming more and more fashionable among young Muslims in the West.[40]*

Sandra M. Bucerius, an associate professor at the University of Alberta who spent five years studying predominantly Muslim Turkish, Moroccan, and Albanian drug dealers in Germany, examines the relationship between social exclusion and immigration policies. Having personally interacted with these young misguided men in cafes and bars, and having even hung out with them in the streets, Bucerius witnessed first-hand the conflicted identity of the young men trying to reconcile their Muslim identity with the contradictory place they have assumed in German society. Her book *Unwanted: Muslim Immigrants, Dignity and Drug Dealing* highlights the constant fear of deportation felt by most second-generation immigrants born in Germany between the 1970s and '90s, who live as "perpetual foreigners."[41]

Unfortunately, as with most discrimination, these are systemic, deeply entrenched, and intergenerational problems. Despite increasing attention and research on such issues, they have not yet entered the mainstream political consciousness and prompted more enlightened policies and practices. Even as far back as fifteen years ago, a study entitled "France and the Unknown Second Generation: Preliminary Results on Social Mobility" showed that while social mobility does exist from one generation to another, the social status of second-generation immigrants remains static and inferior.[42] Today, immigrants are still trying to be French; society won't let them. That was the conclusion of a much anticipated 600-plus page report published by the National Institute of Demographic Studies, which found that second-generation immigrants of mostly African origin faced persistent discrimination and inequities in housing, education, and employment.[43]

In the previously referenced USIP study, Colonel Venhaus gives the example of a young North African who travels to Europe with the hope of finding an egalitarian society that offers him upwards socioeconomic mobility. As the young man dutifully sends money back home, he is consistently dehumanized and reduced to mere cheap labor. One young Moroccan declared, "I was like a slave in France. I could work in the kitchen but was not welcome in the dining room. When I left my neighborhood, people avoided me on the street as if I were unclean."[44]

When a Daesh member of North African descent was asked what had provoked him to join the group, he replied that he was fed up with the hypocrisy of Western governments—proclaiming the importance of human rights and religious freedoms, while relegating Muslims to second-class citizenship. "In Europe, look how we have been treated . . . I wanted to be in the society I grew up with, but I felt, 'You're just the Muslim, you're just the North-African, you will never be accepted.'"[45]

So when the award-winning reporter Souad Mekhennet—who is herself a first-generation German of Turkish-Moroccan descent—challenged this young man, he questioned her, saying, "You really believe that the West respects us? Treats us Muslims equally? . . . I've read your stuff. You interviewed the head of Al Qaeda in the Islamic Maghreb. Why are you just a reporter? Why don't you have your own TV show in Germany? Why are you not making a career in Germany, with all the awards you've won?"[46] He is not entirely incorrect. It's not a stretch to equate the fact that an award-winning journalist with numerous accolades and prestigious fellowships—including being selected a Young Global Leader by the World Economic Forum—is not as celebrated in her home country because of her religion and ethnic background.

CLASH OF CIVILIZATIONS: MOROCCO VS. MOROCCANS

A superficial analysis may lead one to the "clash of civilizations" hypothesis. Or perhaps Moroccans are simply militant by blood? After all, it seems to be *the* problematic immigrant community in France and Belgium, and evidently other European countries. Interestingly, Morocco ranks 122 on the GTI and is among the countries categorized as "suffering no impact from terrorism."[47] This category also includes Norway and Costa Rica. So unless this absurd clash of civilizations is between Morocco and Moroccan immigrants, such reasoning is fallible.

As the Moroccan Professor and political Islam specialist Mohamed Chtatou points out: "This is a European problem. These terrorists were born and raised in Europe, but the European countries had rejected and oppressed them. They do not feel at home neither in Europe nor in Morocco, therefore, face a crisis of identity. And become easy prey for radical Islam. . . . They [extremists] are looking for people experiencing problems with identity, which Europeans do not accept. Then they begin to brainwash, claiming that in fact they have a Muslim identity, and that they will be [sic] Paradise."[48]

Dissonance between Islamic and liberal values could possibly be another line of reasoning and justification. However, when the Bertelsmann Foundation in Germany conducted a cross-country survey involving 14,000 participants, the data showed that most European Muslims strongly believe in democracy and religious diversity.[49] Upon deliberating this fact, it makes a lot of sense. One would imagine that when one immigrates, one chooses a country that is appealing in both the freedoms and opportunities it offers. Especially when framed within the context of Islam's democratic principles of governance embedded in seventh-century Medina. Despite this, according to the Bertelsmann Foundation's research, 61 percent of ethnic Europeans believe that Islam is incompatible with Western liberal values. The study notes,

Yet while many of Germany's four million Muslims are quite open, there is increasing animosity toward them on the part of a majority of the German population. Germany's Muslims suffer from a negative image, presumably shaped by the small minority of radical Islamists who account for less than one percent of all Muslims. Islamophobia is not a marginal phenomenon, but can be found throughout society. When it is considered socially acceptable, it can be used to legitimize discrimination against and exclusion of the Muslim minority. Regular personal contact can help to overcome prejudice against Muslims—but opportunities for such contact are often lacking.[50]

For any individual, community, or society who believes themselves to be either powerless or absolved of contributing to the complex web of radicalization drivers, take note. Perpetual marginalization, loss of dignity and hope, and dehumanization breed extremism. We, as societies that exclude, are effectively pushing individuals to the fringes. There, they find those who accept them, befriend them, and restore their purpose and dignity. I emphasize the "complex web" because it is not as simple as cause and effect. Just like poverty does not equal terrorism, social exclusion does not necessarily result in terrorism. Otherwise, why isn't there a transgender terrorist group? What about refugees—who, amidst the US Immigration debate, have played no role in any jihadist attack in the US since 9/11? Surely they are the epitome of multilayered exclusion and cultural displacement?

EMPATHY

As I pondered why one person radicalizes over another, one story that really touched me was that of Zak Ebrahim—also known as "the terrorist's son." In his moving book, Ebrahim describes an upbringing wrought with domestic abuse, bullying, and intolerant rage.[51] His father, the Egyptian-born El-Sayyid Nosair, shot and killed Meir Kahane, the extremist rabbi who founded the Jewish Defense League, when Ebrahim was just seven years old. Three years later, while in prison, Nosair helped mastermind the 1993 World Trade Center bombing.

Throughout Ebrahim's childhood and adolescence, his family moved more than twenty times, denying him the opportunity to really fit in anywhere. As the perpetual new kid in class, Ebrahim was subjected to the cruelty of teenage bullying and excluded from the stereotypical tightly knit high school cliques. His mother remarried a man who, in his reverence for Nosair's heroism and prestigious status in the "servant of Allah" hierarchy, seemed to be jealous of Ebrahim. The stepfather would exhibit bizarre behavior—including following Ebrahim and subjecting him to scar-inducing beatings.

Here is an individual who is the son of a notorious militant—a legacy, if you will—who is socially withdrawn and suicidal and excluded from Western society. Why didn't he become a suicide attacker or look to militant groups to self-identify? Before meeting Ebrahim, my analysis was that many terrorist- and martyrdom-prone youth come from relatively moderate households—religiously speaking. Even those raised in abusive environments have not witnessed radical

Islam and the first-hand realities and brutality of a terrorist organization like Daesh in the way that perhaps Ebrahim had. With this ignorance comes a naive idealism that lends itself to romanticizing the embrace of the militant brotherhood, compared with their current exclusion. In other words, they had felt greater marginalization from society and family but had not yet become disillusioned with militant Islamist groups. Indeed, after experiencing those realities, many Daesh recruits returned, as the previously aforementioned studies have outlined.

Most influential for Ebrahim, however, was his increased interaction with diversity. Through this antidote to his isolation, he was able to cultivate empathy for the suffering and exclusion of others—namely because of his own hardships. Ebrahim describes a summer job at Busch Gardens, working with a gay colleague who turned out to be "one of the nicest and least judgmental people" he had ever met, and another instance where he realized the friend he had made at a summer youth convention was Jewish.[52] He even notes the irony that watching *The Daily Show* with Jon Stewart—whom he came to see as a positive male role model and *father figure* (let that sink in for a minute)—forced him to confront his bigotry against Jews.

Had his isolation and lack of interaction continued, Ebrahim may have fulfilled an alternative destiny. Instead, his own suffering enlightened him to the fact that we all suffer, and that all human beings have common needs and desires. Through this transcendence, Ebrahim followed a very different path than his father's. He became a voice for moderation, a peace campaigner, and a true Muslim—even though he now self-identifies as agnostic.

Our knee-jerk reaction is to keep rejecting problematic individuals, but intensifying their isolation only aggravates their hatred. Denationalization—or stripping away a person's citizenship—represents this exclusion in its deepest and most extreme manifestation. Aside from dispersing a relatively locally contained problem internationally, denationalization also limits options for humane and legal redress.

Moreover, by becoming their enemies, naturally, we make it easier for them to rationalize harming us. So like-minded rejects and misfits cluster together and find camaraderie in these fringe groups and with societal pariahs. Numerous studies—including a UN study[53]—have found social networks and friendship circles to be the most powerful mechanism through which terrorist recruitment occurs. And yet we continue to alienate. We are ignoring the commonly cited influences for joining Daesh, which frequently include notions of "social injustice" and "unfair access to opportunity."[54] One FTF returnee says this:

I was not thinking about leaving for Syria or anywhere really. But when I went to renew my passport, they told me I couldn't renew it for security reasons. No one would tell me what those reasons were. But without a passport here you are doomed. For example, you cannot get a job because nobody will give you a letter of good conduct, which is needed to get a job. Without a passport, you also cannot buy property, open a business, borrow money, or even get married; you are nobody without a passport. What other options were left for me? I was prepared to put my hands in the hands of the devil. This is why I left for Syria, to see whether life there was better. If it had been, I would have brought my family. But life there was not better."[55]

This demonstrates that although Muslim immigrants in the West may feel socially excluded, they do not represent the greatest source of violent extremists. Even in—and particularly in—their countries of origin, many Islamic militants feel politically alienated and disenfranchised by their respective governments. Before the bloody conflict, Syria's youth were largely apolitical. Through witnessing atrocities and injustices, like most of us, their only hope in humanity became hope in themselves, compelling them to become a force of social and political change. "When I was in my fourth year in university in Syria, I joined a military faction to get rid of a bigger enemy (the regime), even though I did not support that faction's ideology," explained one

Syrian refugee while being interviewed for a West Asia North Africa (WANA) Forum study on radicalization drivers affecting youth in Jordan.[56]

For these reasons, we need to bring the outcasts back into the fold of society—including bringing them to justice and rehabilitation where applicable. Extremists are only capable of reaching violent proportions when they are incapable of or discriminate in their empathy and compassion. This enables them to dehumanize others and rationalize acts committed to achieve noble, or self-actualizing, outcomes. In failing to apply the morals we hold terrorists to, we risk becoming that against which we are fighting.

7

MIRROR, MIRROR

DURING THE ARAB Awakening in 2011, some of the youth activists protesting their governments for greater equality, dignity, and freedom began intimidating the villages in which they lived. For example, they began threatening their neighbors with punitive measures, such as Molotovs, should someone violate an antigovernment "work strike" to try to earn an already meager living. The irony is that in fighting state-imposed oppression, marginalization, and economic inequality, the activists ended up perpetuating and deepening this very injustice.

Most individuals believe themselves to be morally upright, acting in defense of virtue. In reality, both sides of any conflict fail to recognize that they often end up embodying that which they oppose and defiling their moral and religious values in the process. We see this in wars that proclaim to be spreading freedom through repressive means and with activists who have legitimate grievances and are fighting against oppression. As the award-winning author and journalist Barbara Ehrenreich reflects in one of her two dozen books, *Blood Rites: Origins and History of the Passions of War,* "from the point of view of any particular side, in any particular war, the enemy may indeed be seen as a repulsively different Other. But the differences are often almost imperceptible to an outsider. . . ."[1]

Consider this verse from the Quran: "And when it is said to them, 'Do not cause corruption on the earth,' they say, 'We are but reformers.' Unquestionably, it is they who are the corrupters, but they perceive [it] not" (2:11–12). Upon reading this, I interpret my "side" as the "reformers," and Daesh as the "corrupters." Meanwhile, Daesh unequivocally counterinterprets this very same verse. In reality, it is about neither "us" nor "them." The verse was intended for a historical point in time that elapsed some 1,400 years ago. And yet perception is reality, and our fanatic, unwavering, and intoxicating belief in our own self-righteousness is precisely what provokes us to justify violence for a noble outcome.

This unsymmetrical perception can be partially explained by the *fundamental attribution error*, or *correspondence bias*. We overemphasize personal characteristics and the intentions of others, while ignoring the external or situational factors when judging their behavior. In other words, we are inclined to believe that people do bad things because they are bad people; their actions reflect who they are. However, if we are the ones acting less than favorably, we are obviously doing so for a justified reason.

To use a benign example, if one is speeding or cutting people off on the road, it's because one is rushing to school to pick up a vomiting and feverish child, for instance. Seldom does one berate oneself with thoughts like, *I am such an inconsiderate driver. What an arrogant road jerk I am! I could have caused an accident.* Instead, one thinks, *I'm being a protective and compassionate parent. I need to be there for my little boy. He must feel so awful.* We often fail to imagine these situational factors—except when we watch movies. Which is why we can still root for characters who would be considered villains or wrong-doers had we not been given a window into their lives.

Based on empirical data and anecdotal evidence on the push and pull factors driving terrorists, one may empathize with—without condoning—why many have gravitated towards militancy. Nonetheless, I must confess, I struggle to find an iota of humanity in Daesh leaders, and to be unbiased, as it were, in my own judgment. On first reading the harrowing accounts of Yazidi women sex slaves who had escaped the terrorist group, and the indescribably sadistic torture and execution methods, I found myself thinking, *Bin Laden actually seemed moral compared to Baghdadi.* And I am not alone in this assessment.

Before becoming one of the world's most wanted fugitives, many who knew Bin Laden described him as a mild-mannered, humble, and moral individual.[2] Coming from a large family, Bin Laden—one of 29 siblings—was often brought in as the peacemaker and arbitrator for the inevitable large family disputes. His siblings expressed great admiration for him—though they did not necessarily approve of his violent acts.[3]

Paulo Jose de Almeida Santos, a Portuguese Muslim convert who was recruited by Al Qaeda to assassinate Zahir Shah, the exiled king of Afghanistan, recalls the planning of the operation. This was approximately ten years prior to 9/11, and Santos asked Bin Laden what he should do, hypothetically, if the King's grandson happened to be present during the assassination attempt. Bin Laden was furious: "What are you saying? We are Muslims, we do not eliminate children!" Bin Laden added that he would rather have the exiled King return to Afghanistan and risk a civil war than to kill a child.[4] In another interview Santos revealed that, while he was studying synthetic poison at a medical library in Pakistan, there had been some debate over testing the poison's effectiveness on captured spies. When they sought a theological opinion on the matter, apparently the religious cleric almost kicked Santos and furiously declared, "You want to do such tests on human beings? Do you think we are Nazis?!"[5]

Similarly, when asked about killing American civilians Bin Laden answered: "No. The American government is one thing, the majority of Americans don't even vote, they are totally apathetic."[6] Moreover, when it was proposed that Al Qaeda line its pockets through drug trade, Bin Laden condemned destroying families in the West as a means to obtaining money (the Taliban's drug policy bore no such considerations).[7] And yet something pushed Bin Laden to harden his stance and renounce his empathy and compassion for those outside his "in-group."

Ayman Al-Zawahiri—Al Qaeda's current number one—reportedly told Bin Laden that the US would never take him seriously if his demands were reasonable. In other words, wanting foreign troops to withdraw from Saudi Arabia is something most Americans could sympathize with. Instead, Al-Zawahiri urged Bin Laden to issue a *fatwa* (religious edict) targeting all Americans and Jews. Al-Zawahiri reasoned that "The West, led by the US, which is under the influence of the Jews, does not know the language of ethics, morality, and legitimate rights. They only know the language of interests backed by brute military force. Therefore if we wish to have a dialogue with them and make them aware of our rights we must talk to them in a language they understand."[8]

I don't entirely disagree with Al-Zawahiri's assessment. I have read similar sentiments with regards to Conservatives losing elections since George W. Bush because they have been "too nice." Trump's lack of political correctness resonated with many ordinary Americans and may have even been viewed as imperative for the Conservative Party's restoration of power.[9]

In *The Management of Savagery,* which continues to form a cornerstone of the contemporary terrorist curriculum, chief Al Qaeda strategist Abu Bakr Naji similarly favors the excessive use of force over moderation, reasoning that either way, "Our enemies will not be merciful if they overcome us. So it behooves us to make them think a thousand times before fighting us."[10]

Initially, however, Bin Laden was unreceptive to the notion of considering every American to be his enemy. Unfortunately, as Al-Zawahiri predicted, Sandy Berger, the National Security Advisor during the Clinton administration, ignored an Al Qaeda statement calling upon

Muslims to kill Americans and steal their money. Berger even mocked Bin Laden's capability to harm Americans; Al Qaeda responded with the 1998 US embassy bombings in Nairobi.[11]

WHY DO YOU HATE US?

When Americans questioned "Why do they hate us?" following 9/11, the Bush administration claimed that terrorists hated freedom. Bin Laden responded through his "Message to the American People" in 2004 and in another message just days before the 2004 US elections. He asked, incredulously, how, three years after 9/11, the public were still allowing the President to deceive them—obscuring the real causes behind the attacks. Bin Laden added that the attacks were a last resort after he could not take it anymore. [12] Could not take what anymore?

Luckily, Bin Laden was neither making a cryptic declaration nor playing mind games. He broadcast the roots of his anti-Americanism, which dated back to 1982, following the US-backed Israeli invasion of Lebanon: "I couldn't forget those moving scenes blood and severed limbs, women and children sprawled everywhere. Houses destroyed along with their occupants and high-rises demolished ... as I looked at those demolished towers in Lebanon, it entered my mind that we should punish the oppressors in kind and should destroy towers in America."[13]

In another 2004 interview Bin Laden admits he had never actually intended to destroy the Twin Towers but was compelled to act following the accumulated atrocities in Palestine and Lebanon. He continues, saying that the whole world watched as the tragic events unfolded in 1982 (Chapter 3) and rhetorically asks if self-defense can truly be called terrorism.[14] By "the whole world," Bin Laden is referring to the US and its allies, masked by the "unjust United Nations," all of whom he believed to be systematically targeting Muslims.[15]

Bin Laden also qualifies his actions, saying, "What I seek is what is a right for any living being: that our land be liberated from enemies, liberated from the Americans. God gave every living being the instinct to reject invasion by outsiders." [16] As far as Bin Laden—and many other violent extremists—is concerned, the American government had become synonymous with " . . . pictures of one-year-old children with their heads cut off . . . whose members have been amputated . . . the children who died in Iraq, the hands of the Israelis carrying weapons that destroy our children." [17]

Many Muslims—and non-Muslims for that matter—are acutely aware of the Grand Canyon of disregard for non-Caucasian human life. Just as Americans asked "Why do they hate us?" the Lebanese were equally perplexed, asking why Americans hated them in 1982. Once an ally of the US, the Lebanese were shocked to find Made in America shell casings saturating the debris following the devastating bombardments by Israeli forces.[18] Since 1976, Israel has been the largest recipient of US military assistance, and between 1948 and 2013, the US has provided Israel with some US$233.7 billion in aid (after adjusting for inflation).[19] This has not escaped the attention of the Arabs or the Muslim umma.

Al Qaeda's spokesman Suleiman Abu Ghaith wrote of America's arrogance and asked how the world could find it so puzzling that a country that uses terror itself eventually falls victim to its own actions: "For fifty years in Palestine, the Jews—with the blessing and support of the Americans—carried out abominations of murder, suppression, abuse, and exile. The Jews exiled nearly 5 million Palestinians and killed nearly 260,000. They wounded nearly 180,000 and crippled nearly 160,000. Due to the American bombings and siege of Iraq [a reference to the UN sanctions placed on Iraq after the first Gulf War], more than 1.2 million Muslims were killed in the past decade." He continues, saying that leveling the death toll would give Al Qaeda the right to kill four million Americans—including 2 million children—and to exile millions and wound hundreds of thousands.[20] That is equivalent to approximately one 9/11 every day for three and a half years.

In Afghanistan, more than 10,000 civilians have been killed or injured—not since the 2001 invasion, but in just one year: 2017. UN officials only started documenting the casualties in 2009, and since then, over 28,000 civilians have been killed and more than 52,000 wounded.[21] And in Iraq, war and occupation directly and indirectly claimed the lives of about a half-million Iraqis from 2003 to 2011.[22] Imagine instead if half a million Americans had been killed, in America. Or even half a million US soldiers in Iraq during that same period? The numbers are incomparable. US military casualties numbered 4,500, which is less than 1 percent of the Iraqi death toll. And Iraq's population is around ten times smaller.

By no means am I advocating a leveling of the death toll or wishing ill or harm on any civilian or military personnel. But in taking a moment to reflect on the extent of how one 9/11 has been painfully chiseled into the memory and psyche of Americans, can we empathize with the provocation of feelings—without condoning the consequent actions? September 11th continues to be memorialized, and likely will be until the end of time. Most Americans know someone who has been affected or have lost a loved one or a colleague. Everyone living in the US at the time remembers where they were when the planes hit. New Yorkers remember the fear, panic, vulnerability, disorientation, displacement. Running for cover from a deluge of raining debris in lower Manhattan. Unable to find a taxi. ATMs not working. Phone lines are down. *Am I going to die today*? And the worst part was waiting for something worse to happen. I recall twelve of us packed into a walk-in-closet-sized single dorm room in the East Village, watching the news as we strategized whether it would be safer to stay in the city that had already been targeted, or to risk traveling to nearby states and encountering another attack en route.

Months later when I volunteered at Ground Zero, rescue workers were still sorting through rubble and pulling out human remains. Enduring this is sufficiently distressing for those directly and indirectly affected. Now imagine going through this four or five times *a day* for a little under a year. The anguish of watching loved ones killed, drowned, or raped as you try to flee. Imagine fleeing to unimaginable thirst and starvation as you fight for a life whose value in living you have seriously begun to question. These are ordinary civilians, like us. Families, spouses, children, friends—not soldiers. And this is what Iraqis endured for 290 days during the takeover of Mosul.

To dislodge Daesh, Iraqi forces, backed by heavy coalition fire-power, spent more than nine months using "annihilation" tactics in an offensive that was described by US officials as the most intense since World War II.[23] US-led coalition forces carried out more than 1,250 strikes in the city, hitting thousands of targets with over 29,000 munitions. By the time victory was achieved, Mosul's civilian deaths had reached thousands—though the exact numbers have not been acknowledged by the US-led coalition, the Iraqi government, or Daesh. Fortunately for humanity, keeping count are Mosul's grave-diggers, morgue workers, and volunteers who retrieve bodies from the city's eight million tons of rubble—which is three times the mass of the Great Pyramid of Giza.[24]

America has around 325 million citizens in all fifty states. Arabs number around 400 million across twenty-two Arab states. And yet the destruction, disruption, and insecurity the region endures is beyond compare. It is easy to become desensitized and glaze over the numbers of casualties in a part of the world where this has some-how become an expected norm. Ironically, the more "out of the ordinary" an attack is, the more media sensationalism and sentiment of solidarity surrounds it. Peace in the Middle East is an unrealistic and unattainable aspiration. This sort of thing happens all the time, and because of its frequency and greater degree of devastating impact, its significance is somehow diminished.

Alternatively, to reconcile and placate a restless conscience, we proclaim the greater good. Like the US-led offensive on Mosul. Aside from the long-term consequences and new grievances this has planted—which we will no doubt reap in coming years—I wonder how many of us could accept losing the person we loved most in this world because it was speculatively going to make the world safer? And the real ammunition in what is already a heart-wrenching situation is that I am not convinced it *does* make us safer. If victory means a short-term territorial or military defeat then, yes, perhaps. We annihilated the cancer with cell-destructive chemo and radiotherapy but neglected to transform our regimes to ensure the cancerous cells don't return. We overlooked the fragility of our current state, and our increased susceptibility to disease, because in decimating the bad, we also extinguished the good. We are likely to have planted an entirely new slew of grievances for a reinvented Daesh, or some other group, to emerge. One such group—Hay'at Tahrir al-Sham— has already self-assembled in Syria, as a merger between five Islamist organizations.[25]

Moreover, inflaming the blind rage of grief even further is the apathy of the US and its local and international allies for failing to offer any indication that they will undertake a comprehensive survey of the loss of life in Mosul. No significant steps have been taken to compensate the families of the "collateral damage" inadvertently killed by "friendly forces" as the smallest token of acknowledgement that their lives were of value.[26] In December 2017, the Associated Press estimated the civilian casualties in Iraq to be 9,000 to 11,000—nearly ten times higher than previously reported. At least a third of the blood is on the hands of coalition or Iraqi bombardments.[27] And if it were possible to be even more unbelievably and satirically perverse, the survivors are unable to obtain death certificates proving the demise of their loved ones. After unearthing their bodies, which have been reduced to meat and bones under the piles of rubble, they are told "What's this? We need to see faces."[28]

These are the moral double standards that immortalize extremist ideologies and enrich a historical gallery of grievances, which interminably curates injustices and outrage.

SELECTIVE COMPASSION

Many of Bin Laden's statements explicitly point to Western apathy towards Muslim spilled blood as a justification for violence. In his "Message to the Peoples of Europe" Bin Laden says: "In what creed are your dead considered innocent but ours worthless? By what logic does your blood count as real and ours as no more than water? Reciprocal treatment is part of justice, and the one who initiates hostilities is the unjust one."[29] In another interview in 2002, Bin Laden says, "When we kill their innocents the entire world from east to west screams at us. Who said that our blood is not blood, but theirs is . . . ? Who has been getting killed in our countries for decades? More than one million children died in Iraq and others are still dying. Why do we not hear someone screaming or condemning, or even someone's words of consolation or condolence?"[30] Bin Laden also tells them that "security is a vital necessity for every human being. We will not let you monopolize it for yourselves."[31] Without endorsing his actions, Bin Laden's words plainly evoke raw emotion.

Like the many foreign fighters flooding into Syria to join Daesh in defense of the atrocious injustices against their in-group, it is not that Bin Laden *lacked* the capacity for empathy, but rather, that he began to discriminate in his empathy. It is this prejudice that best predicts intergroup violence, according to neuroscientist Emile Bruneau, who researches cognitive biases driving intergroup conflict.[32]

Bruneau's work has attracted interest and funding by diverse institutions, often with opposing agendas, like the United Nations, the US Institute for Peace (USIP), the Soros Foundation, the US Defense Advanced Research Projects Agency (DARPA), and the Office of Naval Research. Having tested the effects and differences between in-group empathy and out-group empathy in three contexts (Americans regarding Arabs, Greeks regarding Germans during the Greek financial crisis, and Hungarians regarding Muslim refugees during the refugee crisis), Bruneau came to an enlightening conclusion.

In all three settings, the participants' feelings of empathy for the suffering of random out-group members correlated with an increase in their willingness to help those out-group members and a decrease in their willingness to harm those members (for example, making donations to civilian victims of drone strikes). However, when participants experienced empathy for the *suffering* of their *in-group* it predicted the opposite: *less* willingness to help random members of the out-group, and *more* willingness to inflict harm on members of the out-group.[33] In other words, violence begets violence.

Sean Hannity asks, in his book *Deliver Us from Evil: Defeating Terrorism, Despotism, and Liberalism,* "How many noble freedom fighters target innocent women and children? How many build torture chambers in the basements of their official buildings?"[34] Collectively, the answer is probably many of them—no matter how unwittingly. In gross violation of fundamental human rights principles outlining the proper conduct of terrorist offense investigations, terror suspects are unlawfully abducted, denied access to a lawyer or fair trial, mentally and physically tortured, and subjected to inhumane and degrading treatment in secret detention sites around the world. This global system, which was largely designed by the US government, totally violates both international and domestic laws. University of North Carolina Chapel Hill Law School students compiled the traumatic comprehensive briefings outlining the narratives of thirty-seven such extraordinary rendition and torture victims.[35]

Among them is Fatima Bouchar, who was four months pregnant when she was wrongfully detained, interrogated, and tortured for many months. Her captors delivered her and her husband to be tortured in Libya in one of Gaddafi's prisons. Bouchar was tortured to the point of threatening her baby's survival. Today, she and her husband have rejected a settlement offered by the UK government because it failed to provide an official apology and semblance of accountability from all the governments involved in Bouchar's treatment. Without the acknowledgment of the suffering she, her husband, and baby were subjected to, a settlement would be meaningless.[36]

Another victim, Sharqawi Abdu Ali Al Hajj, was electrocuted, severely beaten, and threatened with sexual abuse, dogs, and snakes. He was penetrated in the anus, made to wear a diaper, handcuffed and shackled to the wall, placed in solitary confinement in a two-foot-by-three-foot wooden cage with no toilet, and detained at the Dark Prison, where he was subjected to loud music and complete darkness, and was force-fed whenever he refused to eat. As of 2017, Al Hajj had been in US custody for twelve years. One his attorneys, John Chandler, commented on his deteriorating condition, saying, "His health is ruined by his treatment by or on behalf of our country. He can eat little but yogurt. He weighs perhaps 120 pounds. The United States of America has lost its way."[37]

Abu Yusuf, a Daesh leader who supervised the group's hostage program, told a female reporter that the US invasion of Iraq in 2003 had been unjust: there were no weapons of mass destruction, Iraqis were tortured in Abu Ghraib, and the Americans faced no consequences. "Then they're pointing at us and saying how barbaric we are." In his eyes—and no doubt, heart—Abu Yusuf believed his group of freedom fighters would liberate Muslims from oppression by Western powers. "If the U.S. hits us with flowers, we will hit them back with flowers. . .But if they hit us with fire, we will hit them back with fire, also inside their homeland. This will be the same with any other Western country."[38]

Contrary to these gross abominations of humanity, I would venture to say that many, if not most, American soldiers are altruistic in their motivations. To be willing to die for a belief or cause and prevent suffering is a benevolent display of courage and compassion. Even more so when one considers the warrior's honor code that many soldiers strive to embody—in which they hold themselves to the ultimate ethical and moral standards, even in life-threatening situations.

At the US Naval Academy's Department of Leadership, Ethics, and Law, students make a vehement distinction between a *warrior* and a *murderer*, according to Professor Shannon E. French. "Almost without exception, my students insist that a 'warrior' is not a 'murderer.' They can even become emotional in the course of repudiating this (intentionally provocative) potential synonym. It is very important to them to be sure that I understand that while most warriors do kill people, they never murder anyone. Their remarks are filled with contempt for mere murderers," she observes.[39] As far as these soon-to-be naval officers are concerned, murder is committed in cold blood out of hate or without noble reason against the unarmed and innocent. A warrior, on the other hand, knows how to control his anger, only kills in battle when it is unavoidable, and does not take advantage of the weak.[40]

COUNTERTERRORISM BY ANY OTHER NAME

So where does that leave us? Both sides are pursuing what they believe to be moral outcomes using immoral means. Both sides dehumanize the enemy. These cycles do not end with force. They end with justice. Indeed, counterterrorism is terrorism by another name, and it is counterproductive. A UNESCO peace publication, *Blue Dot*, notes that "All forms of violent extremism seek change through fear and intimidation rather than through peaceful means."[41] Should we, then, consider all those who seek change through fear and intimidation rather than through peaceful means to be violent extremists?

Another Security Council Resolution in 2001 "reaffirms its unequivocal condemnation of all acts, methods and practices of terrorism as criminal and unjustifiable, regardless of their motivation, in all their forms and manifestations, wherever and by whomever committed," and "underlines that acts of terrorism endanger innocent lives and the dignity and security of human beings everywhere."[42] We read these security resolutions framing "the others" as terrorists without considering "the other" may be reading them, too, and despairing that humanity and the world has turned their back on them. It is by some remarkable feat of faith, grace, and resilience that the majority of those subjected to these unforgiving circumstances *don't* end up turning to violent extremism.

This is particularly remarkable when it doesn't take a "special type" of individual to commit evil. We are all capable given the right circumstances. The reader may be familiar with the Stanford prison experiment, illustrating what social psychologists like Albert Bandura call *situationism*. Drawing on studies of violence from across the human sciences, Bandura concluded that "it requires conducive social conditions rather than monstrous people to produce atrocious deeds. Given appropriate social conditions, decent, ordinary people can be led to do extraordinarily cruel things."[43] In the experiment, the researchers aimed to test the hypothesis that it was the inherent personality traits of prisoners and guards that primarily caused abusive behavior in prison.

Twenty-four psychologically stable and healthy male college students were recruited for a two-week prison simulation. The participants were predominantly white middle-class and the study intentionally excluded those with criminal backgrounds. They were assigned roles randomly as either guards or prisoners. As their roles developed, some of the "guards" began enforcing authoritarian measures and demonstrating sadistic behavior—ultimately subjecting some prisoners to psychological torture. Some prisoners passively accepted the abuse and became withdrawn, whereas others—at the guards' request—actively harassed other prisoners who tried to stop the torture. This escalation occurred in a matter of just *five days*. It stands to reason that the real-life prison sadism and torture that take place are exponentially more cruel.[44]

Even innocent children are not immune, as the equally renowned "blue eyes brown eyes" experiment demonstrates. The day after Martin Luther King Jr.'s assassination, a third-grade school teacher in

Iowa conducted an exercise to teach her all-white class about discrimination. Jane Elliott designated the blue-eyed children as the superior group, giving them special privileges, such as second helpings at lunch, access to the new jungle gym, and five extra minutes at recess. The blue-eyed children sat in the front of the classroom, and were encouraged to only play with one another.[45]

The brown-eyed children were not allowed to drink from the same water fountain as the blue-eyed children. And Elliott chastised and singled out the brown-eyed students when they made mistakes. At first, the blue-eyed students resisted the notion that they were superior to their brown-eyed peers. That is, until Elliott lied to the children, saying that melanin was linked to their higher intelligence and learning ability. Shortly thereafter, the blue-eyed children—believing they really were "superior"—became arrogant, bossy, and unpleasant to their "inferior" classmates. Their grades even improved, while those of their "inferior" classmates suffered.[46]

We have a tendency to believe such experiments don't apply to us and that we would never falter in such a contrived, or real-life, circumstance. There's a name for this over-optimism: *moral overconfidence*. Nitin Nohria, dean of Harvard Business School, explores this phenomenon in the context of CEOs decimated by front-page scandals, like Enron. Using the controversial Milgram experiment as an example, Nohria shows the gap between how people believe they would behave and how they actually behave, essentially concluding that we are far less virtuous than we think we are.[47]

In the Milgram experiment, study participants are instructed to administer increasing levels of electric shocks to a "learner" who answers incorrectly or not at all. The "teacher" and "learner" are separated in two rooms where they can hear but not see one another. After a certain number of volts, the "learner" bangs on the wall pleading for the "teacher" to stop and complains of his heart condition. Then all responses from the "learner" cease. Since the failure to answer a question is subject to an electric shock, the "teacher" is instructed that he must continue with the experiment. In reality there were no shocks, of course, and only prerecorded sounds of escalating anguish from the "learner." What is interesting is that while some footage shows participant "teachers" in the study becoming exceedingly uncomfortable, what allows them to morally reconcile their actions is to absolve themselves completely of any responsibility by confirming that the authority—and not themselves—will be held accountable.[48]

COMPASSIONATE COUNTERTERRORISM

Captain Wayne Porter, retired former naval chief of intelligence for the Middle East from 2008 to 2011, is convinced that the only solution to terrorism is to deal with its root causes. According to him, "The only existential threat to us from terrorist attacks, real or imagined, is that we stay on the current counter-productive, anarchically organised, money-driven trajectory." Porter, who teaches counterterrorism to military officers at the Naval Postgraduate School, adds, "Our current counter-terrorism strategy, which is no strategy, will destroy our democratic values."[49]

Looking in the mirror with dirt on one's face and then proceeding to clean the mirror is an exercise in futility.[50] Terrorism is an ugly reflection of ourselves. We need to stop cleaning the mirror and start addressing the societies and conditions that are being reflected. To do that, we must start with compassion; that is the true radicalism of our time and the most humane and effective counterterrorism strategy we have at our disposal. But what does compassion actually mean? It is not the often-misunderstood notion of an anemic love that overlooks rampant injustice. Rather, it is the motivation or intention of our actions to prevent suffering.

Rooted in this pure motivation, our actions will be just and compassionate. There's a beautiful parable about the Buddha, who, in one of his lifetimes, was a ferryman transporting 500 saints. A thief jumped aboard the ferry, threatening to kill the saints and steal their belongings. So the ferryman swiftly evaluated the situation and concluded *If the thief kills the saints, he will suffer in hell. If I kill him first, I will save the saints and prevent him from creating terrible karma. And my suffering will be less than his.*[51]

How often are we that indiscriminate in our compassion? It doesn't mean not speaking truth or enforcing justice but simply expanding our sphere of empathy beyond victim or perpetrator, us versus them. Effective counterterrorism necessitates this intentionality and compass of compassion to ensure that in fighting terrorism, we do not become and proliferate that against which we are fighting.

8

COUNTERPRODUCTIVE

HOW DO TERRORIST groups end? According to the Global Terrorism Index (GTI), an analysis of 586 terrorist groups that had operated between 1970 and 2007 found that religious groups represented the highest proportion still active between 2007 and 2017. And whereas military or police defeat was the most successful approach in ending left-wing terrorist groups, the same repressive counterterrorism measures achieved the least success with religious terrorist organizations—contributing to the demise of only 12 percent. Of the 586 groups analyzed, 37 percent were left wing, 37 percent were nationalist groups, 21 percent were religious groups, and 5 percent were right wing.[1]

Another study, by the RAND Corporation, which analyzed 648 terror groups that existed between 1968 and 2006, found that military force led to the demise of only 7 percent overall. The sample also comprised religious, nationalist, left-wing, and right-wing groups. Subsequently, one may question instead, what measures *do* have a success rate greater than 7 percent? According to the authors—one of whom is a US Naval Postgraduate School professor—more than

80 percent of terrorist groups ended after either reaching a political solution (43 percent) or as a result of being penetrated and eliminated by local police and intelligence agencies (40 percent).[2]

When it comes to religious groups, not only is unilateral military intervention costly and ineffective, it has proven to be counterproductive. For example, while military operations weakened Boko Haram and Daesh in 2015—achieving a 10 percent decrease in the total number of deaths in both Nigeria and Iraq—subsequently, Boko Haram expanded into Niger, Cameroon, and Chad, increasing the number of terrorism-related deaths in those three countries by 157 percent. Meanwhile, Daesh and its affiliates almost doubled their international presence, from fifteen countries to twenty-eight. Consequently, in 2015, many nations recorded their highest levels of terrorism in any year in the past sixteen years.[3]

Was the military intervention worth creating a more fatal and less contained permutation of the threat it sought to eliminate? I am not entirely certain how the efficacy of such interventions is measured and evaluated, but failing to map systems-level impact is self-defeating when one considers the wider scope of global human security. By systems thinking, I mean approaching and analyzing components as holistic, interrelated, and interdependent parts of a larger system, and studying the effects of changing one part (e.g., military operations against Boko Haram) on other parts of the system (e.g., surrounding countries). A beautiful example of systems-level impact—renowned among sustainability practitioners—is how the seemingly disconnected action of reintroducing wolves in Yellowstone National Park played a role in affecting the entire ecosystem and contributed to altering the park's geography and the course of its rivers.[4]

Dispersing seeds of terror isn't the only repercussion of military interventions. After conducting extensive interviews with imprisoned violent jihadists in the UK, criminologist Andrew Silke noted that while initially they would attribute their involvement to ideological reasons, after speaking with them, he found "out about . . . what was happening . . . in their personal lives, employment discrimination, yearnings for revenge for the death toll of Muslims." Since this is an unpopular outlook with counterterrorism agencies, he adds that "The government does not like to hear that someone became a jihadist because his brothers were beaten up by police or air strikes blew up a bunch of civilians in Mosul. The dominant idea is that if we concentrate on, somehow, defeating the radical Islamicist ideology, we can leave all of the messy, complicated behavioural stuff alone."[5]

History (and common sense) forewarns us that bombing bases and bunkers may destroy people and targets, but never ideologies, and certainly not grievances. Are we perhaps overlooking the possibility that these tactics bankrupt our security deficit by fueling the anger, humiliation, and injustice that immortalizes the dogmas we are fighting in the first place? Data scientists from the Naval Postgraduate School offer some indication that they do. In a social media study, the researchers compared Twitter feeds from Daesh strongholds before and after US bombings. Before the bombardments, tweets targeted their fury at local enemies in the vicinity—such as mayors, imams, police, and soldiers. As the bombs dropped, the tweets rapidly escalated into an international call for the destruction of Western governments and civilians.[6]

Just as the neuroscientist Emile Bruneau would have predicted, empathy for the suffering of one's in-group correlated with an increased willingness to inflict harm on members of the out-group.[7] Moreover, such actions reinforce the role of a protector—in this case, Daesh—with guardianship over the restoration of justice—or at least retribution. Given that Iraqis rank coalition air strikes as a greater threat than Daesh, according to a Pentagon-funded meta study, one can only imagine the implications of a testosterone-driven adolescence punctuated with daily bombings.[8] In the face of this existential threat and injustice, youth are fed the narrative of a Western crusade against the Muslim umma. Can we reasonably expect these young men not to believe this when their day-to-day experience consistently validates this very belief?

Security measures should seek to ensure human security by enhancing life and reducing—even eliminating—vulnerabilities rather than provoking them. Yet as Iraq's military expenditure rose by 536 percent between 2006 and 2015—the largest increase by any country in the world during that period, according to the Stockholm International Peace Research Institute (SIPRI)—this one-dimensional strategy was paralleled with a rise in civilian deaths.[9] As Dr. Yassir Abd Al-Hussein Al-Darweesh, an Iraqi author, journalist, and researcher, notes in the SIPRI report, "Terrorism is not the disease, but the symptom."

While it is abundantly self-evident to me, as an Arab and Muslim, I acknowledge that my opinions and analysis are subject to skepticism. A Donald Rumsfeld–commissioned report, however, might serve as a more credible source. In 2004, Rumsfeld handpicked and directed a Defense Science Board Task Force to review the impact that the Bush-Cheney administration's policies—specifically the wars in Iraq and Afghanistan—were having on terrorism. Most people in the Middle East could have saved them the time and told them that US foreign policy is, inadvertently, a talent and recruitment funnel for extremist groups. And the task force did indeed come to the exact same conclusions—though they seemed puzzled to find that American intervention in the Muslim World had ". . . paradoxically elevated the stature of and support for radical Islamists, while diminishing support for the United States to single-digits in some Arab societies."[10]

Redirecting a portion of military and security budgets towards "soft power" diplomacy, like development projects and addressing unemployment, may have proven to be a wiser allocation of resources. Despite the absence of a direct causal relationship between poverty and terrorism, recent studies in Nigeria indicate that the mere visibility of USAID programming correlated with decreased levels of support for Boko Haram. Conversely, cutting State Department and USAID spending to pay for military interventions with the intention of defeating terrorism could have precisely the opposite effect.[11]

GOOD GOVERNANCE KILLS TERRORISM

State-imposed brutality, human rights violations, and lack of accountability have proven to be similarly counterproductive to counterterrorism efforts, according to an intensive two-year investigation undertaken by the United Nations Development Programme (UNDP), entitled *Journey to Extremism in Africa: Drivers, Incentives, and the Tipping Point for Recruitment.* After an unprecedented number of former recruits (718) in remote, high-recruitment terrorist hotbeds on the African continent were interviewed, data showed that an overwhelming 71 percent of respondents in the study attributed "government action," including "killing of a family member or friend" or "arrest of a family member or friend," as the catalyst triggering their decision to join terrorist groups. Accordingly, those who expressed a significantly lower degree of confidence in democratic institutions and their potential to deliver progress or meaningful change were the most susceptible to radicalization.[12]

Despite Boko Haram's long-time rejection of secularization, the group's extremism did not turn violent until a government clampdown in 2009 killed their group leader, along with 800 of their members.[13] Political opposition in and of itself is, of course, healthy. However, the departure point from which a resistance turns violent is when victims have no effective legal redress and start to become disillusioned with the established political process. Moral outrage is followed by aggression and the activation of a militarized social identity.

After studying thirty-four campaigns of political violence over 200 years, former CIA officer, psychiatrist, and sociologist Marc Sageman found that in 80 percent of the campaigns he examined, militancy was a response to a community threat. Sageman gives the example of a peaceful school protest over cafeteria food, which escalates with the school administration calling the police and responding with force and violence. The conflict now becomes over the escalation of violence and not over the food.[14] This is why it is necessary to understand the context and point of escalation during the Western-led colonial and imperialist violence, which predated Islamist terror groups.

Journey to Extremism concluded that improved public policy and the delivery of good governance by African governments confronted with violent extremism were far more effective counterterrorism responses than the current disproportionate focus on security interventions.[15] As former UN Secretary-General Ban Ki-moon noted, "Missiles may kill terrorists. But good governance kills terrorism."[16] Another popular counterterrorism measure with an adverse effect on good governance is the use of economic sanctions. Intended to disrupt the financing channels of terrorist organizations, sanctions have, in some cases, been successful in exerting pressure on countries to renounce their support of such militant groups. Sudan's eviction of Osama Bin Laden in 1996 is one such example. However, the overall effectiveness of using sanctions to inhibit terrorism has been mixed.

Sanctions often lend to government and state instability, which in turn promotes a terror-prone environment by unfavorably affecting individuals with no ties to terrorism. As one might imagine, the rulers of countries subject to sanctions are typically neither "law-abiding" nor democratic. Therefore, they can deflect the costs of sanctions onto the broader population. These measures then foment anger and resentment, which may incite retaliatory violence.[17] Moreover, when a weak state cannot, or does not, provide for its people, it provides an opening for other organizations to emerge as ad hoc social welfare providers. Naturally, this increases the political legitimacy and social capital of these fringe groups.

Similarly, state-imposed measures intended to cut terrorism finance also impact local populations. For instance, anecdotally, a peacebuilder working in Somalia recalls how the government literally shut down the ocean to deal with piracy and Al Shabaab activity, and simultaneously stifled the economic livelihood of fishermen. While there may be plenty of fish in the sea, this was of little use to the fishermen who were restricted from access. Subsequently, those without terrorist sympathies previously now had a major gripe against the government, and limited options. I should acknowledge that governments and security forces are under tremendous pressure and often make impossible decisions most of us wouldn't envy. Nonetheless, it is essential that we expand our scope and consideration of unintended consequences, rather than viewing our interventions as siloed and disconnected from a wider web of complexity.

LOVE AMERICA, HATE THE GAME

Rumsfeld's Defense Science Board Task Force was also more than likely surprised to learn that Muslims had no cultural diatribes against the US, nor its ideals of freedom and democracy. Rather, the issue was far less ethnocentric. Muslims hate American policies. In particular, they abhor America's one-sided support of Israel and its prejudice against the legitimate rights of Palestinians. Another source of ire exhausting America's credibility is the hypocrisy behind the US's support of certain authoritarian regimes, while it asserts democracy rhetoric elsewhere. Especially when the US's spreading of liberty and freedom comes with self-serving national interests and at the expense of Muslim self-determination—like the anarchy and suffering ensuing from the occupation of Iraq.

If the top findings of the 2018 Arab Youth Survey are any indication, young people across the Middle East—who are overwhelmingly anti-Daesh—are increasingly viewing America as an adversary. The survey gathered insights through 3,500 face-to-face interviews across sixteen of the twenty-two Arab countries (Bahrain, Kuwait, Oman, Qatar, Saudi Arabia, United Arab Emirates [UAE], Algeria, Egypt, Libya, Morocco, Tunisia, Iraq, Jordan, Lebanon, Palestine, and

Yemen). For the first time in the survey's history, the United States has fallen out of the top five allies named by Arab youth, whereas Russia has assumed the position as the top non-Arab ally for the second year in a row. Russia's influence is notably evident in the Levant (Jordan, Palestine, Lebanon), where 31 percent looked to Moscow as a friend.[18]

What may be counterintuitive for Americans is that from an aspirational point of view, the US comes second (after the UAE) as the country young Arabs would most like to live in and want their own country to emulate. Throughout the survey's history, America has consistently ranked in the top five, which further reaffirms that anti-American sentiment is an opposition towards policies, rather than against its people and culture.[19]

Territorial encroachment is another point of contention shared by Muslim and non-Muslim Arabs. After the controversial 2018 US Embassy opening in the international holy city, a Westernized, highly educated Saudi friend of mine lamented on Facebook, "Jerusalem today, tomorrow Medina, then Mecca." Without entering into a debate on why the embassy move was so heavily contested, suffice it to say that it amplifies a cause worth fighting for and garners considerable public support and outrage for terrorist organizations. It also corroborates Islamic prophecies foreshadowing a degenerate era, before Jerusalem is liberated by the return of the Messiah, following which peace and justice finally prevail on Earth. Daesh adeptly exploits these aggregated resentments and offers a "noble" alternative. Causes like Palestine and Iraq become symbols of oppression and occupation, and every action becomes a direct attack on all Arabs and Muslims.[20]

Having built loyalty among Saddam's Baathists as a prisoner during the US occupation of Iraq, Baghdadi unambiguously claims that where Iraq's rulers failed, the Islamic State will deliver. The government's failures, according to Baghdadi, included the inability to reclaim Jerusalem and not preventing the 2003 US-led invasion that delivered the country into the hands of Shi'ites, who were unwilling to mount a jihad against Alawite minority rule in Syria.[21]

As the Rumsfeld report itself concluded, American diplomacy is not facing a problem of communications messaging, but rather a fundamental problem of credibility.[22]

ELIMINATING THE GRAYZONE

Jiujitsu is known as a "gentler" martial art for employing tactics that neutralize an enemy by using the attacker's own energy or weight against them. It is a tactic that Daesh employs adeptly—particularly pertaining to polarization. When I first came across *The Management of Savagery*, I made an assumption regarding the savagery to which the author refers—that of the United States and the West. In fact, the book outlines in blunt and prescriptive detail a comprehensive strategy for the Islamists to incite a state of savagery and total anarchy and to polarize Muslim and non-Muslim populations until the world is neatly divided into one of antagonistic fundamentalists. They call this "Eliminating the Grayzone"—a tactic that ranks so high on the terror group's agenda, it even graced the cover of the January 2015 issue of their online magazine *Dabiq*.[23]

Gray refers to the space between the stark binary spectrum of black and white—in this case, where diversity, inclusion, mutual respect, and coexistence between Muslims and non-Muslims are safeguarded without coerced conformity. Far-right leaders like Marine Le Pen and Geert Wilders—stoking anti-Muslim sentiments and inciting Islamophobia in their constituencies—inadvertently serve as de facto recruitment officers for terrorist groups. And between burkini controversies in France, Danish cartoons insulting the Prophet Muhammad, and the Dutch documentary *Fitna* in which Quranic verses are juxtaposed with violence and terrorism, opportunities to effortlessly capitalize on friction, hate, and fear are not in short supply.

An example of how this influences violent extremists—which came as a surprise, by the following researchers' own admission—is demonstrated in the findings of a study entitled *Radicalization, Laïcité, and the Islamic Veil*.[24] In this study, William McCants and Christopher Meserole asked this question: Why do individuals radicalize? For the purposes of the research, they used data focusing on Sunni Muslims who actively support violent extremist groups and applied machine learning algorithms to identify the "non-linear" and "interactive" relationships between different factors.

According to the study's standardized foreign fighter scores—that is, those who left their native countries to join groups like Daesh in foreign lands—the top five countries producing radicalized individuals were Tunisia, France, Belgium, Jordan, and Lebanon. The latter two are both Muslim-majority countries bordering Syria, so these were not outliers by any means. Tunisia, however, ranked the highest among the top five, and the other two were France and Belgium. Apart from being Francophone countries, these three nations seemed somewhat more random and unconnected. It turned out "Francophone" was a proxy for something else, the researchers deduced—the French approach to "forced secularism," or *laïcité*.[25]

Both France and Belgium had public national debates around whether or not to ban full-face veils, which they ultimately both outlawed. In Tunisia, Ben Ali's secular regime had banned headscarves from being worn in government offices as far back as 1981, but it was unevenly enforced. After Ben Ali's ouster in 2011, the legacy of the veil dominated political discourse in the lead-up to the October 2011 elections. So the three countries with the highest foreign fighter score that do not border Syria were all Francophone, and all had caustic and divisive national debates about legislation enforcing secularism in the immediate period prior to the onset of the Syrian civil war.

Paradoxically, in seeking to nurture nationalism through homogeneity, such policies and debates essentially became a form of self-sabotage. The nature of this political discourse and the narrative it perpetuates—that it is not possible for one's identity to be both pious and Western—plays right into the hands of terrorist recruiters in sending the message that the West is against Islam. At these starkly contrasting outskirts, you cannot be both Muslim and Western. Wearing a veil or a burka diminishes—even nullifies—your Frenchness. You cannot be both against the *Charlie Hebdo* massacre, which killed twelve people, and against the vulgarity of the satirical paper itself.

Dabiq's magazine cover features a photo of Muslim men holding "Je Suis Charlie" signs and the caption reads "From Hypocrisy to Apostasy, The Extinction of the Grayzone."[26] In this state of extinction, society is polarized and devoid of respect, understanding, compromise, and justice. "We don't negotiate with terrorists" is met with "The West doesn't understand the language of ethics and morality, only force and brutality." This creates an impossible and intractable struggle. Accordingly, we need to cultivate and restore this grayzone and have the moral humility and sobriety to consider the perspective and intentions of our opponents, as opposed to acting with self-righteous intoxication.

Since Daesh allegedly orchestrated and/or inspired several terrorist attacks in the United Kingdom, I imagine the group's leaders were bewildered when Sadiq Khan, the Muslim son of a Pakistani immigrant, was democratically elected mayor of London. If a young immigrant is able to see himself in a leader like Khan, and the possibility—the opportunity—for upwards mobility, equality, and acceptance, it makes for a formidable rebuttal of the "us and them" narrative. Similarly, community and interfaith groups rallying to counter the nefarious "Punish a Muslim Day" (which gamified acts of violence against British Muslims using a rewards system) with #LoveAMuslimDay, rewarding points for kindness towards Muslims, reinforce the grayzone.[27]

So while it may have appeared to be insensitive—inflammatory even—to "build a mosque over Ground Zero," which was neither a mosque nor at Ground Zero, and rather a YMCA-like Muslim community center in downtown Manhattan, true victory for the terrorists was not the proposed construction of the center itself. Rather, victory for the terrorists was in the divisive zoning policy.[28] Had America unanimously embraced the center, Islam, and Muslims— disassociating them from the horrific actions of 9/11—that would have been a truer victory over extremists of all religions, races, and political orientations.

And, reluctant an advocate as I am of "click-tivism," in recognizing our interconnectedness, those in the West can help mitigate polarization through broadcasting their acknowledgment of suffering in Muslim countries. For instance, after the *Charlie Hebdo* attacks, the world marched in solidarity and the ubiquitous #JeSuisCharlie hashtags and photo filters permeated social media. A few months later, when Ankara suffered its third high-fatality attack in five months, there was a deafening silence, prompting many to question *Where is the public outcry: 'Je suis Turkey'?* When we are outraged and show solidarity with Paris, our silence is formidably more deafening when there is no outcry for other mounting Muslim human deaths tolls.

In mitigating fundamentalism, one may adopt one of two approaches: counter-balancing with an equally extremist approach as we wildly see-saw in a constant state of flux; or come to a more moderate center that may be less popular, requires greater compromise, greater concessions and discussions—and quite frankly, takes more work. We are partially responsible for the rise of extreme leaders if we choose to alienate those who attempt to rise in a somewhat lonely middle. We may consider supporting and celebrating candidates who are able to embrace bipartisan agendas. *We are more different than we are alike,* said no one who peacefully and sustainably resolved a conflict, ever.

PART III

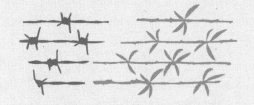

9

SPIRITUAL COUNTERTERRORISM

IN THE WAKE of the attacks on the French satirical magazine *Charlie Hebdo*, which sparked the international hashtag of solidarity #JeSuisCharlie, the onus, UK Secretary of Culture Sajid Javid suggested, was on the Muslim community to do more to tackle terrorism. Saying the attacks had nothing to do with Islam was "lazy and wrong," he added.[1] David Cameron, who was the UK prime minister at the time, echoed the sentiments expressed by his non-practicing Muslim colleague.[2]

They are right. The attacks do have something to do with Islam. Primarily, the ignorance of it. And as Muslims, the onus is indeed on us—principally because we are better-positioned and possess greater religious clout and legitimacy than non-Muslims to cultivate a more holistic understanding of the Quran. So, if we are outraged by the perversion of Islam as the fountainhead of fundamentalism, it is incumbent upon us to leverage Islam as the antidote.

The previously mentioned extensive UNDP study, *Journey to Extremism in Africa,* probed how extremists are able to exploit Islam to justify horrific acts of terror. The problem, they concluded, was not Islam, but rather the ignorance of it.[3] Therefore, it stands to reason that the solution is not "less Islam," but rather a higher-quality religious pedagogy. Quality education overall would synchronously help overcome poverty and unemployment while instilling the critical thinking skills required to deconstruct the context and meaning of violence-oriented scripture and manipulative extremist rhetoric.[4]

But although religious ignorance may hold true for the rank and file, surely the jurisprudence of extremist leaders is intact? In 2014, more than 120 of the world's top Muslim leaders and scholars wrote an open letter to Abu Bakr al-Baghdadi, the leader of Daesh, arguing that the group's practices are not Shariah-compliant. Such allegations are likely to be delegitimized by their source in Baghdadi's eyes—coming from state stooges representing corrupt infidel governments. And with a PhD in Islamic Studies, Baghdadi is persuasively adept at substantiating the group's savagery as lawful. Still, like many who have memorized the 77,800-word Quran—a rich Islamic tradition—mere recitation is a feeble testament to one's profound spiritual comprehension. Millions of Quran memorizers are not even Arabic-speakers—let alone historical experts capable of interpreting the meaning of over 6,000 verses.

Baghdadi is, of course, an Arabic speaker who cherry-picks verses out of context—melding them with questionable *hadith* and the actions of early Muslims into a cacophony of absolute truth. If we conduct earnest self-examinations, we may recognize the tendency to selectively hand-pick information in support of our own narratives to justify peace, compassion, and humanity—as we do with Islam. Not focusing on the Quran in totality hinders our ability to effectively reorient one's passage to violent indoctrination. A holistic approach means embracing and discussing both the relevance and meaning of the Quran's more bellicose verses, because not doing so seriously undermines our credibility.

Consequently, it means avoiding the practice of categorizing and focusing on "good Islam" to counter "bad Islam"—something that preventing violent extremism (PVE) experts have found to backfire and discredit religious preachers and institutions.[5] Such was the case in Nigeria, where the realization came that the long-term defeat of Boko Haram would come neither militarily nor through counternarratives and subsequently catalyzed a pioneering deradicalization program.

Dr. Fatima Akilu, who designed the program, focuses on two critical elements: prevention and rehabilitation. Trained as a forensic psychiatrist, Dr. Akilu has more than twenty years of experience working with offenders. She even counseled John Hinckley Jr., the man who attempted to assassinate Ronald Reagan, while working at a psychiatric hospital in Washington. As she waded into deradicalization work, Dr. Akilu was catapulted into the deep end. Initiating her journey was none other than the chief imam of Boko Haram.

Unlike the many detained "Muslim militants" who had never even seen a Quran before prison, this imam's religious proficiency and cachet endowed him with predictable defiance. Akilu did not attempt to challenge the recalcitrant imam's beliefs. Rather than engage in counternarratives and a tit-for-tat retaliatory debate, she instead canvassed a panoramic view of Islam using the same scripture he used. She taught the Quran within its historical context and the values congruence between Islam and other world religions.

Relearning the holy book in totality, and discovering that its allegories sanctified a wise deference to compassion, forgiveness, and helping others as the pathway to paradise, slowly led the imam to his first major breakthrough. In class, he broke down and began to weep—deeply regretting how he had misled so many people down the wrong path and questioning whether God would ever forgive him. As the spiritual leader of many of the other prisoners, the imam's surprising transformation was instrumental in helping the rest of the group transcend violence.

When I ask whether any forms of exclusion played a role in the radicalization of the detainees Dr. Akilu works with, she emphasizes that the lack of engagement and vacuum of connection is a *massive* theme among Boko Haram joiners. "Religion was never a big factor," she told me. "It was more of a political movement." But those who initially joined for social, political, economic, and identity issues soon found themselves rapidly spiraling into moral destitution.[6]

Although prison deradicalization forms one cornerstone of her work, most of Dr. Akilu's work is on the preventative end. Her foundation, Neem, codesigned an innovative, multilayered early-warning community response mechanism to flag emerging extremist tendencies in consultation with key stakeholders across twenty communities that had produced a large number of Boko Haram recruits. By extrapolating the main reasons youth joined from those communities, Neem was able to create a radicalization index. The have since set up monthly workshops that are organized to equip communities with the tools to identify early signs of radicalization, and, in rural areas far from town and village centers, certain community members are given phones to report unusual behavior.[7]

Moreover, Neem partners with multiple stakeholders to provide youth with alternatives and outlets for expression through different mediums like sports and arts. As well as identifying skills gaps and training, Neem advocates for integration policies that bring government together with society to weave the social fabric and infrastructure around youth, education, employment, gender equality, and working across interfaith communities of Christians and Muslims.

Not many can claim to have successfully deradicalized the chief imam of Boko Haram. I ask Dr. Akilu what the work has taught her. Her most important observation is that in the communities Boko Haram chooses to target, youth have largely been forgotten and left behind. Since Dr. Akilu's undertakings have been exemplified and celebrated as pioneering in international media, I ask how well-funded her efforts are. Sadly, as with most peace-building (and in the social sector more generally), short-term funding cycles and impatient capital disrupt what could otherwise be consistent interventions to sustain long-term change. Peace-building efforts also continue to be fragmented and siloed—meaning that they are disconnected from the bigger whole, sometimes redundant, and create a landscape of interventions that are ten miles wide and one inch deep.

Notwithstanding her financial deficits, Akilu's success in rehabilitation is largely attributed to disarmament through values of compassion and kindness, rather than by engaging in naval or ideological warfare. Others adopting the latter approach have been less successful—despite a greater endowment of resources. In the UK, for example, the controversial Prevent strategy has been criticized for its prejudice, and for making negligible attempts to teach religion in its totality. Rather, its narrative is one that insists on adherence to British values of democracy and human rights over radical religious views. In essence, the perception is that it inadvertently classifies "Britishness," democracy, and human rights as mutually exclusive from Islam, thus feeding sentiments of exclusion.[8]

Described as Orwellian, the program is also said to have pushed law enforcement into the "pre-criminal" space—including discriminatory monitoring, spying, and arbitrary referrals of individuals to deradicalization programs. Singling out the Muslim community, while neglecting to administer the same measures on right-wing radical groups, reinforced the perception that the Muslim umma is being systematically targeted and surreptitiously eliminated. In failing to lead with the British values it was promoting, the program unintentionally bolstered the polarizing narrative peddled by extremist groups—effectively extinguishing the grayzone.[9]

THE MOROCCAN MODEL

One Arab country, which ranked among those "suffering no impact from terrorism" according to the Global Terrorism Index (GTI), has a model worth studying.[10] Especially when, paradoxically, that same country's second-generation immigrants in Europe are among the most vulnerable to violent radicalization. I am, of course, talking about Morocco, which is categorized in the GTI alongside Norway and Costa Rica—the latter being the world's only military-free state. Ranking among the echelons of peace is no easy feat for Morocco, with its 35 million citizens and proximity to Tunisia—a primary exporter of foreign trained fighters (FTFs) to Daesh territories.

Since the 1990s, Morocco has been pioneering religious education and institutionalizing what it deems a moderate and "genuine Islam" that is congenial to the modern world and hallows coexistence with different cultures and civilizations. Deepening spirituality, and cultivating inner transformation and peace from within, through Sufism—or mystical Islam—also elevates the enlightened Moroccan model to another level of consciousness. The reader is undoubtedly familiar with the revered and beloved bestselling Sufi poet Jalaluddin Rumi. A beautiful saying attributed to his enigmatic and sage teacher, Shams Tabrizi, captures the potency of Sufism against insurgent currents of ideology: "If the ka'aba [in Mecca] were suddenly lifted up out of the world, we would see that each person is really bowing [five times a day] to every other person."[11] In honoring the divine in one another, it is impossible for any one of us to reconcile the hate, bigotry, and dogmatism characteristic of violent extremism.

Equally prudent is the recognition by Moroccan authorities that in any form of education, an outstanding curriculum is inconsequential without being delivered by an equally outstanding teacher. Critical to Morocco's success has been its comprehensive reformation and training of imams to guide devotees towards peace and not pathology. In modeling values of inclusivity and equality, the field of spiritual guidance has also opened up to women—*murshidat*—to advise female believers. Graduates of the training are specifically taught to deconstruct extremist discourse and to perform social work.

Since King Mohammed VI's ascension to the throne in 2011, his efforts to revitalize Moroccan Islam have also incorporated two other schools of jurisprudence in addition to Sufism: the Maliki school of Islam, which considers the consensus of the people of Medina in addition to reliance on the Quran and hadith, and the Ashari theological doctrine. Both were chosen for their cultural appropriateness and representation of Morocco's population. Other countries have different intersect nuances and cultural considerations to take into account.[12]

While Morocco's religious paradigm has been effective, and the state has been proactive in targeting inequalities through development programs, it is not without shortcomings. Immunizing the country against the looming threat of homegrown terrorism requires considerable dedication to addressing youth unemployment, socioeconomic and political marginalization, and perceptions of inequality between the French-speaking private-schooled elite and the more economically disadvantaged. "Moderate Islam," without a semblance of societal justice, equality, and dignity, would have proved futile.

In 2005, the government initiated the National Human Development Initiative to lift more than ten million vulnerable people and territories out of poverty and exclusion. And in many cases, the reforms that were intended to create jobs and enhance sustainable human security were designed bottom-up, through comprehensive and broad stakeholder consultations. In parallel, Morocco's vibrant civil society, active private sector, and academia are spearheading counterextremism efforts alongside the government. Projects like *Al Ikram Lil Amal*—Dignity for Hope—work to integrate disadvantaged youth into the labor market and prevent those at risk from falling victim to violent ideologies.[13] Other programs work to rehabilitate and reintegrate former detainees—ensuring that prisons heal and transform individuals and reacclimate them to society. Nevertheless, Morocco's model is by no means perfect nor static, and it must continue to be adaptive and responsive to changing dynamics.

Moreover, while moderate Islam has worked in Morocco, moderation emphatically loses its charm when it is tainted or deemed a proxy for turning a blind eye to either state- or Western-imposed oppression. Moderation can even become a liability. In *The Management of Savagery*, Abu Bakr suggests letting the foolish clerics preach *al wasatiyyah*—the middle way—while extremist organizations entrap the radical idealism of youth.[14]

However, if we reflect on radicalism, we should recognize that it is not necessarily destructive. Winnie and Nelson Mandela were considered radical for their antiapartheid activism. Thomas Jefferson was considered radical in writing the Declaration of Independence and designing a new form of government. Gandhi, Jesus, and many other inspirational and visionary leaders were considered radical extremists during their lifetimes. Questioning deeply held conventional beliefs and systems and venturing to disrupt the status quo are instrumental parts of advancing human progress. Radical energy can yield transformative change when driven by compassion and the service of the societal whole—victim and perpetrator. One social entrepreneur I encountered brings this radical love to life through his—for lack of a better term—"de-radicalization programs."

GOD IS LOVE

Searching for innovative case studies in what seems to be a nascent and perhaps under-reported field, I came across Basit Jamal, who repurposes the power of Islam as the remedy for violent extremism. Jamal unconventionally blends teachings that appeal to a multitude of Islamic sects—including Shia, Wahhabi, Sunni, and Sufi—through his reliance on one absolute source of Islamic authority: the Quran. Unlike extremist preachers who discourage and even disparage questioning and critical thinking, Jamal invites his learners to reflect on, ponder, and deliberate what they are reading and the context in which it was written. In cultivating and deepening one's spirituality in tandem with religious knowledge, Jamal has facilitated the transition of thousands of mindsets from one of "kill your enemy" to one of "turn your enemies into friends."[15]

Unique to Jamal's methods are an intimate understanding of the biases, perceptions, and recalcitrance of an extremist—namely because he used to be one. Jamal does not conform to the typical profile of other radicals described in the previous chapters. He was well adjusted and was neither socially nor economically excluded. He grew up in a stable, affluent family in India. At school, he was in a mixed environment and was a star athlete with a love for science and zero interest in religion. However, at university, things began to change. Politicized Islamic groups amassed supporters by lambasting Israeli and American foreign policies and the global persecution of Muslims. They staunchly believed conspiracy theories like the Jews (Mossad) had orchestrated—or at least facilitated—9/11 to make Muslims look bad. Contradictorily, despite the alleged conspiracy to defame Muslims, they still celebrated the attacks as a triumph for the umma.

Any and every opportunity that could be appropriated by these groups to reaffirm their narrative and spread their ideology was exploited. In turn, this meant totally ignoring anything that nourished the grayzone. Jamal recounts an incident where Muslims were not allowed to pray in a US airport; the other American travelers came to their defense, insisting on their religious liberties. This example of interfaith solidarity was not stockpiled in the extremist ammunition depot.[16]

Experiencing what many of us experience in our formative college years—soul-searching, self-discovery, and reinvention—Jamal was gradually drawn in. While Jamal shared the sentiments of injustice and moral outrage towards Western treatment of Muslims, he was not personally persecuted as a Muslim minority in India. What Jamal was, however, was initially ignorant of the Quran. Fortunately, his interest in science led him to question everything—something he was strongly discouraged from doing by his politico-religious group.

However, his cognitive abilities were belittled and he was told that the Quran was too complex for him to understand.

Grounded in a sound pedagogy, Jamal rebelled intellectually, asking himself, *Why wouldn't I understand?* He clandestinely studied the Quran unsupervised and came across many scholars who contradicted his radical beliefs. In his quest to prove them wrong, he probed further. Sincere in his search for truth, Jamal found that the more he researched, the more he recognized that those other scholars were, in fact, correct. After all, extremism is a weakness of one's conviction, and the search for absolute truth is a true testament of faith. Ultimately, Jamal's accumulation, depth, and breadth of religious knowledge fortified him against the tides of violent extremism.

Jamal runs various trainings in villages and schools, and has even been invited to prisons. To scale his impact, he also trains peer-educators to deliver his three-day program in their own communities. As a recipient of the prestigious Ashoka fellowship for social entrepreneurs, Jamal receives a basic stipend, but his work remains grossly underfunded. As though this obstacle wasn't challenging enough, his monetary sources add an additional layer of complexity. Receiving government funds would corrode his credibility as a "stooge of the state." Western philanthropy would brand him "an agent of the infidels." And Muslim foundations—with their sectarian inclinations—make his "non-denominational" work much more difficult to categorize.[17]

I ask how he would approach the deradicalization of someone like Baghdadi. As with Dr. Akilu, his cardinal rule is never engage in debating specific points or try to use a counternarrative that can backfire. In other words, "Don't contradict them; instead show them a new path." Ultimately, Jamal views himself as someone who simply facilitates a return to an authentic understanding of Islam, but only they—the individual—can break their own belief system. Instead, he teaches irrefutable stories and examples from the Quran that demonstrate love, kindness, and forgiveness—ones that extremists cannot contradict because in doing so, they would be contradicting the Quran itself.

This is of paramount importance. Moses walked on water, Jesus could heal the sick, and Muhammad received revelations over a period of twenty-three years composing the intricate word-smithery of the Quran. Each prophet's miracles were specific to their era. Magic and sorcery in the time of Moses, medicine in the time of Jesus, and poetry during the advent of Islam. The Prophet Muhammad's disbelievers were challenged to come up with a similar literary work, with none rising to the occasion. Moreover, due to the Islamic belief that the original teachings of Judaism and Christianity were tainted and altered by mankind over time, the Quran's miracle was that it would remain intact and lend itself to memorization.

Although Islamic understanding has metamorphosed over time, hadith are subject to questions of reliability by many, and sects and schools of jurisprudence have fragmented, no matter what, the Quran remains the immutable North Star. So, Jamal tells me, if someone can demonstrate the Quran as an unambiguous book of love and show extremists that they don't have to engage in violence to be close to God, "if you can open a door to God that implores you to forgive and have compassion and mercy and kindness—all the attributes of God himself—it's a huge relief for them to abandon their hate."[18]

One such story he narrates from the Quran is that of Habil and Qabil (Abel and Cain), the two sons of Adam. Committing the very first murder on Earth, Cain kills Abel, and before he does so, Abel tells him that he (Abel) would never lay a hand on him (Cain) for God loves the pious. This parable is recounted as an example of what it means to be pious—to choose not to seek revenge nor wrong one's brother. Even if, and when, one's own brother is about to kill one, one should be like Abel. Another parable from the Quran that Jamal uses is that of the Prophet Yusuf, whose jealous brothers threw him in a well and abandoned him. Later, Yusuf was captured, sold as a slave, and imprisoned by a non-Muslim king. When the King and his kingdom were in danger of famine, Yusuf, who had the gift of prophetic dream interpretation, warned the ruler and advised him on how to save his people.[19]

Similarly, Jamal shares the story of Pharaoh—one of the most nefarious tyrants named in the Quran. While acknowledging that Pharaoh deserved be killed, the Quran asks one to be kind to Pharaoh, giving him a chance to perhaps be reminded of or to fear God. Put another way, the Quran teaches that it is better to try to convince or warn someone of the consequences of their ethical deviations and to let them consider that there is always a chance that even the most wicked can repent and change. Although Jamal does not make the explicit link for them, when the extremists equate their enemies with the evil "Pharaoh"—as they commonly do—recalling these paradigms of forgiveness reframes their understanding of what it means to be Muslim. Especially given that the Quran enjoins one to turn an enemy into one's dearest friend through kindness.[20]

Upon hearing these stories of persecution, and of how the prophets respond with love instead of retaliatory violence, many radicals are relieved to tears, comprehending for the first time that God is love. Their pledge is to God regardless, and Islamic teachers excel at instilling a potent fear of defying God. Thus, to be afforded the self-permission to abandon hate removes this Herculean burden from their hearts.

Another fundamental point is that while Jamal veers away from debate, not discussing the relevance and meaning of the more violent and bellicose verses of the Quran would undermine his credibility. Instead, he explains the context and concept of *fitna* and the meaning of religious persecution during the advent of Islam. Muslims were prevented from freely practicing religion; they could not construct mosques; they were tortured and even slaughtered for their monotheism. It was in this context that the Prophet Muhammad was permitted to fight or "wage jihad" in self-defense—as a very last resort after years of oppression, famine, murder, and ultimately migration from Mecca to Medina. Despite the existing discrimination against Muslims today, they are comparatively free from the religious persecution defined in the Quran, according to Jamal.

While I agree with him, I would be remiss in not recognizing my own bias and lack of humility for believing that, irrespective of all these injustices, a good Muslim should have the moral fortitude to emulate the prophets and model their forgiveness and kindness. My family was not bombed in Mosul. I was not wrongfully detained and tortured at a notorious torture facility while pregnant. Nor was I targeted in a group killing by drone for simply being a Muslim male of military age who happened to attend a funeral or wedding. And thankfully, I am not an Iraqi who watched her country descend into anarchy as foreign forces exploited natural resources, and humiliated, tortured, and killed my fellow citizens. Considering the rule of proportionality in jihad, it is understandable how a terrorist may be led to justify leveling the uneven death toll.

To be clear, the stipulations of jihad are distinctly outlined in the Quran and have been egregiously violated by terrorist groups claiming offensive or even defensive warfare. Unlike terrorism, jihad should be used as a last resort after every other method of reconciliation has been exhausted, and wounded enemy soldiers are to be treated as one's own. Property damage (including places of worship), forced conversions and executions of non-Muslims, conquering territories for economic (and *ego-nomic*) gain, sex slavery, and indiscriminate killing of soldiers and non-combatants all contradict the rules of jihad.[21]

Nonetheless, while I vehemently reject terrorism, unless we change the current conditions that blur these very fine lines between persecution and justified self-defense—beginning with an acknowledgment of the reality facing many Muslims in conflict zones—we limit our ability to contain the terrorist threat. Acknowledging does not signal sanction; it is possible for one to say, *I understand these conditions* without condoning the methods used in seeking resolution. Naturally, if we disapprove of current tactics, we must also offer just and accessible alternative forms of settlement.

In closing our conversation, I ask Jamal's thoughts on the refusal of Muslim imams to perform traditional Muslim prayers for the deceased perpetrators of the London Bridge attack in 2017—asserting that the "indefensible attackers" were not true Muslims. At first blush, mainstreaming such practices elicits hope that one could evaporate the ambiguity around the idea of a holy death and deter otherwise justifiable suicide attacks.[22] His response was that the extremists would simply apostatize the imams, counting them among infidel governments. He did acknowledge the need for these types of gestures to alter the global perception of the Muslim community but ultimately discounted their influence on terrorists.

Based on the work of Dr. Akilu and Jamal, I am inclined to believe that while semantics might be important for *us*, semantics are less relevant as a counternarrative to dissuade terrorists. For example, one emerging suggestion has been the use of the word *fasadis*—seditionists—as opposed to jihadis to delegitimize the belief that joining a terrorist organization is ordained holy war. Theoretically, this sounds like a reasonable hypothesis. But such divisive language that engages in criticism and debate adds nothing to reconstructing an understanding of Islam that is rooted in the values that render violent extremism obsolete—namely, peace, love, compassion, and kindness; and service to God, Earth, mankind, and all sentient beings. Organizations working on religious countermessaging campaigns on and offline should be particularly prudent about this point and place greater emphasis on narrative rehabilitation.

The efficacy of Jamal and Dr. Akilu, and the work of others who use comparable methods across the Muslim world, equally reinforces my conviction that defeating what is essentially positioned as a "holy war"—albeit one that shrouds a political agenda—requires a one-upmanship of moral authority. If someone is truly God-fearing, they will simply be unable to reconcile violence or "evil" without the delusion of sanctimoniously fighting injustice. Ceasing to exemplify this injustice is the talisman that neutralizes the dogma touted by extremist groups.

Justin Welby, the Archbishop of Canterbury, said the onus was on religious leaders to take responsibility for addressing acts committed in the name of faith. "Throughout history, religious tradition and scriptures have been twisted and misused by people" to justify violence.[23] As Muslims, for example, we have expected the disappointingly silent Aung Sang Su Kyi to condemn the horrific genocide against the Rohingya in Burma. But perhaps even more crucial than condemnation is for Muslim imams and clerics (and all multifaith religious leaders, for that matter) to emphasize our interdependence and for them to teach—not simply tolerance—but radical love, radical inclusion, and radical compassion.

And in this quest, the imams must reframe their roles from teachers to facilitators, inviting questioning and reasoning that induces faith, not fear. The tools of critical inquiry would have profound implications on education, economic development, and sociopolitical progress across the Muslim world. And in enabling the reconstruction of one's own narratives, unlike the Miligram experiment, individuals would be less likely to outsource their humanity and moral responsibility to fallible and misguided human beings.

10

RADICALIZING
INCLUSION

BENJAMIN FRANKLIN FAMOUSLY said, "An ounce of preven-
tion is worth a pound of cure." Of course, he wasn't talking about preventing and countering violent extremism—or P/CVE, as it's known.
He was talking about fire safety. In our current approach to counterterrorism, it is as though we are dealing with a raging fire. Fueling
it are accumulating grievances, lit by a history of deeply entrenched
injustices and violations. We become angry at the fire. We want to
annihilate it. So, to punish the fire, we spray it with gasoline. We bomb
it. We shower it with kindling and a fusillade of injustice until the
fire burns higher. We drive it out so it burns elsewhere. All we really
needed was water to pacify the fire: "Darkness cannot drive out darkness; only light can do that."[1]

In favoring a more humane, yet scientific, approach to counterterrorism, I must acknowledge that evidence and attribution of
efficacy in the field of P/CVE is difficult. How does one prove that
one's interventions deterred someone from radicalizing in a world of

complexity, where a multitude of crosscutting variables, externalities, and personal elements interact? Rigorous monitoring and evaluation, and long-term assessments—and investments—in this field are scant. Yet I would argue that until military interventions are subject to the same rigor, impact monitoring, and evaluation that the peace-building organizations operating on shoe-string budgets are, there is little evidence substantiating the long-term return on investment (ROI) or social return on investment (SROI) of military interventions either. In fact, arguably, quite the opposite.

Successfully killing a terrorist or bombing a target would be considered an "output" in the social sector as opposed to a successful "outcome." Consider the example of training 500 underprivileged youth with job skills. If half of the youth are subsequently unable to find jobs due to ethnic discrimination and become increasingly frustrated with the lack of opportunity they have to put their skills to use, clearly, this would not constitute "success." A more desirable outcome, for instance, would be that 88 percent of trainees were subsequently able to find employment and tripled their income, on average. So vital are such considerations that most peace-builders analyze the projected impact of their interventions and operate according to the conflict-sensitivity principles of "Do No Harm" to outline how they intend to mitigate unintended negative consequences.[2]

Failing to evaluate the long-term outcomes of military interventions, and the negative repercussions on socioeconomic and political dynamics, one could argue, is societally irresponsible, and perhaps even absurd. Particularly when peace-builders vying for restricted grants and funding need to comply with "do no harm," while the considerably more cataclysmic military interventions are not subject to such exacting standards. If—in some parts of the world more than others—we are demanding that businesses be more ethical and responsible in mitigating their social and environmental impacts and are urging them to contribute a net positive to society, shouldn't we subject militaries and the security sector, with actual human lives in their hands, to more scrupulous standards? And greater social responsibility is equally about the occupational mental and physical health and safety of the military's own employees—the brave women and men who serve with altruistic and honorable intentions, more often than not.

Thus, if we think of traditional counterterrorism interventions as a symptomatic cure, then addressing the root conditions of violent extremism and building societal immunity are most certainly the more desirable "prevention." Accomplishing this requires us to acknowledge that "there is no route to peace. Peace is the route," to invoke Mahatma Gandhi. In other words, wisdom and common sense should compel us to act in accordance with the outcomes we seek and to model the inclusive and virtuous values and ideals we endeavor to uphold.

Fortunately, there is a dawning recognition among state actors for an inclusion-inclined preventative approach to violent extremism. A gap, however, between policy and practice persists. In researching inclusive approaches to security, policy recommendation papers abound ad nauseam—eclipsing the visibility of actual practitioners working on the ground. Many in the international community seem to be talking about it, but fewer are working on it—or at least directing the necessary resources for mainstreaming implementation. Nevertheless, globally renowned heavyweights lending this field their political clout are helpful in mobilizing P/CVE.

At the sixteenth meeting of the United Nations Counter-Terrorism Centre (UNCCT) Advisory Board in 2018, Secretary-General António Guterres affirmed, "Military and security measures against terrorism are important, they are essential, but we also need to address the underlying conditions that are conducive to young men and women being lured by terrorism and violent extremism. No one is born a terrorist, and nothing justifies terrorism, but we know that factors such as prolonged unresolved conflicts, lack of the rule of law and socioeconomic marginalization can all play a role in transforming grievances into destructive action."[3]

Among the UN's building blocks for preventing violent extremism (PVE) are promoting a rule of law, human rights, gender equality, youth engagement, participatory decision-making and civic engagement, and fighting corruption. Or, put another way, the basic foundations of human development and good governance. The UN's PVE strategy also underscores the importance of engaging in dialogue with alienated and at-risk groups, providing them with effective socioeconomic alternatives to violence, and reintegrating former extremists.[4] In essence, to prevent violent extremism, the consensus of the international community is to ensure justice and social, political, and economic inclusion.

Tony Blair, the former British prime minister who had offered his unqualified support to George W. Bush before the 2003 Iraq invasion, saying, "I will be with you, whatever," has made similar recommendations.[5] Today, Blair's foundation works to counter extremism, among other issues related to global stability. In a report entitled *Turning Point: A New Comprehensive Strategy for Countering Violent Extremism,* Blair urges the US and its allies to align their policies with their values. He recommends an urgent expansion of the CVE ecosystem, saying that pledging $US1 billion annually to global efforts would catalyze a surge in investment from other public, private, and social sector stakeholders. Long-term success, the report notes, must be achieved through "winning the battle of ideas, for it is ideas that can turn the disenchanted into murderers willing to kill innocent victims."[6]

Amidst knee-jerk responses to terrorism, we would be wise to remember that terror is a tactic, and that there are complex reasons driving individuals towards violence. Each must be dealt with accordingly. Martyrs with a death wish are differently motivated than second-generation cultural castaways marooned between a European identity that marginalizes them and a motherland that rejects them. Boko Haram devotees motivated by status symbols like cash and a motorcycle differ from politically repressed Arabs with historical and present-day political grievances. Just as there is no one predictor or cause of terrorism—a tactic that lacks causal coherence—"one-bomb-kills-all" solutions are likely to disappoint.

One certainty is, however, that social, economic, and political inclusion are far more powerful antidotes. Why? Simply because, humanizing counterterrorism forces us to confront the underlying issues and conditions rather than the symptoms. It is the only gateway to sustainably ending terrorism. Lofty and utopian as that goal may sound, when human lives—and the quality of those lives—are at stake, one would hope that we would aspire for moonshot targets.

WHAT INCLUSION DOES TO RADICALS

Given that reaching a political settlement represents one of two primary ways in which terrorist groups end, according to research by RAND, the GTI, and others, we may consider successful examples of governments that integrated terrorist groups into the political process. For instance, the Irish Republican Army (IRA) desisted from terrorist activity following the Good Friday Agreement, which addressed governance issues and constitutional changes regarding the status of Northern Ireland within the UK, and the respective relationships between Northern Ireland, the Republic of Ireland, and the UK. In El Salvador, the Farabundo Martí National Liberation Front (FMLN) began disarmament following the 1992 Chapultepec Peace Accords; and in Mozambique, that same year, the Resistencia Nacional Mozambicana (RENAMO) signed a peace agreement with the government. For the latter two countries, enduring inequality has made for a tenuous peace.

Yet for each of these cases, a negotiated settlement was possible, owing to narrowly defined achievable goals. Establishing a transnational Islamic caliphate, on the other hand, is highly implausible given the unlikelihood that the governments of Muslim majority nations would be willing to negotiate—let alone yield.[7] I will come back to what it means to create the caliphate—or how we might "reimagine the caliphate"—but for the time being, we may consider how political accommodation and inclusion can end, or hinder, support for terrorist organizations on the supply side (i.e., the recruits). Especially when an increase in religious piety correlated with a decrease in support for terrorist organizations in one Muslim-majority nation.

In Indonesia—which is home to the world's largest Muslim population, numbering around 225 million people—political pluralism has been a safeguard for violent extremism, even as the country has paradoxically become more overtly religious. According to a 2012 Pew Survey, over 70 percent of Indonesian Muslims support enforcement of Shariah on a national level.[8] Secularism is not the counterextremism antidote here, but the support of democracy seems to be. Despite their shortcomings, post-Suharto presidents compellingly demonstrated the virtues of "the rule of the people," by protecting the rights of religious and ethnic minorities and minimizing the role of the military and religion in politics, unlike their dictatorial predecessor.

They also allowed Islamist groups into the political sphere—rather than banning them. In some cases, presidents found common ground with Islamist agendas on issues like anticorruption and poverty alleviation—and adopted them as their own. Another crucial factor was that by allowing Islamists into government, they allowed them to publicly fail and dismantled any romanticized notions surrounding their savior status. Without ever having the chance to actually serve in office, Islamists can make idealistic promises while preserving an immaculate reputation.[9]

Surely enough, given the opportunity to enter into politics, Islamists did not succeed in remaining scandal-free. One case, dubbed "Beefgate," exposed Luthfi Hasan Ishaaq, the former Chairman of Indonesia's largest Islamist party, the Prosperous Justice Party (PKS), for being guilty of bribery and money laundering after he accepted kickbacks in return for influencing the agriculture ministry to increase a company's beef import quota.[10] Another member of parliament (MP) from the PKS—who ironically helped pass a controversial antipornography law—resigned after he was caught watching explicit videos on his computer during a parliamentary session.[11] Given the innumerable examples of spiritual incongruence exhibited by "Muslim" terrorists outlined in previous chapters, these incidents should not be totally astonishing.

Rather than asking what Islamists will do to politics, one may ask this question instead: What can political inclusion do to Islamists? One group of researchers investigated the influences of democracy on Islamists in their report "Zealous Democrats: Islamism and Democracy in Egypt, Indonesia and Turkey."[12] Among the findings is the transition from a Shariah state to Shariah values, which is to say that the focus on a set of values and principles takes precedence over a physical Islamic state. Relevant to this emphasis on values is the focus of constituents on the moral differentiation between Islamist groups and their secular counterparts—not just in terms of messaging, but rather, that they practice what they preach. In Indonesia, for instance, the moral incongruence between the words and actions of Islamist politicians diminished their ability to project superiority over secular groups. Moreover, constituents are interested in good governance rather than Islamic governance, therefore this leads to a modest secularization of Islamist policy agendas—not in the sense that policies are incompatible with Islam per se, but rather that they are focused on secular issues like anticorruption and poverty, as opposed to religious issues like segregation of the sexes.[13]

One should caution, however, against an unbridled zeal for democracy as a universal panacea. Indonesia has had a richer experience with participatory politics, and a different history and demographic makeup than other Muslim nations.[14] Moreover, despite the absence of flagrant injustice and persecution, Indonesia's sociopolitical conditions are neither perfect nor static. Given that radical Islam endorses both anti-Chinese sentiment and economic nationalism in Indonesia—where most of the top fifty richest Indonesians on the Forbes lists are ethnic Chinese—inhibiting the threat of violent extremism invariably hinges on more than just political participation.[15] "To deal with radicalism and extremism, we need to deal with economic inequality," Joko Widodo, Indonesia's current president, told the managing editor of *Foreign Affairs* in a 2014 interview.[16]

RADICAL IDEALISM: DYING FOR A CAUSE

Inclusion of Islamic politicians is vital. Equally, if not more important, however, is constructively harnessing the radical idealism of youth. Research on youth unemployment, injustice, and violence, conducted by the humanitarian organization Mercy Corps, draws our attention to the fact that half of the world's population is under thirty, with youth "forming the backbone of many paramilitary and terrorist organizations."[17] One major recurrent recommendation—based on interviews and surveys with youth in Afghanistan, Colombia, and Somalia—is the importance of providing youth with a meaningful outlet in which to voice their opinions and contribute to public reforms on issues of corruption, predatory justice systems, and exclusive governance structures.[18]

Capitalizing on the energy of youth—their literal willingness to die for a cause—is something extremist groups strategically conspire to exploit. And for those very same youth, we fall short of engaging them and reframing how we view them—from adversaries, to partners in peace. Instead, we see them either as burdens—a "youth bulge"—or as beneficiaries who need saving. I recall speaking at a session entitled *Youth, Economics and Violence* at the Salzburg Global Seminar in 2015, where then-UN Youth Envoy Ahmad Alhendawi was also participating. To be assigned as an envoy implies one must resolve some sort of crisis, Alhendawi noted—as though youth are a problem to tackle.[19] It's true: we have a Middle East Envoy, an Envoy to Syria, an Envoy for Refugees, and we are placing youth in the same category.

As one peace-builder who tirelessly advocates for the inclusion of youth in this field tells me during an informal discussion, "We often blame the young people committing violence—it's not the children's fault. Blame sits on the shoulders of the institutions who have failed at delivering the social contract they promised to uphold. We need to recognize ourselves as part of the problem; as corporate executives, government leaders, and civil society—we are all complicit in the injustice." We should instead recognize the superpowers and core competencies of youth, as extremist groups do so astutely. We must view them as positive disruptors with unfulfilled potential, and a desire to meaningfully contribute to society, and we must facilitate the opportunities for them to do so.

One may wonder with skepticism whether youth even possess sufficient political maturity to adopt serious issues of national concern. During the UN panel *Inclusion: An Essential First Step in Preventing Violent Extremism,* Aslam Souli, vice president of Tunisia's National Youth Initiative Against Terrorism, observes that community dialogues on the most pressing issues for youth tended to reveal discontent with the lack of local services, bad governance, inequality, and corruption. "Believe me . . . the issue of violent extremism comes at number 10 or 11. Violent extremism is only a symptom."[20]

One particularly unique model for youth political engagement comes from the nonprofit organization Search for Common Ground's (Search) Palestine country office. *The President*—a Palestinian reality show created by Search's media division that has been dubbed *American Idol* meets *The Apprentice*—debuted in 2016 with 1,200 competitors and an impressive 40 percent Palestinian viewership.[21] Contestants were required to hold election rallies, critique current ministers, and present their political platforms on real-life issues. With 70 percent of Palestinians under the age of thirty, frustrations with economic decline and self-serving politicians, corruption, and nepotism can dangerously veer into violent manifestations.[22] Waad Qannam, the inaugural winner of the show and the son of refugees from East Jerusalem says, "I felt that that moment was the key to giving the youth a chance to participate in Palestinian politics."[23]

From reality television to the real world, where more than 50 percent of the population is under thirty but less than 2 percent of elected legislators are of that age group, the "Not Too Young To Run" campaign was launched to promote political participation of young people across the globe. Nigeria's 75-year-old president was the first to sign the bill, reducing the presidential age limit from 40 to 35, and governorship positions from 35 to 30. That is not to suggest positive discrimination in favor of youth without merit. Rather, it is to endow youth with opportunity and unbiased access to political participation.[24] Similarly, UN Security Youth Resolution 2419, which was cosponsored by 75 member states, advocates for the inclusion of young people in shaping the peace process as a present imperative, versus a future prospect.[25]

Youth-led initiatives are equally if not more important in giving youth greater agency. Christian Cito Cirhigiri, a peace journalist and activist from the Democratic Republic of the Congo (DRC) and founder of Peacemaker 360, has undertaken the formidable challenge of working to prevent his country from collapsing into civil war. Facilitating a bottom-up nonviolent movement is his way of credibly channeling youth frustrations against the government. Through uniting youth that represent different religious backgrounds, Peacemaker 360 simultaneously supports interfaith dialogue and a peaceful democratic transition in Congo, whereas strengthening social cohesion enhances the long-term functioning of democratic institutions in the country.[26]

Cirhigiri is not an anomaly. Diametrically opposed to terrorist groups, thousands of young people are engaging in what can be life-threatening work because they *feel* they are doing God's work, rather than being told to do God's work, as Saji Prelis, Director of Children and Youth at Search, notes in a conversation.[27] He shares the example of Pakistani human rights activist Gulalai Ismail, who at sixteen years old, set up Aware Girls to train young women on mobilizing and igniting the political engagement of other women. Nobel Peace Prize laureate Malala Yousafzai, who was shot by the Taliban for her advocacy for female education, attended the group in 2011 and currently sits on the board.[28] Gulalai's experience, while less internationally recognized than Malala's, has been marred by death threats, gun shootings, and other forms of harassment and intimidation. Local Taliban have placed her and her family on their hit list—forcing them to relocate.[29]

As the following chapters share in greater detail, these are the organizations and individuals who critically need our support to survive and thrive, and whose already fragile work is impaired—if not totally incapacitated—by the military or state violence we impose. Moreover, if we are to reasonably expect youth to be constructive in their radical activism—that is, to build rather than destroy—shouldn't we as policymakers and militaries endeavor to do the same? To build, not destroy. And yet, as the adage goes, whoever has a hammer sees every problem as a nail.

11

CAN'T WE ALL
JUST BELONG?

PERSISTENT IN THEIR recruitment efforts, Daesh has been known to invest hundreds of hours to ensnare just one individual in their web of terror. Fortunately for Kyrgyzstan, one peace-building organization in the Central Asian nation outperforms them by investing more than 1,500 hours to identify the 3 to 4 percent of youth who are most at risk of violent radicalization. Through grassroots discussions, they ask illuminating questions revealing grievances, frictions, and fears, like "How do you see your community in the next five years?" They speak to schools, juvenile detention facilities, influencers, and opinion leaders to identify the most isolated and vulnerable. They study what makes the concept of a caliphate resonate and deconstruct the language and rhetoric used by terrorist recruiters.[1]

Ultimately, what they have learned is that terror groups bait their victims with three simple promises: a just society, brotherhood and belonging, and equality for the disenfranchised. Since the fall of the Soviet Union, ethnic conflicts, political divides, and religious tensions have increased societal friction in Kyrgyzstan. Nepotism is pervasive—inflaming existing inequalities. And many youths whose parents leave to work in more financially lucrative cities like Moscow—some 2,500 miles away—are left vulnerable to the fraternity of terrorist groups.

Through the Youth as Agents of Peace and Stability program, the 3 to 4 percent of young people most at risk are transformed from young problem-makers into emerging community builders. Applying this peace-building approach yields tremendous dividends for the country's long-term trajectory. In one testimonial, a seventeen-year-old, beaming at his own reinvention, says, "Before I was known for being good at fighting, now I am popular for my social work."[2] Facilitating an individual's personal transition from societal menace to altruist is also effective in other Muslim-majority countries like Malaysia and Indonesia, where members of law enforcement bond with detainees through jointly helping slums and orphanages. Police officers reinforce the message that this is what being a good Muslim is about—helping others. And the experiences cultivate empathy and reconnect extremists to society.[3]

Similarly in Iraq, Fatima Al-Bahadly, founder of the Firdaus (paradise) Foundation, teaches youth that God created them not to kill or die but to dedicate their lives to worship, work, and service of society. When the frustrations of unemployment shockingly enticed her own son to join Daesh, Al-Bahadly walked from camp to camp in Salah al-Din province, speaking with over 3,500 youth in an attempt to reengage them. Al-Bahadly redefines the nature of heroism paraded by militia groups as constructive action for the betterment of communities, rehabilitating derelict schools, and replanting trees. "I tell them jihad is not spilling blood on the streets, it is giving blood in hospitals." So far, she has managed to disarm around 150 young men—including her own son.[4]

Conscious of the void and the stark absence of alternatives to satisfy the primitive human needs of heroism, Jordanian social entrepreneur

Suleiman Bakhit created *Hero-Factor*: a comic portraying positive role models for young Arabs and promoting heroism as an antidote to extremism. *Hero-Factor* also features stories of prominent Islamic historical figures—delegitimizing and rivaling historically inaccurate narratives peddled by Islamic extremists. If this sounds too simple or ineffective, I can assure you that the extremists don't think so.

I reached out to Bakhit just before the 2018 World Economic Forum at Davos, which we were both scheduled to attend. Only one of us showed up. A couple of months later, I received an apologetic message from Bakhit, who had been attacked and targeted by extremist groups (again) because of his work, and had to undergo several surgeries. If a comic book can provoke such a backlash, perhaps we should pay more attention to what truly threatens extremist groups.

ALL YOU NEED IS LOVE

Both absurd in its simplicity and logical in its psychology, sometimes, to deradicalize an individual, all you need is love. Black September, for example, was at one time one of the most ruthless and feared terrorist organizations in the world, infamously known for the kidnapping and massacre of eleven Israeli athletes during the 1972 Munich Olympics. The group was also responsible for assassinating Jordan's prime minister, Wasfi al-Tal. As al-Tal lay on the marble floor of the Sheraton Hotel in Cairo, dying, one of the assassins reportedly knelt beside him and licked his flowing blood.[5]

Black September was purposefully established following the loss of the West Bank to Israel in the 1967 Six-Day War and the expulsion of Palestinians from Jordan in September 1970. The elite terror unit had one primary mission: to highly publicize and prioritize the Palestinian cause on the global agenda. And it worked. Yasser Arafat, leader of the Palestinian Liberation Organization (PLO), was invited to address the UN General Assembly, and shortly thereafter, the PLO was granted special observer status. After it had served its purpose, however, Black September became somewhat of a liability. How does one shut down a cold-blooded maniacal group of around 100 unrestrained young men?

The answer, it turned out, was by marrying them off. After hand-picking the most attractive young Palestinian women they could find and enlisting them on a "mission to a greater cause" at the request of their leader, Yasser Arafat, the PLO arranged a mixer in Beirut. In addition to anticipated matrimony, the PLO offered financial incentives. Those who married would be paid US$3,000, would be given an apartment in Beirut furnished with kitchen essentials like a gas stove and a refrigerator, and a television, and would be offered a nonviolent role with the PLO.[6]

Couples that conceived within a year would be rewarded with an additional US$5,000. Remarkably, it worked. The Black Septemberists fell in love and reprioritized what mattered most to them, and what was not worth losing: their wives and their children. In validating their "sobriety," former terrorists who were asked by the PLO to travel abroad for nonillicit activities refused—fearing that they would be arrested en route and deprived of their families.[7]

Having children doesn't always yield this result, but for one extremist on the other end of the hate spectrum, it was a pivotal moment. I was initially intrigued by an article describing Arno Michaelis's encounter at a McDonald's, where a black woman working at the cash register noticed a swastika tattooed on his middle finger. With all the unconditional love in her eyes, she told him "You're a better person than that. I know that's not who you are." Michaelis literally ran away and never went back to that McDonald's again.[8]

When I reached out to Michaelis to learn more about his experiences, he pointed out that for an extremist to validate his or her worldview, society must reflect their hostility, leading to mutual dehumanization. So when people responded to him with hate they were behaving exactly as he wanted them to behave. He was in control. However, when people defied his hostility with kindness and compassion, it forced him to question his own savagery—instead of his perceived savagery of "the others." He recounts another incident where he was hung over and hungry at work and a black colleague extended his hand and said, "Hey skinhead, do you want half my sandwich?"[9]

In isolation, these encounters are insufficient to totally disarm someone, but an aggregation of kindness is humanly difficult to reject in the long run. And although Michaelis would get drunk and surround himself with others who shared his ideology to reinvigorate his white supremacist rhetoric, he was unable to submerge his surfacing recognition. "Once you realize, it's not exactly something you can un-know," he tells me.[10]

Based on his personal experience, and having worked with innumerable violent Islamists and right-wingers, Michaelis insists that their actions are *always* designed to provoke hostility. A white supremacist must make Jews and people of color hate whites. Similarly, Muslim extremists, like Daeshites, must make non-Muslims hate Muslims to continue perpetuating their narrative. Otherwise, the lines between "us and them" blur into union.

I ask how influential Michaelis's own feelings of exclusion were in feeding his extremism. "It's a prerequisite," he says, definitively. "You cannot function without exclusion to perpetuate the suffering you're going through."[11] Thus, it becomes a psychological paradox. To end your suffering, you need connection with society, but because your ideology reaffirms the belief that society hates you and has forsaken you, your salvation becomes your source of anguish. And even though Michaelis didn't fall neatly into the category of an at-risk young white American—having come from a nice suburb of Milwaukee—he actively convinced himself society had abandoned him.

As I listened to Michaelis's insights on *incels*—involuntary celibates who are unable to find a sexual or romantic partner despite desiring one—I contemplated the parallels with sexually frustrated youth joining Islamist extremist groups. And although the white power movement didn't necessarily articulate it in this way, essentially they framed their ideology around three main types of exclusion, according to Michaelis: those feeling rejected by society were glorified as white warriors that no one appreciated; unemployment was caused by the Jews, who were bringing in the Mexicans to take all the jobs; and if you didn't have a girlfriend, the Jews were also at fault for putting black men like Michael Jordan on billboards and elevating their heartthrob status among white women. Laughable and ridiculous as these theories may be to some, it would be unproductive not to take seriously the underlying sentiments they substantiate.

Ultimately, for Michaelis, his serial encounters with kindness, and the fear of losing his daughter due to either his own incarceration or death, jolted him to do a 180. Today, he helps counsel people trying to exit extremist movements. Typically, these are individuals who, like substance abusers, have already hit rock bottom and have made a conscious decision not to pursue a path of self-destruction. With one exception: Chris Buckley, whom Michaelis met while filming a documentary on the Ku Klux Klan (ironically, the documentary never aired because the channel was concerned it "humanized the Klan").[12]

Buckley, the former Klansman, left for Iraq following 9/11 to counterattack Muslims. Daring his enemy with KKK symbols and *kafir* (infidel) tattooed on his body, Buckley hated Muslims, blacks, Jews, and homosexuals. Eventually, Michaelis convinced Buckley to meet Heval Mohamed Kelli, a Muslim Kurdish refugee who fled Syria after 9/11 to come to the US.

Kelli climbed the professional ladder—initially working as a restaurant dishwasher and eventually becoming a cardiologist. Today, he owns a black Mercedes sedan and a house on a pond—having achieved the American dream. Buckley, on the other hand—who served his country at war—lives in refugee-like conditions and spiraled into drug addiction through a common gateway of painkillers after breaking his back in an accident. The sad irony of those living like refugees in their own country is not lost on the emotionally intelligent Kelli, and he has made it his mission to interact with and spotlight these *Hillbilly Elegy*-type forgotten and excluded parts of America—a message made more powerful by his identity as a Muslim refugee.[13]

THE POWER OF EMPATHY

I cannot over-emphasize how consequential empathy is to this type of work. Judy Korn, a German social entrepreneur who rehabilitates Neo-Nazi and Muslim extremist youth incarcerated for hate crimes, does so by teaching them empathy. Since 2001, Korn's organization, the Violence Prevention Network (VPN), has worked with more than 500 such cases in Germany. Her track record is impressive, showing recidivism rates of 30 percent, compared with 80 percent for all juvenile offenders in Germany.[14]

In addition to empathy, Korn's main ingredients for resilience against extremism are teaching youth to develop self-awareness and self-reflection skills; the ability to question personal justifications for criminal behavior; building reliability and dependability in personal relationships; and gaining self-esteem through balancing self-acceptance with constructive self-criticism.[15] VPN also adopts a preventative approach by protecting vulnerable children from the claws of Daeshite recruiters. With the influx of refugees in her home city of Berlin, Korn's *Al Manara* program—or lighthouse—targets the 4,000 unaccompanied refugee minors who are dangerously at-risk.[16] At an investment of around EUR 10,000 per person per year, Korn's program is far less costly than military interventions—both fiscally and in terms of human loss of life.[17]

Given that extremism is religion-agnostic, various other programs and organizations, like Exit, utilize the same tools to help Neo-Nazis abandon white supremacism as they employ to deradicalize young Swedes belonging to violent Islamist groups. Robert Örell, who works for Exit and is a former Neo-Nazi himself, reflects on what drove his own extremism, noting that as a "loser" in school, "I never did well. The group made me believe that I was superior, they welcomed me and channeled my anger." He says, "They were able to give explanations to the wrongs and injustices polarizing the world. Us and them. Right and wrong." The best candidates for groups like this are the weakest: victims of bullying or marginalization, with difficult family situations—perfect for brainwashing.[18] In this sense, radicalization is less about recruiting supporters and more about mobilizing enemies. For Örell, he ultimately found the brotherhood, protection, and status he was seeking by joining the military.

One program Örell has collaborated on with a local theatre uses storytelling and sharing personal narratives to help antagonistic groups empathize, humanize, and relate to one another. During a series of around twenty half-day sessions, the participants explore group dynamics and in-depth identity work. In the process of self-discovery, what many have noted as a particularly powerful realization is hearing the reflections of their own feelings mirrored by the "other," as well as the role they personally play through their actions, and the consequences of those actions in perpetuating the same feelings of exclusion that they suffer from. Exit has been operating for twenty years and Örell's dedication has enabled more than 700 reformed extremists to escape a cycle of violence.[19]

Scientific research also substantiates the empirical evidence on empathy. A renowned social neuroscientist, Tania Singer, initiated "Project ReSource" at the Max Planck Institute for Human Cognitive and Brain Sciences in Leipzig, Germany. By engaging 300 volunteers over the course of the nine-month project, Singer was able to detect structural changes to the brain in MRI scans after just one week of training on mindfulness, compassion, and perspective taking, which corresponded with enhanced prosocial behaviors! Singer posits that incorporating such training into school curricula could build more cohesive interconnected societies that are more resilient to extremism.[20]

THEY ARE "OUR TERRORISTS"

Mayor Bart Somers of Mechelen is perhaps one of the most enlightened politicians I have encountered. Recognizing that all violence starts with disconnection, his Belgian city has adopted a policy of integration rather than segregation as an armor of resilience against terrorism. Whereas Daesh managed to poach the highest number of foreign fighters of all the European countries from Belgium, in Mechelen, not a single person was successfully enlisted to join. A remarkable feat considering the small city is home to 20,000 Muslims—more than Hungary and Slovakia combined—and is straddled between Antwerp and Brussels, where foreign fighter rates are high. Mayor Somers, who was awarded the biennial World Mayor Prize, estimates that according to the regional average, twenty-five residents should have left Mechelen in pursuit of violent jihad.[21] So how does Mechelen do it?

When you speak about radicalization, you need to have empathy and intuitive thinking, he tells me. Violent extremists try to provoke an emotional response to engage recruits. They demonstrate compassion to convince marginalized individuals their unfavorable circumstances and feelings of frustration are not their fault—but society's. With the group, one goes from zero to hero. Mayor Somers, who has read extensively on the topic, and also bases his city's policies on decades of experience, observes similarities in the pathways of isolation architected by such groups—whether they are violent Islamists or cults. "It always begins with isolating an individual from society—for example, telling them they shouldn't have non-Muslim friends. Gradually, even their Muslim friends are not *real* Muslims, so you should abandon those too. Then your family is also no good."[22]

Emphasizing the importance of prevention, the Mayor underscores how much more difficult, costly, and energy intensive deradicalization is compared with prevention. "You need to be there at the moment people are still psychologically open to reasoning. We are recruiting people to our society before extremists recruit them."[23] What does it mean to be there early enough to recruit citizens to society?

For a start, the city focuses on mutually reinforcing elements of policing and community dialogue. Since 9/11, Somers diligently transformed a neglected Belgian city into a paradigm of inclusion and social integration through targeted preventative measures aimed at bolstering social cohesion. Immigrants view themselves as full citizens, rather than societal rejects or second class. Urban renewal and revitalization projects have upgraded rundown neighborhoods melding socioeconomic classes and promoting class-based integration between immigrants and the affluent.

Community programs are subsidized, including a center offering social and recreational services ranging from counseling to soccer. Youth workers assist children with homework, and even school dropouts receive assistance to complete their studies. One prevention counsellor says, "The challenge is to make them [youth] feel part of the community and that means giving them real opportunities to develop as members of the community with rights—but also with duties."[24] Immigrants see themselves as meaningful contributors to society, rather than as a burden, and that this society is for them. Of paramount importance to the mayor is bringing people together on an individual level, rather than only a community level—personalizing and deepening their interactions. And he believes all cities should have a Minister of Society tasked with ensuring that citizens live together in harmony, without isolation or alienation.

I must emphasize that the mayor is not against military interventions per se, and policing is key to his city's strategy. However, he recognizes the serious imbalance in funding between the two approaches. "The prevention work doesn't cost so much money—you just have to do it and redirect funds to reduce the segregation," he says.[25] Thus, it's a matter of political will (rather than dollars or Euro bills). Nonetheless, while a city must respect the rule of law and create safety, police cannot be viewed as the enemy. Key to this is the interaction of police

at the community center—no doubt refashioning their image as punitive law enforcement to being stewards and custodians of community
well-being. Even the mayor himself drops into the center from time
to time. Consequently, citizens don't see the state as a place they don't
belong, or perceive it as hostile.

If the mayor can ensure safety, clean roads, and access to parks,
even the older generations witnessing the transformation of their city
won't come to view it as a decline or loss; rather, they see it as a net
positive. Identity in Mechelen doesn't look away from diversity, he
tells me. Indeed, Mechelen is safer, cleaner, and more diverse, with
50 percent of its citizens coming from a foreign background, and it
has the highest concentration of Moroccans in Belgium. Whether in
a corporation or in a city, diversity without inclusion can be deeply
destructive. So in Mechelen, they don't leave people out; they build a
wall around their children to ensure they don't lose a single generation to violent extremism. This inclusive narrative is critical.[26]

After the 2016 Brussels airport bombing, the mayor tells me how
he visited the biggest mosque in his city. Knowing what the Muslims must have been feeling—as I did living in New York during
9/11—fearing the stigma and anger that would be directed towards
them, Mayor Somers spoke tremendously reassuring words. "I'm
your mayor and you're my citizens, and unfortunately, you have been
twice-victimized." He was referring to their vulnerability to the threat
of terrorism as Belgian citizens, and again as Muslims with a hijacked
identity, making them feel unsafe. "But if someone discriminates
against you, I will be by your side," the mayor assured them.[27]

That evening, politicians condemned the terrorists and their horrific acts—reinforcing a polarizing "us and them" narrative and calling
for them to be thrown out of the country. At such a poignant moment,
the mayor took a morally courageous stance. While he enforced the
need to bring the terrorists to justice and vehemently condemned
the attacks, he said, "but even if they're terrorists they are our terrorists. They were born and raised in our societies, they went to our

schools, they are our problem."[28] It was the first time, in such a difficult moment, that someone had embraced them as humans. Many Muslim youth watching the interview were reduced to tears by this demonstration of indiscriminate compassion.

Essentially, Mayor Somers created a city that is worthless in terms of prospective terrorist talent and grievances to exploit. Vilvoorde, for instance, provided Daesh with twenty-eight recruits—despite being half Mechelen's size. In 2014, Vilvoorde adopted Mechelen's model of resilience. Miraculously, two years later, the Daesh-bound departures stopped.[29] So if this approach is both more humanistic and effective, why aren't we seeing its application across more European cities?

Part of the challenge lies in its misfit with bipartisan politics because both build on polarization. That is, the left sees discrimination and the right sees criminalization. Neither views cities as non-homogenous, composed of diverse citizens. In some respects, they are somewhat embodying a Western Salafist approach. And yet the mayor argues that many rights and equalities were introduced in opposition to our traditions and habits—like gender equality and LGBT rights because of the fundamentalist values democratic societies are built upon.

Other European cities, like Helsinki, Vienna, Aarhus, and Rotterdam, have also worked to foster a sense of political participation and inclusion—particularly of newcomers and the attitudes towards them. There's even a "Strong Cities Network" comprising a global web of mayors, policymakers, and practitioners united in building social cohesion and resilience to counter violent extremism. So to summarize using a warrior-like ethos: to prevent violent extremism, we should endeavor to leave no man behind.

GENDER INCLUSIVITY AND SECURITY

Mayor Somer's approach to community-based interventions and the crucial role of policing in responding to terrorism forms a key component of PAIMAN Alumni Trust's (PAIMAN) theory of change. This is based on evidence that police—as a permanent presence in local communities—are better positioned than the military to respond to violent extremism in a more humanistic and community-focused way. Studies also indicate that female police officers in particular are less likely to use excessive force—though they will not hesitate to use it where necessary—and are more adept at deescalating potentially violent confrontations than their male counterparts. Furthermore, as one researcher notes, "A community that promotes tolerance and inclusivity, and reflects norms of gender equality, is stronger and less vulnerable to violent extremism."[30]

The potency of gender inclusion in security is notably more significant in a country like Pakistan, where PAIMAN is based. The nonprofit's work has evolved since 2004, from empowering mothers with the critical thinking skills to recognize and disrupt the radicalization of their children, to working with the Taliban to help them reconcile their multiple identities and cultures as Pakistanis, Pathans, and Muslims.[31] Included in this process is psychosocial care for returnees, religious literacy education, livelihood-skills training, and civic education.

Rather innovatively, PAIMAN has also expanded their purview to fundamentalist fashion—unravelling numerous lethal prêt-à-porter suicide vest production lines. First, they deglamorized what seamstresses believed to be their contributions to a higher cause by educating them on the true meaning of jihad. Then they steered the women's stitching skills towards more durable dressmaking, versus a one-time wear.[32] Through community empowerment and activating civic engagement, PAIMAN is able to neutralize extremism through strengthening the community's social fabric—making it bullet- and suicide-bomb proof.

PAIMAN has trained 4,300 women and 14,000 men, and has deradicalized, rehabilitated, and reintegrated almost 1,300 extremists and at-risk individuals. To build social cohesion, they formed a coalition of women representing madrassa teachers, multifaith activists, and leaders of religious political parties. The coalition promotes inclusion, equality, interfaith dialogue, and a platform for expression allowing all voices to be heard—regardless of religious beliefs. Interfaith understanding is celebrated through the observance of multireligious festivals. And in invoking the principles of the Medina Charter, the coalition stands up for one another in the face of violence perpetrated against any one faction of the community.[33]

SPORTS AND DEVELOPMENT

Community-building approaches would be lacking without underscoring the universally commended role of sports in development and in dismantling intergroup segregation and individual isolation. I can perhaps think of no recent symbol more powerful to illustrate the unifying power of sports than the 2018 Champions League match between Real Madrid and Liverpool in Ukraine.

I won tickets to the final—which I gifted my brother so I could focus on writing this book! Like a textbook description of globalization, in the sports pubs and bars of Kiev were middle-aged British men dressed in Pharaoh garb, swigging pints of Danish beer. Slurring their speech, the men promised to convert to Islam if Mohamed Salah—Liverpool's star player who is both an Arab and a Muslim—won the match! Liverpool fans have even created chants like "If he's good enough for you, he's good enough for me, if he scores another few, then I'll be Muslim too!"[34]

Even in the sectarian quagmire that is Iraq, soccer was a powerful unifier during the country's victory in the 2007 Asian Cup quarterfinals. One man told the *New York Times* that the Iraqi team was the only thing uniting the war-torn nation: "When the Iraqi team wins a game, the people in Karkh, who are Sunnis, get happy. The people in Rusafa, who are Shia'as, get happy ... The team includes all the Iraqi sects, but they are all Iraqis and they are our brothers ... I hope that the Iraqi politicians would look at these simple football players who managed to unite the Iraqi people and learn from them."[35]

And without even reaching the Champion's League level, sports and e-sports are a huge untapped resource for PVE efforts towards youth engagement and connecting disparate groups. Australia's "More Than a Game" program uses soccer to engage young males at risk of radicalization due to personal experiences of marginalization. Sport is used as a platform to build social cohesion and address issues of cultural identity and nonviolent expression, and the youth are also mentored as part of the fortification against extremist ideologies. An evaluation of the initiative, which is a joint effort between the federal police, a sports club, and city councils, found it increased community resilience and cross-cultural awareness, fostered social inclusion and trust, and was especially effective in engaging at-risk youth in civic engagement and responsibility.[36]

All of the initiatives outlined here are relatively low-cost and low-hanging fruit; they should be a fundamental component of good governance. To reiterate the opening of this chapter, Daesh invests hundreds of hours getting to know individuals on a personal basis—understanding their grievances, empathizing with their personal problems, and successfully framing their narrative to enlist them in the cause. We should question how much we value the diverse and distinct individuals that, together, are the make-up of a terrorist group, and the amount of time and resources we devote to personalizing our prevention programs for something that many of us name as our most urgent global threat.

12

SHOW ME THE MONEY

WHEN MUHAMMAD YUNUS, the father of microfinance and founder of Grameen Bank, was awarded the Nobel Peace Prize in 2006, it validated the proposition that peace is inextricably linked to poverty and that poverty is a threat to peace. I am uncertain as to whether many people would have consciously made that link without hearing his acceptance speech. In it, Yunus applauded the world's moral audacity for adopting a historic millennium development goal in the year 2000—to halve poverty by 2015. However, one year after the turn of the century came September 11, followed by the invasion of Iraq—effectively derailing the world from the pursuit of this dream.[1]

At the time of Yunus's speech, the US alone had spent over US$530 billion on the war in Iraq. To put this number in perspective, today, Iraq is seeking less than 20 percent of that amount—US$88 billion—for post-war reconstruction. To date, it has been allocated only US$30 billion.[2] In his speech, Yunus continued by saying, "I believe terrorism cannot be won over by military action.... We must address the root causes of terrorism to end it for all time to come. I believe that putting resources into improving the lives of the poor people is a better strategy than spending it on guns. . . . The frustrations, hostility and anger generated by abject poverty cannot sustain peace in any society. For building stable peace we must find ways to provide opportunities for people to live decent lives."[3]

Although poverty doesn't cause terrorism, as Chapter 5 illustrates, we should recognize that a vacuum of hope and dignity among young people makes them considerably more vulnerable to terrorist recruitment—especially when ignited by flagrant injustice. This chapter highlights examples of development-based interventions that have successfully deterred terrorist recruitment, including some of the pitfalls of poor implementation. Secondly, in keeping with one of the main intentions of this book, these examples capture the endemic challenge impeding the scale and impact needed for preventing and countering violent extremism (P/CVE)—inadequate funding, in addition to the underdeveloped role of the private sector in P/CVE.

TERRORISM ACCELERATOR

To borrow from the entrepreneurship space, if we were to map Daesh's business model on the ubiquitous Business Model Canvas (see the following figure), our Customer Segments would be Syrians and Iraqis—for obvious geographic reasons—and foreign fighters, who are predominantly youth traveling to join the militant group from other countries and children who are often recruited against their will.

To win its differently motivated Customer Segments, Daesh deceptively promises community and belonging, meaningful purpose, religious purification, and adventure and status, along with financial incentives. Although its talent retention is poor, pervasive grievances massively boost its talent attraction and recruitment efforts. Comparatively, traditional counterterrorism interventions—which may cut off terrorist financing and revenue streams—don't satiate the needs of recruits whatsoever. More ominously, these tactics reinforce Daesh's polarization strategy and mirror the group's terrorization of civilian populations.

Daesh Business Model Canvas[4]

Key Partners

- Global affiliates like Boko Haram give them an expanded presence in Nigeria, Niger, Chad, and Cameroon. Others are in Uzbekistan, Libya, Egypt (Sinai Peninsula), Saudi Arabia, Yemen, Algeria, Afghanistan, Pakistan, and the North Caucasus.
- Members in Morocco, Lebanon, Jordan, Turkey, and Israel, but no official branches in those areas.
- Allegedly relies on Turkey to smuggle large amounts of oil sent by tankers via smuggling routes across the border.

Key Activities

- Terrorize and intimidate civilian populations, mobilize supporters, and polarize Muslims away from their governments and towards Daesh.
- Recruit and train fighters.
- Provide welfare and public services and jobs.

Key Resources

- Media apparatus & propaganda
- Territorial & asset control for extortion
- 40,000 fighters & affiliates that expand its global support base
- Adept at exploiting grievances & polarizing populations

Value Proposition

- Inclusion and belonging
- Purpose, adventure, and status
- Jobs and economic freedoms

Customer Relationships

- Customer acquisition through fear and intimidation (Iraq and Syria)
- Customer acquisition through appealing to grievances

Retention is poor

Channels

- Sophisticated media apparatus in 23 languages, online and offline propaganda
- Radicalization hotbeds; areas with significant grievances and where youth have been left behind.

Customer Segments

- Syrians and Iraqis
- Foreign fighters
- Children

Cost Structure

- Value driven: Daesh will invest a lot of time and resources to radicalize and recruit just one individual.

Revenue Streams

- Looting, extortion, kidnapping, and robbery
- Taxing agriculture and livestock production and other third parties
- Donations and fundraising

Essentially, through military brute force, we are trying to win our Customers by bombing them, killing their families, humiliating them, denying them dignity, exacerbating unemployment and a tenuous economy, instigating socioeconomic and political flux, and failing to acknowledge—let alone properly compensate for—the collateral damage. Even if one terrorist group is militarily weakened, by not neutralizing existing grievances, we simply allow new groups to enter the vacuum and present their alternatives to the disaffected. In short, our current approach is a violent extremism incubator and accelerator.

On the other hand, if it's not already clear, a robust counterterrorism incubator and accelerator needs to eliminate the grievances and injustices leveraged by extremist groups—not amplify them. And it should present alternatives that fulfill the Value Proposition presented by Daesh, such as providing opportunities for inclusion and belonging, dignity, economic empowerment, and purpose. One successful precedent is Iraq's Sunni Awakening Councils, which had been lauded for reducing violence in Iraq following the US-led invasion.

The councils were composed of Sunni tribesmen who were formerly allied with Al Qaeda in fighting *against* US and Iraqi forces. Through financial incentives (and the disillusionment of group members with Al Qaeda's extremism), the US military gained the support of thousands of former insurgents who subsequently denied Al Qaeda the physical space to operate within their spheres of control. Within one year, the councils successfully transformed the huge province of Anbar into one of most secure parts of Iraq.[5] Unfortunately, in 2008, the Iraqi government, then led by Iraqi Prime Minister Nouri al-Maliki, assumed stewardship for the 50,000-member group and promised to pay them. Maliki's unwillingness to integrate the councils into the security forces and general discrimination led to predictable resentment and mistrust.[6] Moreover, his concerns that the former insurgents may establish an armed Sunni opposition somewhat manifested as a self-fulfilling prophecy, having left them with the options of unemployment or joining Daesh in its war against the government.[7]

PUTTING PEACE TO WORK

Fifteen years ago, research on development-based interventions to deter terrorist recruitment was sparse. However, in 2003, with the support of Department of Defense federal funding, RAND examined the effectiveness of social and economic development policies on inhibiting a resurgence of terrorist violence in three country case studies where terrorism was perceived to be a viable response or form of retaliation against economic and social injustices. Their primary conclusions were that social and economic development policies can weaken local support for terrorist activities and discourage terrorist recruits. However, alone, they do not eliminate terrorism. Moreover, inflated expectations of inadequately funded social and economic development policies are likely to renew support for terrorism. And finally, the efficacy of development policies to inhibit terrorism hinges on their implementation.[8]

Development initiatives attempting to mitigate local perceptions of government repression and ethnic bias were examined in Northern Ireland, where the Catholic Irish were denied access to economic, social, and political opportunities for religious and ethnic reasons; in Mindanao, where supporters of the Islamic Moro National Liberation Front (MNLF) claimed that the Christian-dominated central government ignored their needs and used violence to suppress Muslim dissent; and in the more convoluted Palestine, where supporters of Fatah and the Palestinian Liberation Organization (PLO) justified the use of terrorism against an occupier (Israel) that had forced them out of their rightful territory into refugee camps where they lacked the most basic needs.[9] With the exception of the latter, these cases represented friction between a government and its own citizens.

Mindanao, for instance, has been plagued with high threats of terrorism and violent crime for decades and has fought the government of the Philippines for independence. In 1996, then-President Fidel Ramos reached a peace agreement providing for an Autonomous Region of Muslim Mindanao (ARMM), which also included provisions for social and economic development. The second largest island in the Philippines is a top agricultural producer and considered the major "breadbasket" of the country. Therefore, it seemed natural to look to banana and asparagus plantations to validate the hypothesis that peace pays.

Encouragingly, private investment in the plantations did indeed provide surrounding communities with a viable alternative to violence and resulted in a remarkable 100 percent employment rate. Potential terrorist recruits opted to reap the advantages of preserving peace over sowing violence and discord.[10] Unfortunately, inadequate funding caused the initiative to degenerate. As social and economic aid dwindled—at only $6 per person per year over a period of five years—the meager sum aggravated existing religious tensions and economic inequality.

In particular, most of the development funds were directed towards Christian-concentrated neighborhoods, which predictably fomented resentment among Muslim districts. Through the UN and the World Bank, the international community had also pledged approximately US$500 million for peace and development, targeting small-scale projects such as medical equipment and training, community-based cooperatives, and farming initiatives. However, given that Mindanao lacks proper road and transportation infrastructure, many towns are isolated—meaning that most of the projects tended to focus on the semideveloped and less impoverished areas. By widening inequality, these measures amplified perceptions of discrimination.

To further expand on "what not to do," the large-scale development programs in Mindanao were designed and executed with a blatant disregard for community needs. Aside from failing to consult local stakeholders, the programs were used as money-making schemes lining the pockets of investors who neglected long-term needs in favor of making a quick buck. Accountability mechanisms were also lacking, which meant that much of the development aid allocated to Mindanao was misappropriated through bribery and kickbacks.[11] Out of approximately US$100 million in government-pledged support intended to rapidly increase access of the most poor, vulnerable, and conflict-affected areas to basic economic and social infrastructure, services, and employment opportunities, an overwhelming majority of the funds went toward administrative costs, leaving approximately only US$18 million a year for development projects.

As one might expect, these circumstances—coupled with inflated hopes and expectations that were not met—renewed support for local terrorist groups.[12] Failures of the Mindanao project are largely attributed to poor execution rather than potential efficacy. Similarly, in Palestine, a misallocation of funds was to the project's detriment. Over half of the Palestinian Authority's expenditures were allotted for the police and civil service, with the remainder heavily concentrated on large-scale infrastructure projects, such as an airport and the Gaza port, in addition to a high-profile apartment high-rise called Karameh Towers. Many Gazans live in refugee camps and suffer from inconsistent access to food and water. In addition, the average annual income in Gaza fluctuates between US$600 and US$1,200.[13] Therefore, infrastructural development schemes were irrelevant to the everyday lives of those communities, and at US$30,000 per unit, the Karameh Tower apartments were priced far beyond the means of most Gazans.

Northern Ireland, on the other hand, had a more positive experience because the United Kingdom set aside a considerable budget to provide nondiscriminatory access to social and public welfare services. Between 1997 and 2001, the amount averaged US$869 million annually and the EU added a further US$48 million towards these efforts. So the total aid package amounted to approximately US$543 per person per year—far more substantial than the meagre US$6 in Mindanao.[14]

Development policies contributed to an expansion of a business elite in Northern Ireland and a new middle-class that had formerly lent its support to terrorists. Consequently, the community recognized the economic benefits of peace and worked to inhibit local support for terrorist activities.[15] Investments also prioritized equalizing access to, and quality of, education, health, housing, infrastructure, and urban development. So there was no perceived discrimination or exacerbation of religious tensions between Catholics and Protestants.[16] Most importantly, all programs were designed with the involvement of local residents, with proportional representation of Catholics and Protestants jointly working on implementation. Consequently, this eliminated any doubt that the programs were underhanded, skewed, or manipulated in any way.[17]

Fundamental to the success in Northern Ireland and other similar programs and case studies is one critical and imperative feature: the most effective policy implementations are those that are developed in consultation with local community leaders. This multi-stakeholder consultation and co-creation process parallels another growing business discipline—design-thinking or human-centered design, which ensures product or service development that is locally attuned to customer needs. Such an approach also organically builds trust, which is another imperative for program efficacy.

FIGHTING FUNDAMENTALISM THROUGH FARMING

It took one social entrepreneur in Nigeria several years to earn the trust of a demographic susceptible to extremism and unexpectedly seed peace through farming. I came to learn of Kola Masha through the Skoll World Forum for Social Entrepreneurship at Oxford University—an annual gathering where changemakers, Nobel Laureates, social scientists, and redefined "billionaires" with the intention of impacting one billion people come home to a like-minded and like-hearted tribe. At this "Davos of Social Innovation," notable personalities like Muhammad Yunus, Richard Branson, and the late "King of Data" Hans Rosling have been among the forum's delegates.

Masha—whose social enterprise Babban Gona won the distinguished 2017 Skoll Award—asks rhetorically, "Why has it become so easy for disgruntled individuals to raise a mini-army? Because young people have limited economic opportunities."[18] According to Masha, youth in Nigeria face a staggering 50 percent unemployment rate—which means one in two young people are unemployed. One might wonder, however, when Boko Haram is offering cash and a motorcycle, how does Masha get at-risk youth to ditch their symbols of status for tractors?

It turns out youth are much more practical. Most would prefer to stay in their hometowns, he tells me.[19] They only leave in pursuit of economic opportunities, which are largely absent in rural areas. So to dissuade the youth from leaving to join insurgencies—which is typically their last resort—Masha arms the young men and women with the ability to earn more than enough to take care of themselves and their families. Babban Gona's business model is designed to dramatically increase farmer income through crop yield optimization, microcredit, and economies of scale. Although it's difficult to capture specific data on former extremists who have renounced Boko Haram—not something they would want to openly divulge, I am told—Masha narrates a story of one of his members that encapsulates the downwards spiral that has entrapped so many Nigerian youth.

In search of better opportunities, this young member left his community to become a motorcycle taxi driver. City life was rough. He endured days of hunger, waiting in the rain for customers and in constant fear that his only asset—his tattered motorcycle—would be stolen or simply break down. And many like him indeed plummeted into destitution, making them the perfect recruits to fill vacancies as motorcycle getaway drivers for Boko Haram's merciless kidnappings and robberies. Instead, through the alternative Babban Gona pro-vided, this young man was able to turn his life around in two years. He has earned enough money to purchase his own retail store, he bought his mother three goats, and now he owns not one motorcycle but two. His dignity dividend is priceless.

Initially, Masha's greatest challenge was trust building. It took several years, but once Babban Gona reached an inflection point—proving its model, and earning the social license to operate—growth accelerated. Babban Gona doesn't screen its members by age and is open to everyone, but around 45 percent of its 20,000 farmers are under the age of thirty-five, and it has helped increased their net income by three and a half times. The social enterprise has also disbursed 16,000 profitable loans with a remarkable 99.9 percent loan repayment rate.[20]

Estimated numbers of Boko Haram militants vary, but they run in the thousands. Masha, meanwhile, is targeting an army of 1 million farmers by 2025 at a cost of less than US$1 billion—or US$1,000 a person.[21] Once a community has succumbed to extremism, it can be very difficult to solve, resulting in the loss of at least one or two generations before restabilizing, Masha tells me. By targeting communities teetering on the border of violent extremism, Masha's organization creates an economic buffer that also maintains both human and food security.

As with most impact trailblazers, Masha's current formidable challenge is funding. Today, in the conflict-afflicted and food insecure region of North-East Nigeria, it is virtually impossible to get investments from the private sector, and government interventions are very costly. Had investments in preventative initiatives like Masha's been made ten years ago, they would have constituted a fraction of today's security budgets and the opportunity cost of economic decline.

INVESTING IN PEACE AND PROSPERITY

Achaleke Christian Leke, a peace activist and the National Coordinator of Local Youth Corner Cameroon, promotes peace and countering violent extremism through a "Prison-preneurship" program, which reintegrates young violent offenders into society by building their vocational and entrepreneurial skills in addition to leadership and peace-building skills. His organization works in eight prison facilities in six regions, with 300 young people directly benefiting.[22] Doing as terrorist groups do, Achaleke allows the young offenders to reinvent themselves into heroes and she-roes. More than 5,000 young Cameroonians have benefitted from his youth-led organization's programs on peace-building, countering violent extremism, leadership development, and national integration.[23] Unfortunately for the likes of Achaleke—who was named Commonwealth Young Person of the Year in 2016—entrepreneurship promotion barely skims 1 percent of the US Foreign Aid budget, according to calculations by Steven R. Koltai.[24]

In a *Harvard Business Review* article, Koltai argues in favor of allocating greater amounts of overseas assistance towards entrepreneurship, noting that job creation promotes stability.[25] Merely the awareness and visibility of such initiatives can increase the hope and confidence of local populations—dissuading their support for extremist groups. Studies have suggested as much; the visibility of USAID programs appears to be correlated with people's increased confidence in their government (and positive views of the US) and with decreased support for extremist groups. For example, in Nigeria, 78 percent of people who said USAID-funded programs were "visible" or "very visible" reported being "confident" or "very confident" in their government. Of those who said they were confident in the government, 87 percent were unsupportive of extremist groups.[26]

Unfortunately, current meager allocations of foreign aid are disproportionately focused on supporting micro and small enterprises, rather than larger companies with the wherewithal to employ thousands, or for-profit social enterprises, like Babban Gona, that stabilize economies and markets and reinforce long-term incentives for maintaining peace. It's a bit of a catch-22 because, as Masha rightly notes, who would invest in a North-Eastern Nigerian venture fund? Or, for that matter, a Syrian high-impact entrepreneurship accelerator?

Businesses don't appear to fully appreciate the mutually beneficial roles they can play in maintaining peace. Nestle, for instance, is Babban Gona's biggest client. In creating shared value—that is, driving profits through serving societal or environmental needs—Nestle helps Masha's farmers increase their incomes by enhancing their crop yield and quality, which are important agricultural inputs for the Nestle supply chain of nutritional products. I cannot help but wonder, however, why they are not measuring the impact these efforts have on maintaining peace and security and the averted cost of business disruptions caused by violence and volatility. If they did, it could provide a powerful business case and incentive for other corporations to view investments in peace as worthwhile economic endeavors.

While the Shared Value approach of driving economic competitiveness through serving societal needs is nascent in the peace-building field, its potential is already being explored by international nongovernmental organizations (NGOs) like Mercy Corps and Search for Common Ground (Search)—a 2018 Nobel Peace Prize nominee and, in full disclosure, a former client of mine. In Sri Lanka, for instance, Search is facilitating the intermarriage between business-friendly and people-centered solutions in urban settings. Search convenes small businesses; large enterprises like luxury housing developers, hoteliers, and the banks funding such projects; and young people, civil society, local communities, and government. Together, they address the vulnerability and division engendered by this rapid urbanization.

With billion-dollar projects looking to commercialize the beautiful Indian Ocean island of Sri Lanka, many people are left displaced. And the businesses involved seem totally indifferent to local communities; people are uprooted and relegated to lower-quality housing at an accelerated pace, increasing friction between the local people and the incoming businesses. We know that tourism's contribution to GDP in countries with terrorist attacks is half that of countries without terrorist attacks.[27] So in Sri Lanka, recognizing that violence and insecurity are the nails in the coffin of a burgeoning tourism sector, the stakeholders work together to improve the lives of young people and address their grievances through a business model that has social capital. This means that the business model is financially sustainable while earning the social license to operate in the long-term.

Up until Search came on the scene, large companies and hoteliers had previously tried—and failed—to engage marginalized communities, and municipalities were somewhat disconnected from local needs. Search, on the other hand, was viewed as a credible convener because of its peace-building expertise and social clout from working with grassroots communities and civil society, with the backing of private-sector capital. While it's too early to capture meaningful data or success metrics, the beginnings are promising and those involved in the project have noted that in some ways, Search is offering Sri Lankan youth what Daesh claims to offer: a sense of agency and purpose, status, and a meaningful opportunity to engage in improving their individual and societal circumstances.

SOCIAL IMPACT BONDS

Social finance is another emerging sector with the potential to close the peace-building investment gap. Social impact bonds (SIBs), for instance, are already being used to address social problems like recidivism in Europe and America.[28] Similar to a pay-for-success model, SIBs are a public-private partnership where the government pays an intermediary to manage a social issue with the objective of improved social outcomes and public-sector savings. Investors provide the operational costs for the intermediary's program and are paid a financial return on their investment if predetermined targets are achieved.

To use a hypothetical example with arbitrary numbers for illustrative purposes, let us say that the Nigerian government secures investors to fund a five-year program designed by a collaborative of peace-builders and other multi-stakeholder actors at a cost of US$5 million. A successful outcome is defined as reducing the economic costs of violence in Nigeria by 30 percent. If the interventions reach their target, investors are paid a 10 percent return on government savings.

For example, if costs of violence are indeed reduced by 30 percent, saving the Nigerian government US$100 million in terms of costs to tourism, the national economy, public health expenditure, costs of disruptions, destructions of public property, and so on, investors would be paid US$10 million. This means they would have doubled their initial US$5 million investment.

Although there are evident challenges in proving causality with violent extremism, peace innovation in the finance sector could have profound implications for providing the rigor required to monitor and evaluate the effectiveness of interventions preventing violent extremism and to calculate the consequent social and economic byproducts of those interventions. Not to overlook the fact that literal investments in peace—whereby institutional investors receive both a financial and social return on their investments—also unlock the type of finance needed for capital-intensive solutions like Masha's. What also remains unexplored in this scenario—and with SIBs in general—is the potential role of militaries as investors, or co-investors, to secure more favorable and less fatal circumstances in conflict settings. Certainly food for thought . . .

When I listen to Masha's challenges, one thing strikes me. He has an MBA from Harvard, a Masters in Mechanical Engineering from MIT, and a Skoll Award—considered a Nobel Prize in the social innovation sector. And he—like so many social entrepreneurs and positive-change agents—struggles to prove his interventions pay off and are worthy of greater resource allocations. One can only imagine the frustrations of the less globally connected. And whereas military interventions don't need to prove efficacy to merit funding, the social sector struggles to prove that its interventions make a difference, while frugal and short-term funding cycles make this a largely unattainable ideal. When one considers the comparative return and social return on investment between soft and hard power interventions, it becomes clear that we need to reevaluate the economics of peace.

13

PEACE PAYS AND MORALITY TRUMPS

AMONG THE GLITZ and glamour of beauty pageants, the clichéd question asking what the world needs most is almost always answered with the equally stereotypical "world peace." I wonder if we have relegated this to an unobtainable utopian ideal that no longer warrants serious pursuit. Utopian as this goal may be, our dominant perceptions of peace and justice are contrastingly substandard. Traditionally, we tend to perceive peace and justice as merely the absence of war and humanitarian violations. In other words, we assume that peace can only be maintained by a threat of coercion. Yet a perennial threat of coercion indicates an omnipresent source of discontent—which is likely to result in interminable violence. This somewhat unambitious and less desirable state is known as *negative peace*.

Positive peace on the other hand, is defined as the attitudes, institutions, and structures that create and sustain peaceful societies, which also lead to other positive outcomes, such as thriving economies, greater inclusion, and higher levels of resilience. According to the Global Peace Index, this optimum environment conducive to the flourishing of human potential was improving from 2005 until a plateau in 2013 and was followed by a subsequent deterioration.[1] In 2016, violence and conflict peaked as we saw record levels of terrorism, the highest number of global battle deaths for 25 years, and the largest number of refugees and displaced people since World War II.[2] Right now, we are facing a historic decline in global peace.

In addition to obvious social ramifications, not investing in positive peace comes with costly implications for the global economy. Violence cost the world US$14.76 trillion in purchasing power parity (PPP) terms in 2017, which is equivalent to 12.4 percent of the global GDP. Since 2012, the total economic impact of violence has increased by 16 percent.[3] Non-OECD countries with declining positive peace saw their GDP growth per annum to be 1.45 percent lower on average than those that showed improvements in positive peace. Similarly, domestic currency depreciated by 0.4 percent and credit ratings were more likely to be downgraded when countries experienced deteriorations in positive peace—falling, on average, by 4.5 points on a 0 to 22 scale. Consequently, foreign direct investment (FDI) is less than half in less peaceful countries, while interest rates are higher and less stable.[4]

Governments—and the US in particular—should also heed the economic impact of wars on terrorism, given an Al Qaeda legacy strategy to accelerate imperial overstretch and induce the collapse and bankruptcy of the United States. Over-extending America beyond its financial and military means, Daesh believes, will lead to the demise of the world's superpower.[5] By the end of April 2018, US public debt had exceeded US$21 trillion.[6] Waging wars has also led to an unsustainable overstretch of human resources in a military empire spanning nearly 800 military bases in around 80 foreign countries.[7] Given the 500,000 deployable troop limit, personnel deficits set up the US military to simply "drop from exhaustion," as it tries to be everywhere, all the time.[8]

One could also posit that compelling Arab countries to overspend on security is intended to accelerate the downfall of Middle East governments—paving the way for Daesh's regional expansion. Between nationalist uprisings, sociopolitical discontent, regional conflicts, and terrorist threats, per capita military expenditures in the Arab states have grown two and a half times between 1990 and 2014.[9] Meanwhile, these government security expenditures divert funds from socially and economically uplifting programs, thereby feeding grievances, polarization, and an environment of negative peace at home.

While we have been limited in ascertaining the ROI of military counterterrorism interventions on long-term peacefulness outcomes, using conservative assumptions, we know that the cost-effectiveness ratio of peace-building is 1:16, according to data generated from the Institute for Economics and Peace. This means that for every dollar invested in countries where there is conflict, the future cost of conflict would be reduced by US$16.[10] Yet while our global military spending sits at US$1.7 trillion—which represents almost 11.5 percent of the total cost of violence[11]—paradoxically, peace-building and peacekeeping expenditures represent just 2 percent of global economic losses from conflict.[12] When one US$4,000 rocket launcher would be enough to fund a three-day peace-building workshop for 160 youth, one may question how we are evaluating the choices we make to ensure human security.[13] According to calculations by Search for Common Ground's (Search's) vice president of programs, Lena Slachmuijlder, one year of the US Department of Defense's budget would keep Search alive for 15,000 years.

Back in 2007, Phillip H. Gordon, an American diplomat and foreign policy expert, calculated that just one week's worth of military spending in Iraq could boost America's moral authority beyond comparison. Based on 2007 figures, the war in Iraq was costing around US$375 million a day. One week's worth of spending (US$2.6 billion) would have been enough to fund all of the following, with US$1 billion left to spare: the entire budget of the Middle East Partnership

Initiative (around US$100 million); the entire public diplomacy budget for the Muslim world (US$150 million); opening a new American cultural center in every Arab country (US$400 million); scholarships to US universities for 10,000 Middle Eastern universities (US$400 million); and an expansion of the Peace Corps by 10,000 volunteers (US$400 million).[14]

Even more perplexing is that within the social sector itself, 336 foundations made 2,908 grants totaling just US$350.7 million for peace in 2015, according to the Peace and Security Funding Index.[15] Of this amount, US$13 million went towards countering violent extremism (CVE). By comparison, that same year, 22,893 grants totaling US$2.4 billion were made by foundations for human rights—even though peace is a prerequisite for other social and environmental issues like human rights, health, and education—all of which are disrupted and exacerbated by conflict.[16] All things considered, how much can we afford to invest in peace? At a 2018 UN Security Council meeting in April 2018, Kessy Ekomo-Soignet, executive director of URU, a youth-led organization in the Central African Republic, proposed that at least US$1.8 billion—one dollar for every young person on the planet—be invested in youth to underscore their role in building peace and the prevention of violent extremism.[17] It's a drop in the ocean.

Ultimately, we need greater proportionality in investments for positive peace. If we were to allocate just 1 percent of all global defense spending, which was US$1.7 trillion in 2018 according to the Stockholm International Peace Research Institute (SIPRI), that would provide us with a more meaningful budget of US$17 billion.[18] Ultimately, if these are not investments and social venture risks we are willing to make, then we need to seriously ask ourselves: do we really want peace?

HOW DO WE KNOW PREVENTION WORKS?

Search's vice president of programs, Lena Slachmuijlder, shares a quick anecdote on her attendance of a war conference.[19] A military speaker presents the use of a special helicopter with smaller wings for tactical maneuver during counterterrorism operations. Following this, the peace-builders presenting their P/CVE work are bombarded with skepticism regarding efficacy. It does seem rather unfair given the disproportionate budget allocations and the lack of long-term social risk assessments and outcome-based design, monitoring, and evaluation (DME)——rigor required of well-endowed militaries relative to the peace-building sector operating on limited budgets.

To defeat terrorism, we must first recognize that it is only winnable if it is not a "war." By the same token, we need to believe it is preventable. One may consider the analogy of the advent of medicine. Unable to comprehend that ailments could be cured—much less prevented—our unenlightened predecessors attributed their afflictions to medieval witchcraft outside their purview. We need an evolution of political consciousness to recognize that violent extremism *is* preventable.

True as it may be that proving we averted violent radicalization on an individual level is more difficult, we can measure whether peace-building interventions decreased support for militant groups or diminished activities by non-state actors to undermine counterterrorism efforts. We can evaluate the effectiveness of interventions in alleviating the societal grievances and injustices that lead to violence and vulnerability to terrorist recruitment. Levels of collaboration, trust, and communication between communities and security forces can be measured. Most importantly, we can prove efficacy when it comes to the markers of healthy societies and good governance that lead to greater positive peacefulness.

One demonstration of program efficacy was achieved in 2017 at the conclusion of a three-and-a-half-year project in Nigeria, where an unconventional alliance between security forces and Search led to greater stability and enhanced intelligence gathering. Search has been operating since 1982 and oversees twenty projects in fifteen countries across Asia, Africa, and the Middle East specifically focused on PVE. For this project—dubbed "The Plateau Will Arise! Phase II (PWA

II): Consolidating an Architecture for Peace, Tolerance and Reconciliation"—Search utilized consensus-based advocacy training, conflict transformation training, and human rights monitoring and reporting and facilitated multi-stakeholder dialogue to engage all levels of society. All of this training was conducted for community members, local and state governments, and security services.[20]

Given that mistrust and fear of security forces overwhelmingly impedes open communication channels between civilians—whose role in thwarting terrorist attacks, violence, and crime is critical—a key objective of PWA II was activating the role of communities in safeguarding their own security. Encouragingly, end-line survey data showed that an average of 91.5 percent of community respondents expressed improvements in their relationships with security forces and 79.1 percent with government. Overall, the security situation in all communities improved: 68.9 percent in Jos North noted great improvement, followed by Barkin Ladi (61.7 percent), Bokkos (53.2 percent), and Langtang North (43.6 percent).[21]

Search's approach seeks to use conflict as a point of departure to build more resilient socially cohesive communities through improving communication between disagreeing parties and addressing underlying grievances that may lead to violence. This differs somewhat from attempting to "eliminate conflict"—which, to some degree, is a natural and even necessary part of life. Accordingly, respondents attributed conflict trainings to be a major factor in the increased communication and information sharing with security agents. One participant cited them as transformational, explaining that, "Before the trainings, I saw them [security] as enemies. We now report issues to them."[22] As examples of improved relations with security agents, surveyed households named instances of increased amicability and mutual greetings, greater approachability to voice complaints, faster response times to distress calls, security agents playing football (soccer) with local community members, and increased youth involvement in security services.[23]

Given the critical time-sensitivity of intelligence in preventing escalation and conflict—particularly in rural areas with limited connectivity and no security presence—the Early Warning System (EWS) formed another instrumental mechanism contributing to this project's successful outcome. Developed in PWA Phase I, the EWS included trainings to engage civilians in community-wide protection and to support information sharing. Unfortunately, although 73 percent of interview respondents found the EWS to be effective, its efficacy waned in direct correlation with reduced funding, because of its contingency on the use of cell phone data.

Of note for militaries is the importance of responsiveness to complaints regarding the behavior of soldiers and addressing threats to credibility. For security agents to function optimally, communities need to believe that the agents have their best interests at heart. Another localized initiative spearheaded by Search in Niger addressed this through reinstating the cultural tradition of camel racing, which had been halted during the country's instability. Celebrating the renewal of these activities consequently reestablished trust between local communities and the military and similarly enhanced communication and information sharing critical to security.

In both examples, Search worked with local militaries, who frequently have greater operational legitimacy and a better understanding of their environment to deal with insurgent groups than foreign militaries do. In avoiding the perils of economic and military overextension, foreign militaries should place a greater emphasis on the capacity building of national security forces. A light foreign military footprint—or none at all—displaces the precipitating impact such a territorial intrusion is likely to have on terrorist recruitment.[24]

MORAL ECLIPSE

In assuming that individuals are predisposed to positive self-identification, and that one feels an inherent sense of obligation to fight against the unjust victimization of one's in-group, might we consider an alternative scenario, in which Daesh lacks the credibility to claim itself as the defender of Muslim persecution? What would it look like if we usurped the custodianship of justice and rendered their narrative obsolete? If we pause to consider the elements that make joining Daesh so compelling, we could learn how to beat them at their own game and reroute prospective militants.

In essence, we have discovered that the caliphate itself is relatively unenticing. Based on the previously mentioned UN Counter-Terrorism Centre study, establishing an Islamic State ranks low on the list of priorities, with just 16 percent of foreign fighters giving this as a reason for joining Daesh.[25] Rather, individuals are lured by what a caliphate promises to offer. Namely: justice, dignity, equality, and belonging. Is it unreasonable, or deemed to be an inferior recourse, that we endeavor to accommodate these human needs, particularly when these elements are the foundations of good governance and also mirror the democratic ideals of the US and many Western nations? Could it even be a desirable recourse, given that American culture excels at fostering belonging—be it through platoons, fraternities, or team sports?

Could we outperform Daesh by creating the caliphate ourselves, metaphorically speaking, through providing the social, economic, and political inclusion they allege to offer? I am proposing neither the creation of a literal Islamic territorial empire nor that we engage in a power struggle. Rather, I am suggesting that we expand our purview beyond the professed end goal of establishing a caliphate, and instead examine the outcomes it promises. For example, we don't pursue wealth for the sake of wealth, but rather for the material and immaterial freedoms it can provide us.

If we agree that "All forms of violent extremism seek change through fear and intimidation rather than through peaceful means,"[26] in continuing to pursue change through fear and intimidation, our methods are indistinguishably similar. Revered spiritual leaders like Muhammad,

Jesus, and Moses succeeded in winning hearts, minds, converts, and disciples precisely because they inspired with indiscriminate love and compassion—not terror. They won us over with their unwavering moral North—and not in spite of it. We may find our ethical armor to be a more powerful shield against terrorism in the long run.

REPETITION IS INSANITY

What we have learned, in summary, is that violent extremism is neither an affliction nor personal pathology. Anyone is capable, given the right constellation of circumstances, to assume the custodianship of justice and what they believe to be noble ends. Total immunity to this moral ambiguity is highly dubious, given the evidence that, even in the most benign settings, children are capable of this moral decay, as demonstrated in the brown-eyes blue-eyes experiment.

Superficial examination may have initially led one to surmise causality between Islam and violent extremism. Yet based on overwhelming evidence, studies, and interviews conducted by diverse organizations, including multilaterals, military institutions, academia, think tanks, and nonprofits, this hypothesis is flimsy at best. Islam is largely used as a moral justification for sociopolitical and economic grievances, or for spiritual redemption—as evidenced by the numerous religiously ignorant, Islamically incongruent "jihadists."

Nevertheless, to diminish an individual's ability to justify their actions with delusions of Islamic devotion, we must work to rehabilitate Islamic comprehension with positive messaging. Whereas counternarratives seek to refute Islamist propaganda through point-by-point rebuttals—which can backfire—what is critically needed is an emphasis on narrative restoration that canvases a more expansive and contextualized understanding of Islam. Such an understanding must simultaneously avoid sidestepping combative scripture—which undermines credibility—while remaining deeply rooted in the unadulterated values of Islam. Unlike the hadith, teaching irrefutable parables from the Quran that demonstrate love, kindness, and forgiveness cannot be contradicted, because in so doing, a Muslim would be blasphemously contradicting the immutable Quran itself.

Muslim imams must be involved on a local level to ascertain how content should be presented for cultural resonance. Education specialists must ensure these teachings engage students. Former violent extremists with a better understanding of the terrorist psyche can provide insight into messaging for prison rehabilitation and deradicalization programs. I hope those currently working in the counternarrative space—particularly online—will consider the wisdom of the likes of Jamal Basit and Dr. Akilu.

If for no other reason than the fact that historically, military interventions have led to the demise of only 7 percent of terrorist organizations since 1968—with the *least* amount of success in defeating religious groups—we should seriously reexamine our current counterterrorism approaches. These interventions are having the opposite effect they were intended to have by feeding polarization and validating extremist propaganda used by organizations like Daesh— that the West is insidiously ethnically cleansing the Muslim umma, which both justifies the use of terror as "proportional" jihad and subsequently provides a recruitment pipeline for terrorist groups.

Slaying the enemy with force has also led to the proliferation of new grievances, regenerating like a hydra. For every beheading of the beast, several more sinister mutations emerge. Meanwhile, any form of physical destruction leads to more tenuous economies and creates more hospitable social conditions in which terrorism can thrive, while the positive countereffects of peace-builders are impaired or totally incapacitated. And so we find ourselves buckled into a ceaseless cycle of violence.

If love and marriage can offset Black September; a policy of inclusion is working in the city of Mechelen; and neuro-scientific research substantiates the impact of compassion and mindfulness training— showing structural changes to the brain in MRI scans after just one week—we owe it to ourselves to abandon self-imposed limitations and preconceived notions on what counterterrorism solutions should and could look like.

BUILDING NEW MODELS

One of my favorite quotes, which is attributed to the polymath American inventor and futurist Buckminster Fuller, has profoundly impacted the way I think about my own work and theories of social change. He said, "You never change things by fighting the existing reality. To change something, build a new model that makes the existing model obsolete."[27] In terms of the *ultimate* outcome, I would venture to say that we are all aligned: eradicate violent extremism to save lives and enhance the quality of life. Where we diverge is on the approach—fighting the old, versus building the new.

For me, building the new means remodeling our societies to become more resilient to violent extremism. The tools and principles I propose to architect social change—while familiar—represent a remix and reconfiguration of largely siloed disciplines and stakeholders. This reinvented approach seeks to leverage the tools of capitalism, coupled with the disruptive force of social innovation, and falls at the intersection of warfare and welfare. By no means is it intended as a conclusive panacea; I can only endeavor to share what I have learned, all of which is guided by my interdisciplinary and multisector background, working on interconnected sustainable development issues like peace, climate change, and inclusive economic growth.

Firstly, in my observations working with (peace-building) nonprofits, innovation is desperately needed to address financial deficits in the field more generally, and for P/CVE in particular. Short-term funding cycles instituted by donors disrupt what could otherwise be consistent interventions to sustain long-term change. Donors could benefit from greater social returns by adopting a patient capital approach and even jointly funding social outcomes together in alliance with other donor groups. This means investing more and in longer-term outcomes and multiyear project cycles that allow profound transformations to take root and flourish. Put another way, donors cannot expect "large-scale impact"—which for many, implies reaching at least one million people—with a budget of US$100,000. Even this inadequate figure is on the higher end of what many peace-builders have to work with—some receive under US$1,000![28] Often, this results in less effective project design that is informed by donor requirements and short-term time-frames, rather than maximizing impact and long-term gains.

Some may view a more capital-intensive approach as risky. Therefore, we may reframe a traditional donor approach into a venture philanthropy approach. If one considers the high engagement of venture capitalists in providing nonfinancial assets like technical expertise and networks to improve the odds of startup success and growth, we may question why such an enterprising model has not gained greater popularity in the social sector,[29] whereas, paradoxically, competition—which is at the heart of capitalism—is incentivized, as nonprofits vying for grants need to prove they can "do it all" to win limited and restricted grants. In reality, such monumental social change often necessitates collaboration between multiple peace actors, each with their niche and core capabilities.

Another paradox is that while peace-builders are required to apply rigorous design, monitoring, and evaluation—or DME—the military does not. It may seem strange to suggest as much, but in a way, military institutions may need to view themselves as agents of social change—beyond their surface-level mission of "winning wars." Rather than viewing this as a punitive measure, enforcing a DME approach on militaries—where feasible—can help them better assess long-term risks and implications, thus bringing to light potential unintended sociopolitical, economic, and environmental consequences likely to adversely affect near-term and long-term security. Somalia's ocean embargo, which affected local fishermen (Chapter 8,) is one such example of an action taken to maintain security that backfired. If a DME approach is adopted, we could prevent damaging, unintended consequences and bolster the conditions for peace from an entirely different dimension.

This includes applying the principles of "do no harm": a widely adhered-to, systematic conflict sensitivity framework for effective operations in conflict settings and in the mitigation of negative impacts.[30] Such principles take into account the highly meandering, nonlinear path to change—one that is influenced by numerous seemingly unrelated and yet interdependent elements. Recognizing all of these parts of the system, how they interrelate and interact, and identifying the ones with the greatest influence—positive or negative— incontestably leads to better-informed decision-making.[31] *Systems mapping*, as this practice is known, can provide an additional layer of intelligence and foresight for those operating in conflict settings— including militaries and governments.

COLLECTIVE IMPACT

When asked to name my role models and heroines during interviews, I am always reluctant. While individuals deserve to be celebrated, often the notion of glorifying a single person diminishes the collective heroism of the entire ecosystem that was integral to advancing change. In a frustratingly fragmented social sector, the ascendancy of collaborative models has strongly characterized my own approach to work. Beyond buzzwords like "multi-stakeholder," the meaning of *collaboration* is more akin to integration and synchronization, rather than a convening of disparate parts.

A model for social change that does justice to this interconnected and collaborative approach of collective heroism is a framework known as *Collective Impact*. Mark Kramer, who, incidentally, I also met at the Skoll World Forum on Social Entrepreneurship, developed this model, with his colleague John Kania, at FSG—a social impact advisory firm Kramer cofounded with the renowned business strategist and Harvard professor Michael Porter.

Dismantling these endemic silos for P/CVE work is imperative for meaningful change—both in practice and in the open source sharing of critical data and knowledge within the P/CVE multi-stakeholder community. However, given that this uncharted path makes for strange bedfellows (peace-builders, military, and multinational corporations), it may require an element of persuasion and an appetite for innovation. In keeping with Collective Impact best practices, first and foremost, there needs to be an alignment of diverging interests and a common agenda for change.

Secondly, this unlikely alliance—which should also include the more traditional stakeholders, like communities, government, vulnerable groups, and civil society—needs to come to a consensus on the articulation of the problem and what constitutes a successful outcome. Common success metrics and other indicators need to be defined to capture this collective impact. Moreover, in avoiding the redundancy and fracturing of efforts, this model must foster mutually reinforcing activities.[32] And finally, as delicate as this balancing act may be between multiple partners, the dynamics and flux of navigating social change means that the model needs to be adaptive, responsive, and continuously self-corrective through feedback loops, data analytics, and insights.

So far, the Collective Impact framework has largely been applied to comparatively less precarious issues like health, education, and housing. And while there is no predetermined recipe or prescription without a locally specific in-depth diagnosis, as an operational template, the framework's application could enhance peace and security in vulnerable settings. One such promising example is the tourism sector pilot in Sri Lanka, described in the previous chapter (which blends both Shared Value and Collective Impact frameworks).

MORALITY TRUMPS

My primary impact intentions in writing this book were to celebrate the undervalued efforts of the thousands of lion-hearted peace-builders working with limited means and tenacious spirit for our collective benefit, and to mobilize greater support and resources for P/CVE. In nudging the international community to refresh its outlook on traditional counterterrorism solutions, I am cautiously optimistic that with such a reconfigured approach, one that leverages the unique strengths of different actors and disciplines, we may find a winning powerhouse for a more peaceful world.

In closing, I must stress that each component of architecting social change is a science that should not be attempted by a naively well-meaning yet unqualified individual. To paraphrase one of my favorite humanitarian mavericks, Dan Pallotta, who challenges our notions of "doing good" versus "feeling good," if someone is about to operate on you, would their "good intentions" sufficiently compensate for their lack of surgical training?[33] Of course not. Designing for social change is no different.

Nevertheless, as the numerous case studies and examples illustrate, we are all fundamental to the functioning of inclusive societies in our respective roles as businesses, entrepreneurs, policymakers, and members of society. And while I hope that the stories featured in this book have moved and inspired you, and that you consider supporting one of the many organizations deeply engaged in this work, there is perhaps one more potent antidote to fighting fundamentalism. That is, that we labor to cultivate the inner transformations needed to effect outer change.

If we can recognize that the root causes of most global threats we face—including conflict—are the values and conditions that allowed these problems to exist in the first place, we must dismantle our own internalized models and mindsets, or we risk regenerating the very conditions we sought to overcome. Accordingly, if a fundamentalist is one who is unyielding in their attitudes and opinions, and one who divides the world in binary terms, we may ask ourselves: *Am I personifying or perpetuating a form of fundamentalism and exclusion in my interactions with "the other"?* While it may be tempting, for instance, to find creative ways to humiliate an enemy or opposition—be it in war or politics—as Basit Jamal teaches from the Quran (and incidentally, a similar quote has been attributed to Abraham Lincoln), "The best way to destroy your enemy is to make him your friend."

Terrorism in and of itself is not an ideology; it is a tactic. Fighting it disconnects us from this reality. Would we declare war on ballistic missiles? Humanizing counterterrorism, on the other hand, forces us to confront the underlying issues and conditions—the disease, rather than the symptoms. We owe it to ourselves to adopt a more human-ized, values-first approach to counterterrorism. Resonant with this notion of soft diplomacy is the one thing former violent extremists, and veterans, have repeatedly told Lena Slachmuijlder at Search that they most regret: their narrow perception of "power." True strength, they come to realize in hindsight, is in the ability to not use force. At 72 years old, another former US president, Thomas Jefferson, had a similar epiphany when he wrote, "I hope our wisdom will grow with our power, and teach us, that the less we use our power, the greater it will be."[34] One can only hope.

──────NOTES──────

Introduction

1. David Cortright and George A. Lopez, *Uniting Against Terror: Cooperative Non-military Responses to the Global Terrorist Threat* (Cambridge, MA: The MIT Press, 2007), 37.

2. Seth G. Jones and Artin C. Libicki, *How Terrorist Groups End: Lessons for Countering al Qa'ida* (RAND Corporation, 2008), *www.rand.org/content/dam/rand/pubs/monographs/2008/RAND_MG741-1.pdf*.

3. Arie Perliger and Daniel Milton, "From Cradle to Grave: The Lifecycle of Foreign Fighters in Iraq and Syria," Combatting Terrorism Center at West Point, November 11, 2016, *https://ctc.usma.edu/from-cradle-to-grave-the-lifecycle-of-foreign-fighters-in-iraq-and-syria/*.

4. Hamed El-Said and Richard Barrett, *Enhancing the Understanding of the Foreign Terrorist Fighters Phenomenon in Syria* (United Nations Office of Counter-Terrorism [UNOCT], July 2017), *www.un.org/en/counterterrorism/assets/img/Report_Final_20170727.pdf*.

5. *Global Terrorism Index 2017* (Institute for Economics and Peace, November 2017), *visionofhumanity.org/app/uploads/2017/11/Global-Terrorism-Index-2017.pdf*.

6. Keith Proctor, "Youth and Consequences: Unemployment, Injustice and Violence—Afghanistan, Colombia, Somalia," Mercy Corps, February 13, 2015, *www.mercycorps.org/research-resources/youth-consequences-unemployment-injustice-and-violence?source=WOW00088&utm_source=release&utm_medium=media%20relations&utm_campaign=youth%20conflict%20report*.

PART I

1. Who Is the Terrorist?

1. Naif Al-Mutawa, "Superheroes Inspired by Islam," (TEDGlobal Conference, July 2010), Accessed online, *www.ted.com/talks/naif_al_mutawa_superheroes _inspired_by_islam?language=en.*

2. Al-Mutawa, "Superheros Inspired by Islam."

3. Trevor Noah, "Prince Harry and Meghan Markle's Royal Wedding" (Live at the O2 London May 21, 2018), YouTube, *www.no-ads-youtube.com/video/ trevor-noah/prince-harry-meghan-markle-s-royal-wedding-live-at-the-o2-london- trevor-noah?v=njfl_bwFBoI.*

4. Miriam Valverde, "A Look at the Data on Domestic Terrorism and Who Is Behind It," *PolitiFact*, August 16, 2017, www.politifact.com/truth-o-meter/ article/2017/aug/16/look-data-domestic-terrorism-and-whos-behind-it/.

5. Europol, "European Union Terrorism Situation and Trend Report (TE-SAT) 2016," *EU Terrorism Situation and Trend Report*, November 1, 2016, *www .europol.europa.eu/activities-services/main-reports/european-union-terrorism -situation-and-trend-report-te-sat-2016.*

6. Feliks Garcia, "White Nationalist Movement Growing Much Faster Than Isis on Social Media," *Independent*, September 4, 2016, *www.independent.co.uk/ news/world/americas/white-nationalist-movement-twitter-faster-growth-isis-islamic -state-study-a7223671.html.*

7. Alan Strathern, "Why Are Buddhist Monks Attacking Muslims?" *BBC News*, May 2, 2013, *www.bbc.com/news/magazine-22356306.*

8. Alan B. Krueger and Jitka Maleckova, "Does Poverty Cause Terrorism? The Economics and the Education of Suicide Bombers," *The New Republic Online*, June 24, 2002, *https://newrepublic.com/article/91841/does-poverty-cause-terrorism.*

9. James Michael Lutz and Brenda J. Lutz, *Terrorism: Origins and Evolution* (New York: Palgrave Macmillan, 2005) 26–27.

10. Walter Laqueur, "Terrorism: A Brief History," *EJournal USA Foreign Policy Agenda* 12 (2007): 21.

11. "Joseph Stalin: Created Worst Man-made Famine in History," *History: Fast Facts*, April 19, 2016, *www.youtube.com/watch?v=_aF_sRXVdoU.*

12. Rupert Colley, "Yakov Stalin—A Summary." *History in an Hour*, March 18, 2013, *www.historyinanhour.com/2013/03/18/yakov-stalin-summary/.*

13. Laqueur, "Terrorism: A Brief History," 22.

14. Brian Michael Jenkins, "The 1970s and the Birth of Contemporary Terrorism." *The Hill,* July 30, 2015, *http://thehill.com/blogs/pundits-blog/homeland-security/249688-the-1970s-and-the-birth-of-contemporary-terrorism.*

15. Timothy Naftali, *Blind Spot: The Secret History of American Counterterrorism,* Interview with Timothy Naftali, C-SPAN, July 21, 2005, *www.c-span.org/video/?188136-1/blind-spot-secret-history-american-counterterrorism.*

16. Christoph Reuter, *My Life is a Weapon: A Modern History of Suicide Bombing* (Munich: Bertelsmann Verlag, 2002).

17. "Tamil Tigers: Suicide Bombing Innovators," NPR: *Talk of the Nation,* May 21, 2009, *www.npr.org/templates/story/story.php?storyId=104391493.*

18. Lutz, *Terrorism: Origins and Evolution,* 39.

19. Abdel Bari Atwan, *The Secret History of Al Qaeda* (New York: University of California Press, 2006), 92.

20. Arnaud Blin and Gerard Chaliand, eds. *The History of Terrorism: From Antiquity to Al Qaeda.* Trans. Edward Schneider. (New York: University of California Press, 2007). 221–23.

21. Alix Langone, "Police Swamped with 1,200 Calls About Suspicious Packages: The Latest on the Austin Bombings," *Time,* March 20, 2018, *http://time.com/5205181/austin-bombings%20/.*

22. James Alan Fox, "How Do We Prevent Future Stephen Paddocks? After Vegas, Way Forward Fraught with Problems," *USA Today,* October 3, 2017, *www.usatoday.com/story/opinion/2017/10/03/how-do-we-prevent-future-stephen-paddocks-way-forward-fraught-problems-jameslan-fox-column/724856001/.*

23. Laqueur, "Terrorism: A Brief History," 20.

24. Richard F. Grimmett, "Instances of Use of United States Armed Forces Abroad 1798–2008," Congressional Research Service, March 10, 2011, *https://fas.org/sgp/crs/natsec/R41677.pdf.*

25. IPPNW-Germany, "Body Count: Casualty Figures after 10 Years of the 'War on Terror,'" PSR: Physicians for Social Responsibility, March 19, 2015, *www.psr.org/blog/resource/body-count/.*

26. Micah Zenko and Jennifer Wilson, "How Many Bombs Did the United States Drop in 2016?" Council on Foreign Relations, January 5, 2017, *www.cfr.org/blog/how-many-bombs-did-united-states-drop-2016/.*

27. Jack Serle, "Obama Drone Casualty Numbers a Fraction of Those Recorded by the Bureau," The Bureau of Investigative Journalism, July 1, 2016 *www.thebureauinvestigates.com/stories/2016-07-01/obama-drone-casualty-numbers-a-fraction-of-those-recorded-by-the-bureau.*

28. Bruce Hoffman, *Inside Terrorism* (New York: Columbia University Press, 2006), 43.

29. Robert Windrem, "US Government Considered Nelson Mandela a Terrorist Until 2008," NBCNews.com, November 2, 2015, *www.nbcnews.com/ news/world/us-government-considered-nelson-mandela-terrorist-until-2008 -flna2D11708787*.

30. League of Arab States, "The Arab Convention for the Suppression of Terrorism," Adopted by the Council of Arab Ministers of the Interior and the Council of Arab Ministers of Justice (Cairo, Egypt, April 1998), *www.unodc .org/images/tldb-f/conv_arab_terrorism.en.pdf.*

31. "Information on More than 180,000 Terrorist Attacks." Global Terrorism Database, University of Maryland National Consortium for the Study of Terrorism and Responses to Terrorism: A Center of Excellence of the U.S. Department of Homeland Security, July 2018, *www.start.umd.edu/gtd/*.

32. *Global Terrorism Index 2017* (Institute for Economics and Peace, November 2017), *visionofhumanity.org/app/uploads/2017/11/Global-Terrorism-Index-2017.pdf.*

33. *Global Terrorism Index 2017* (Institute for Economics and Peace).

34. *Global Terrorism Index 2017* (Institute for Economics and Peace).

35. *Global Terrorism Index 2017* (Institute for Economics and Peace).

36. *Global Terrorism Index 2016* (Institute for Economics and Peace, November 2016), *http://economicsandpeace.org/wp-content/uploads/2016/11/Global-Terrorism -Index-2016.2.pdf.*

37. Lorenzo Vidino, Francesco Marone, and Eva Entenmann, "Fear Thy Neighbor, Radicalization and Jihadist Attacks in the West," ICCT: International Centre for Counter-Terrorism - The Hague, Publications, June 14, 2017, *https://icct .nl/publication/fear-thy-neighbor-radicalization-and-jihadist-attacks-in-the-west/*.

38. Vidino, Marone, and Entenmann, "Fear Thy Neighbor."

39. The Soufan Group, "Foreign Fighters: An Updated Assessment of the Flow of Foreign Fighters into Syria and Iraq," December 2015, *soufangroup.com/ wp-content/uploads/2015/12/TSG_ForeignFightersUpdate_FINAL3.pdf.*

40. Thomas Hegghammer, "The Rise of Muslim Foreign Fighters: Islam and the Globalization of Jihad," *International Security* 35, 3 (Winter 2011/12): 53–94, *www.belfercenter.org/sites/default/files/files/publication/The_Rise_of_Muslim _Foreign_Fighters.pdf.*

41. The Soufan Group, "Foreign Fighters."

2. Make the *Umma* Great Again

1. Alexander LaCasse, "How Many Muslim Extremists Are There? Just the Facts, Please," *Christian Science Monitor*, January 13, 2015, *www.csmonitor.com/*

World/Security-Watch/terrorism-security/2015/0113/How-many-Muslim-extremists-are-there-Just-the-facts-please.

2. Laylá Abū Zayd, *Life of the Prophet: A Biography of Prophet Mohammed* (Beruit: Dar Al-Kotob Al-Ilmiya, 2011), 90.

3. Ṣaff al-Raḥmān Mubārakfūrī, Tabassum Siraj, Michael Richardson, and Badr Azimabadi, *When the Moon Split: A Biography of Prophet Muhammad* (Riyadh: Darussalam, 2002), 61–70; Hazrat Mirza Bashiruddin Mahmud Ahmad, Khalifatul Masih II, *Life of Muhammad*, 7th ed. (UK: Wakalat-e-Tasnif, 2014).

4. Lesley Hazleton, *The First Muslim: The Story of Muhammad* (New York: Riverhead Books, 2014), 142.

5. Barnaby Rogerson, *The Prophet Muhammad: A Biography* (London: Abacus, 2003) 157.

6. Yasmeen Qadri, "Democracy in Islam: Myth or Reality," Paper presented at Law-Related Education, State Bar, Austin, Texas, February 6, 2004, *https://theisla.org/wp-content/uploads/resources/Qadri-Democracy_in_Islam.pdf.*

7. Qadri, "Democracy in Islam."

8. Qadri, "Democracy in Islam."

9. Qadri, "Democracy in Islam."

10. Qasim Rashid, "Anyone Who Says the Quran Advocates Terrorism Obviously Hasn't Read Its Lessons on Violence," *The Independent*, April 10, 2017, *www.independent.co.uk/voices/islam-muslim-terrorism-islamist-extremism-quran-teaching-violence-meaning-prophet-muhammed-a7676246.html.*

11. Maysam J. Al Faruqi, "Umma: The Orientalists and the Quranic Concept of Identity," *Journal of Islamic Studies* 16, 1 (2005): 2–3.

12. Gilles Kepel, *Jihad: The Trail of Political Islam* (New York: Belknap Press, 2002), 38.

13. Ibn Taymiya, *A Muslim Theologian's Response to Christianity: A Translation of Ibn Taymiyya's Jawab al- Sahih li-man Baddala din al-Masih*, trans. Thomas F. Michel (New York: Caravan Books, 1985), 56–57.

14. Taymiya, *A Muslim Theologian's Response to Christianity*, 57.

15. Kishwar Rizvi, "Destruction of Mosul Mosque Desecrates History," CNN, June 24, 2017, *https://edition.cnn.com/2017/06/24/opinions/destruction-mosul-mosque-opinion-rizvi/index.html.*

16. John L. Esposito, *Unholy War Terror in the Name of Islam* (New York: Oxford University Press, 2002), 45.

17. Natana J. DeLong-Bas, *Wahhabi Islam: From Revival and Reform to Global Jihad* (New York: Oxford UP, Incorporated, 2004), 8.

18. DeLong-Bas, *Wahhabi Islam*, 17.

19. DeLong-Bas, *Wahhabi Islam*, 225.

20. DeLong-Bas, *Wahhabi Islam*, 30.

21. Malise Ruthven, *A Fury for God: The Islamist Attack on America* (London: Granta, 2002), 72–98.

22. Gilles Kepel, *Jihad: The Trail of Political Islam* (New York: Belknap Press, 2002), 314.

23. Robert Irwin, "Is This the Man Who Inspired Bin Laden?" *The Guardian*, UK edition, November 1, 2001.

24. Ruthven, *A Fury for God*, 86.

25. Ruthven, *A Fury for God*, 84–85.

26. Ray Takeyh and Nikolas K. Gvosdev, *The Receding Shadow of the Prophet: The Rise and Fall of Radical Political Islam* (New York: Praeger, 2004), 159.

27. Takeyh and Gvosdev, *Receding Shadow of Prophet*, 161.

28. Salim T. S. Al-Hassani, ed. *1001 Inventions. Muslim Heritage in Our World*, 2nd ed. (Manchester: Foundation for Science, Technology and Civilization, 2006).

29. Thomas Walker Arnold, *The Preaching of Islam* (New York: Charles Scribner's Sons, 1913), 2.

30. Peter Adamson, *Al-Kindi (Great Medieval Thinkers)* (New York: Oxford University Press, 2006).

31. Ehsan Yarshater, ed., "Avicenna," *Encyclopaedia Iranica*. 2006. Accessed May 2009, *www.iranicaonline.org/articles/avicenna-index*.

32. Arnold, *Preaching of Islam*, 2.

33. Toby E. Huff, *The Rise of Early Modern Science: Islam, China, and the West* (Cambridge, UK: Cambridge University Press, 1993), 67.

34. Huff, *Rise of Early Modern Science*, 117.

35. George Saliba, *Islamic Science and the Making of the European Renaissance* (Cambridge, MA: The MIT Press, 2007), Chapter 7.

36. "Self-Doomed to Failure," *The Economist*, July 6, 2002: 24–26.

37. Soumitra Dutta, Bruno Lanvin, and Sacha Wunsch-Vincent, Eds., *Global Innovation Index: Energizing the World with Innovation* (Ithaca, NY: Cornell University, INSEAD, and WIPO, 2018).

38. Thomas L Friedman, *The World Is Flat: A Brief History of the Twenty-First Century* (New York: Farrar, Straus and Giroux, 2005), 561.

39. "Self-Doomed to Failure," 24–26.

40. Friedman, *The World Is Flat*, 564.

41. "Saudi Arabia Tops Arab World with Registration of 664 Patents in 2017," *Al Arabiya*, English edition, April 17, 2018, Accessed June 23, 2018, *https://english .alarabiya.net/en/business/technology/2018/04/17/Saudi-Arabia-tops-Arab -world-with-registration-of-664-patents-in-2017.html*.

42. Friedman, *The World Is Flat*, 565.

43. Assaf Moghadam, *The Globalization of Martyrdom Al Qaeda, Salafi Jihad, and the Diffusion of Suicide Attacks* (Baltimore: Johns Hopkins University Press, 2008), 150.

44. UNDP, "Arab Human Development Report 2016: Youth and the Prospects for Human Development in a Changing Reality," UNDP: United Nations Development Programme, Regional Bureau for Arab States, *www.arab-hdr .org/reports/2016/english/AHDR2016En.pdf*.

45. Abdel Bari Atwan, *The Secret History of Al Qaeda* (New York: University of California Press, 2006), 109.

3. Post-Colonial Hangover

1. Peter Mansfield, *A History of the Middle East*, 2nd ed. (London: Penguin Books Ltd., 1991), Chs. 9–10.

2. Benjamin R. Barber, *Jihad vs. McWorld* (New York: Times Books, 1995), 11.

3. Matthew Weaver, "Isis Declares Caliphate in Iraq and Syria," *The Guardian*, US edition, June 30, 2014, *www.theguardian.com/world/middle-east-live/2014/ jun/30/isis-declares-caliphate-in-iraq-and-syria-live-updates*.

4. Mansfield, *A History of the Middle East*, chs. 9–10.

5. Beverley Milton-Edwards and Peter Hinchcliffe, *Conflicts in the Middle East since 1945* (New York: Routledge, 2007), 3.

6. Milton-Edwards and Hinchcliffe, *Conflicts in the Middle East*, 12.

7. Ilan Pappe, *The Ethnic Cleansing of Palestine* (London: Oneworld, 2006).

8. "By Hook and by Crook: Israeli Settlement Policy in the West Bank," B'Tselem: The Israeli Information Center for Human Rights in the Occupied Territories, July 2010, *www.btselem.org/publications/summaries/201007_by _hook_and_by_crook*.

9. Tom H Hastings, *Nonviolent Response to Terrorism* (Boston: McFarland and Company, Inc., 2004), 135.

10. Sean Hannity, *Deliver Us from Evil: Defeating Terrorism, Despotism, and Liberalism* (New York: HarperCollins, 2004).

11. BBC, "United States of America Timeline," *BBC News*, January 10, 2012, *http://news.bbc.co.uk/2/hi/americas/country_profiles/1230058.stm*.

12. Erika G. Alin, *The United States and the 1958 Lebanon Crisis: American Intervention in the Middle East* (Lanham, MD: University Press of America, 1994).

13. Alin, *United States and Lebanon Crisis*.

14. Hastings, *Nonviolent Response to Terrorism*, 40.

15. Mansfield, *History of the Middle East*, 223.

16. Mansfield, *History of the Middle East*, 223.

17. Steven Hiatt, *A Game as Old as Empire: The Secret World of Economic Hit Men and the Web of Global Corruption* (Oakland, CA: Berrett-Koehler Publishers, 2007), 14.

18. Hiatt, *Game as Old as Empire*, 14.

19. Jillian Schwedler, "Islamic Identity: Myth, Menace, or Mobilizer?" *SAIS Review* 21, 2 (2001): 10.

20. Hiatt, *Game as Old as Empire*, 15.

21. Daniel Yergen, *The Prize: The Epic Quest for Oil, Money, and Power* (New York: Free Press, 2008).

22. Hiatt, *Game as Old as Empire*, 70.

23. Hiatt, *Game as Old as Empire*, 133.

24. Hiatt, *Game as Old as Empire*, 231.

25. CNN, "Study: Bush, Aides Made 935 False Statements in Run-up to War," CNN Politics, January 24, 2008, *http://edition.cnn.com/2008/POLITICS/01/23/bush.iraq/*.

26. Fouad Zakariyya, *Myth and Reality in the Contemporary Islamist Movement*, Trans. Ibrahim M. Abu-Rabi (London: Pluto Press, 2005), ix.

27. Ray Takeyh and Nikolas K. Gvosdev. Takeyh, *The Receding Shadow of the Prophet: The Rise and Fall of Radical Political Islam* (New York: Praeger, 2004), 14.

28. Abdel Bari Atwan, *The Secret History of Al Qaeda* (New York: University of California Press, 2008), 40.

PART II

4. Islam Made Me Do It

1. The White House, "President Trump's Speech to the Arab Islamic American Summit," Statements and Releases, Foreign Policy, May 21, 2017, *www.whitehouse.gov/briefings-statements/president-trumps-speech-arab-islamic-american-summit/*.

2. Thích Nhất Hạnh, *Peace Is Every Step: The Path of Mindfulness in Everyday Life* (New York: Bantam Books, 1991).

3. Hamed El-Said and Richard Barrett, *Enhancing the Understanding of the Foreign Terrorist Fighters Phenomenon in Syria* (UN Counter-Terrorism Centre [UNOCT], July 27, 2017), *www.un.org/en/counterterrorism/assets/img/Report_Final_20170727.pdf*.

4. Esther Addley, Nazia Parveen, Jamie Grierson, and Steven Morris, "Salman Abedi: From Hot-Headed Party Lover to Suicide Bomber," *The Guardian*, US edition, May 26, 2017, *www.theguardian.com/uk-news/2017/may/26/salman-abedi-manchester-arena-attack-partying-suicide-bomber*.

5. Agence France-Presse, "Orly Airport Attack: Drugs and Alcohol Found in Gunman's Blood," *The Guardian*, US edition, March 19, 2017, *www.theguardian.com/world/2017/mar/20/orly-airport-shooting-drugs-and-alcohol-found-in-gunmans-blood*.

6. Kim Willsher, "Nice Attacker Grew Beard in Week Before Truck Rampage—Prosecutor," *The Guardian,* US edition, July 18, 2016, *www.theguardian.com/world/2016/jul/18/nice-attack-premeditated-mohamed-lahouaiej-bouhlel-beard-prosecutor*.

7. Stephen Burgen and Ian Cobain, "Barcelona Attack: Four Suspects Face Court after Van Driver Is Shot Dead," *The Guardian*, US edition, August 22, 2017, *www.theguardian.com/world/2017/aug/21/police-searching-barcelona-van-driver-shoot-man*.

8. Natalia Drozdiak and Matthew Dalton, "Two Suspects Sold Bar in Brussels Not Long Before Paris Attacks," *The Wall Street Journal*, November 18, 2015, *www.wsj.com/articles/two-suspects-sold-bar-in-brussels-not-long-before-paris-attacks-1447863006*.

9. Mary Anne Weaver, "The Short, Violent Life of Abu Musab Al-Zarqawi," *The Atlantic*, June 8, 2006, *www.theatlantic.com/magazine/archive/2006/07/the-short-violent-life-of-abu-musab-al-zarqawi/304983/*.

10. Fox News, "Hasan Called Himself 'Soldier of Allah' on Business Cards," Fox News, January 7, 2015, *www.foxnews.com/us/hasan-called-himself-soldier-of-allah-on-business-cards*.

11. Peter Bergen, *United States of Jihad: The Untold Story of Al-Qaeda in America* (New York: Broadway Books, 2015), Kindle.

12. Bergen, *United States of Jihad.*

13. Bergen, *United States of Jihad.*

14. Christoph Reuter, *My Life Is a Weapon: A Modern History of Suicide Bombing* (Princeton, NJ: Princeton University Press, 2006).

15. Toby Harnden, "Seedy Secrets of Hijackers Who Broke Muslim Laws," *The Telegraph*, 6 October 6, 2001, *www.telegraph.co.uk/news/1358665/Seedy-secrets-of-hijackers-who-broke-Muslim-laws.html*.

16. Reuter, *My Life Is a Weapon*.

17. Malise Ruthven, *A Fury for God: The Islamist Attack on America* (London: Granta, 2002), 122.

18. Ruthven, *A Fury for God*, 122.

19. Reza Aslan, *How to Win a Cosmic War: God, Globalization, and the End of the War on Terror* (New York: Random House, 2009).

20. Davide Lerner, "It's Not Islam That Drives Young Europeans to Jihad, France's Top Terrorism Expert Explains," *Haaretz.com*, August 20, 2017, *www.haaretz.com/world-news/europe/it-s-not-islam-that-drives-young-europeans-to-jihad-terrorism-expert-says-1.5477000*.

21. Mark Mazzetti and Eric Schmitt, "In the Age of ISIS, Who's a Terrorist, and Who's Simply Deranged?" *The New York Times*, July 17, 2016, *www.nytimes.com/2016/07/18/world/europe/in-the-age-of-isis-whos-a-terrorist-and-whos-simply-deranged.html?_r=0*.

22. Associated Press in Detroit, "Flint Airport Stabbing Suspect Was Not on Radar of Canada or US Authorities," *The Guardian*, US edition, June 23, 2017, *www.theguardian.com/us-news/2017/jun/23/flint-airport-stabbing-suspect-amor-ftouhi-lone-wolf*.

23. Vikram Dodd and Matthew Taylor, "London Attack: 'Aggressive' and 'Strange' Suspect Vowed to 'Do Some Damage,'" *The Guardian*, US edition, June 20, 2017, *www.theguardian.com/uk-news/2017/jun/19/several-casualties-reported-after-van-hits-pedestrians-in-north-london*.

24. Abdel Bari Atwan, *Islamic State: The Digital Caliphate* (London: Saqi Books, 2015), 20–21.

25. *Global Terrorism Index 2017* (Institute for Economics and Peace, November 2017), *visionofhumanity.org/app/uploads/2017/11/Global-Terrorism-Index-2017.pdf*.

26. Sami Aboudi, Omar Fahmy, and Kevin Liffey (ed.), "Bomber Planning to Attack Mecca's Grand Mosque Blows Himself Up: Ministry," *Reuters*, World News, June 23, 2017, *www.reuters.com/article/us-saudi-security-idUSKBN19E2BL*.

27. Justin Whitaker, "Dalai Lama: There Is No 'Muslim Terrorist' or 'Buddhist Terrorist,'" UHRP: Uyghur Human Rights Project, September, 18, 2016, *uhrp.org/news/dalai-lama-there-no-%E2%80%9Cmuslim-terrorist%E2%80%9D-or-%E2%80%9Cbuddhist-terrorist%E2%80%9D*.

28. The White House, "Trump's Speech to Arab Islamic American Summit."

29. Khalid Aziz, "Country Paper on Drivers of Radicalism and Extremism in Pakistan," Friedrich Ebert Stiftung, December 2015, *library.fes.de/pdf-files/bueros/pakistan/12144.pdf*.

30. Alan Travis, "MI5 Report Challenges Views on Terrorism in Britain," *The Guardian*, US edition, August 20, 2008, *www.theguardian.com/uk/2008/aug/20/uksecurity.terrorism1*.

31. Lisette Thooft, "Karen Armstrong: 'There Is Nothing in the Islam That Is More Violent than Christianity,'" *Nieuw Wij*, January 18, 2015, *www.nieuwwij.nl/english/karen-armstrong-nothing-islam-violent-christianity/*.

32. Thooft, "Nothing in Islam."

33. El-Said and Barrett, "Enhancing Understanding of Foreign Terrorist Fighters."

34. Robyn Scott and Lisa Witter, "Can Nigeria Teach Us How to Build Defences against Terrorism?" World Economic Forum, Global Agenda, January 18, 2016, *www.weforum.org/agenda/2016/01/can-nigeria-teach-us-how-to-build-resilience-against-terrorism/*.

35. *Global Terrorism Index 2017*, (Institute for Economics and Peace).

36. El-Said and Barrett, "Enhancing Understanding of Foreign Terrorist Fighters."

37. Arie Perliger and Daniel Milton, "From Cradle to Grave: The Lifecycle of Foreign Fighters in Iraq and Syria," Combatting Terrorism Center at West Point, November 11, 2016, *https://ctc.usma.edu/from-cradle-to-grave-the-lifecycle-of-foreign-fighters-in-iraq-and-syria/*.

38. Perliger and Milton, "From Cradle to Grave."

39. Perliger and Milton, "From Cradle to Grave."

40. El-Said and Barrett, "Enhancing Understanding of Foreign Terrorist Fighters."

41. El-Said and Barrett, "Enhancing Understanding of Foreign Terrorist Fighters."

42. Souad Mekhennet, "What Are the Root Causes of Islamic Terrorism?" *Global Agenda*, World Economic Forum, January 18, 2016, Accessed in 2017, *www.weforum.org/agenda/2016/01/what-are-the-root-causes-of-islamic-terrorism/*.

5. Poverty of Hope

1. David Gold, "Economics of Terrorism," CIAO: Columbia International Affairs Online, New School University, May 8, 2009, *www.files.ethz.ch/isn/10698/doc_10729_290_en.pdf*.

2. Abu Bakr Naji, *The Management of Savagery: The Most Critical Phase the Umma Will Experience* (2004), 111, *https://www.cia.gov/library/abbottabad-compound/20/207DE0C1094BC68A7061C96629DD5C1A_adara_twahsh.pdf*.

3. Dan Ackman, "The Cost of Being Osama Bin Laden," *Forbes*, September 14, 2001, *www.forbes.com/2001/09/14/0914ladenmoney.html#14d363f132a3*.

4. Mabruk Kabir, "Empowering a New Generation of Female Entrepreneurs in Afghanistan," The World Bank, End Poverty in South Asia, March 15, 2017, *blogs.worldbank.org/endpovertyinsouthasia/empowering-new-generation-female-entrepreneurs-afghanistan*.

5. Zuri Linetsky, "Jobs, Not Bombs, Will Win the War on Terror," *Foreign Policy*, March 14, 2017, *foreignpolicy.com/2017/03/13/this-poll-proves-that-trumps-counterterrorism-strategy-will-fail-africa-nigeria-boko-haram/*.

6. Linetsky, "Jobs, Not Bombs."

7. Linetsky, "Jobs, Not Bombs."

8. Hamed El-Said and Richard Barrett, *Enhancing the Understanding of the Foreign Terrorist Fighters Phenomenon in Syria* (UN Counter-Terrorism Centre [UNOC]), July 27, 2017), *www.un.org/en/counterterrorism/assets/img/Report_Final_20170727.pdf*.

9. El-Said and Barrett, *Enhancing Understanding of Foreign Terrorist Fighters*.

10. Arie Perliger and Daniel Milton, "From Cradle to Grave: The Lifecycle of Foreign Fighters in Iraq and Syria," Combatting Terrorism Center at West Point, November 11, 2016, *ctc.usma.edu/from-cradle-to-grave-the-lifecycle-of-foreign-fighters-in-iraq-and-syria/*.

11. Neven Bondokji, Kim Wilkinson, and Leen Aghabi, "Trapped Between Destructive Choices: Radicalisation Drivers Affecting Youth in Jordan," WANA Institute, February 21, 2017, *wanainstitute.org/en/publication/trapped-between-destructive-choices-radicalisation-drivers-affecting-youth-jordan*.

12. Peter Byrne, "Anatomy of Terror: What Makes Normal People Become Extremists?" *New Scientist*, August 16, 2017, *www.newscientist.com/article/mg23531390-700-anatomy-of-terror-what-makes-normal-people-become-extremists/*.

13. Forbes International Contributor, "The World's 10 Richest Terrorist Organizations," *Forbes*, December 12, 2014, *www.forbes.com/sites/forbesinternational/2014/12/12/the-worlds-10-richest-terrorist-organizations/*.

14. El-Said and Barrett, "Enhancing Understanding of Foreign Terrorist Fighters."

15. Jessica Stern, *Terror in the Name of God Why Religious Militants Kill* (New York: Ecco, 2003), 212–17.

16. Stern, *Terror in Name of God*, 212–17.

17. Shanta Devarajan et al., *Economic and Social Inclusion to Prevent Violent Extremism* (Washington, DC: World Bank Publications, Economic Monitor, October 2016).

18. Shawn Teresa Flanigan, "Charity as Resistance: Connections between Charity, Contentious Politics, and Terror," *Studies in Conflict and Terrorism* 29, 7 (2006): 641–55, *http://dx.doi.org/10.1080/10576100500522579.*

19. Ismat Sarah Mangla, "Why Do American Muslims Fare Better Than Their French Counterparts?" *International Business Times,* November 18, 2015, *www.ibtimes.com/why-do-american-muslims-fare-better-their-french-counterparts-2189449.*

20. Africa Center for Strategic Studies, "Extremism: Root Causes, Drivers, and Responses," November 20, 2015, *http://africacenter.org/spotlight/extremism-root-causes-drivers-and-responses/.*

21. *Global Terrorism Index 2017* (Institute for Economics and Peace, November 2017), *visionofhumanity.org/app/uploads/2017/11/Global-Terrorism-Index-2017.pdf.*

22. Keneshbek Sainazarov, Central Asia Program Director, Search for Common Ground, conversation with author via Skype, June 20, 2018.

23. "White Right: Meeting the Enemy," *Exposure,* Season 7, Episode 2, directed by Deeyah Khan, written by Gareth McLean, featuring Deeyah Khan, Brian Culpepper, and Pardeep Kaleka, aired December 11, 2017, viewed on Netflix, *www.netflix.com/search?q=white%20right&jbv=80994804&jbp=0&jbr=0.*

24. Byrne, "Anatomy of Terror."

25. Byrne, "Anatomy of Terror."

6. Dis-Integrated

1. Eric Hoffer, *The True Believer: Thought on the Nature of Mass Movements* (New York: Harper and Row, 1966), 44.

2. Philip Rucker and Julie Tate, "In Online Posts Apparently by Detroit Suspect, Religious Ideals Collide," *The Washington Post,* December 29, 2009, *www.washingtonpost.com/wp-dyn/content/article/2009/12/28/AR2009122802492.html.*

3. Colonel John M. "Matt" Venhaus, US Army, *Why Youth Join al-Qaeda,* United States Institute of Peace (USIP), 2010, *www.usip.org/sites/default/files/SR236Venhaus.pdf.*

4. Venhaus, *Why Youth Join al-Qaeda.*

5. Venhaus, *Why Youth Join al-Qaeda.*

6. "Jihad Cool," *Wikipedia: The Free Encyclopedia,* April 4, 2018, *https://en.wikipedia.org/wiki/Jihad_Cool.*

7. Abdel Bari Atwan, *Islamic State: The Digital Caliphate* (Oakland, CA: University of California Press, 2015), 20.

8. "The Real Housewives of ISIS," *Revolting*, BBC, January 5, 2017, *www .youtube.com/watch?v=fKL9b5-DL4A*.

9. Marc Sageman, *Turning to Political Violence: The Emergence of Terrorism* (Philadelphia: University of Pennsylvania Press, 2017).

10. Venhaus, *Why Youth Join Al Qaeda*.

11. Mitchell D. Silber and Arvin Bhatt, *Radicalization in the West: The Homegrown Threat* (New York: City of New York Police Department, 2007).

12. Silber and Bhatt, *Radicalization in the West*.

13. Peter Bergen, *United States of Jihad: The Untold Story of Al-Qaeda in America* (New York: Crown, 2016).

14. Bergen, *United States of Jihad*.

15. *Homegrown: The Counter-Terror Dilemma*, directed by Greg Barker, HBO Documentary Films, aired on February 8, 2016, *www.imdb.com/title/tt5497132/*.

16. Bergen, *United States of Jihad*.

17. Bergen, *United States of Jihad*.

18. Johannes Hirn, *Will Box for Passport*, photo essay of Tamerlan Tsarnaev, 2009. See *www.huffingtonpost.com/2013/04/19/tamerlan-tsarnaev-boxing-photos_n _3118629.html*.

19. Josie Jammet, "The Fall of the House of Tsarnaev," *Boston Globe*, December 15, 2013, *www.bostonglobe.com/Page/Boston/2011-2020/WebGraphics/Metro/ BostonGlobe.com/2013/12/15tsarnaev/tsarnaev.html*.

20. Neven Bondokji, Kim Wilkinson, and Leen Aghabi, "Trapped Between Destructive Choices: Radicalisation Drivers Affecting Youth in Jordan," WANA Institute, February 21, 2017, *wanainstitute.org/en/publication/trapped -between-destructive-choices-radicalisation-drivers-affecting-youth-jordan*.

21. Manal Omar, "Why Women Are a Not-So-Secret Weapon for ISIS," CNN, 31 March 31, 2017, *edition.cnn.com/2017/03/31/opinions/female-fighters-isis -behind-the-mask-omar-opinion/index.html*.

22. Sageman, *Turning to Political Violence*, 6.

23. United States Senate, "Zachary Chesser: A Case Study in Online Islamist Radicalization and Its Meaning for the Threat of Homegrown Terrorism" (PDF), Majority and Minority Staff Senate Committee on Homeland Security and Governmental Affairs, February 2012, *www.hsgac.senate.gov/imo/ media/doc/CHESSER%20FINAL%20REPORT(1)2.pdf*.

24. Emma Green, "How Two Mississippi College Students Fell in Love and Decided to Join a Terrorist Group," *The Atlantic*, May 1, 2017, *www .theatlantic.com/politics/archive/2017/05/mississippi-young-dakhlalla/524751/*.

25. Glennon Doyle Melton, "One Teacher's Brilliant Idea to Stop School Shootings Has Nothing to Do with Guns," *Business Insider,* February 17, 2018, *www.businessinsider.com/one-teachers-brilliant-idea-to-stop-future-school-shootings-has-nothing-to-do-with-guns-2018-2.*

26. *Global Terrorism Index 2016* (Institute for Economics and Peace, November 2016) *http://economicsandpeace.org/wp-content/uploads/2016/11/Global-Terrorism-Index-2016.2.pdf.*

27. Arie Perliger and Daniel Milton, "From Cradle to Grave: The Lifecycle of Foreign Fighters in Iraq and Syria," Combatting Terrorism Center at West Point, November 11, 2016, *https://ctc.usma.edu/from-cradle-to-grave-the-lifecycle-of-foreign-fighters-in-iraq-and-syria/.*

28. Perliger and Milton, "From Cradle to Grave."

29. Sarah Lyons-Padilla, "Can Discrimination Contribute to Feelings of Radicalization?" *American Psychological Association,* August 5, 2017, *https://www.apa.org/news/press/releases/2017/08/discrimination-radicalization.aspx.*

30. Sarah Lyons-Padilla, "I've Studied Radicalization—And Islamophobia Often Plants the Seed," *The Guardian,* US edition, June 13, 2016, *www.theguardian.com/commentisfree/2016/jun/13/radicalisation-islamophobia-orlando-shooting-florida-muslims-trump.*

31. Alex Nowrasteh, "Immigration and Crime—What the Research Says," *Cato Institute,* July 14, 2015, *www.cato.org/blog/immigration-crime-what-research-says.*

32. "U.S. Muslims Concerned about Their Place in Society, But Continue to Believe in the American Dream: 1. Demographic Portrait of Muslim Americans," Pew Research Center: Religion and Public Life, July 26, 2017, *www.pewforum.org/2017/07/26/demographic-portrait-of-muslim-americans/#fn-28360-8.*

33. "Islamic, Yet Integrated: Why Muslims Fare Better in America Than in Europe," *The Economist,* September 6, 2014, *www.economist.com/united-states/2014/09/06/islamic-yet-integrated.*

34. Silber and Bhatt, *Radicalization in the West.*

35. "Muslims Widely Seen as Facing Discrimination," Pew Research Center: Religion and Public Life, September 9, 2009, *www.pewforum.org/2009/09/09/muslims-widely-seen-as-facing-discrimination3-2/.*

36. Youssef Chouhoud and Dalia Mogahed, "American Muslim Poll 2018: Full Report," ISPU, April 30, 2018, *www.ispu.org/american-muslim-poll-2018-full-report/.*

37. Nowrasteh, "Immigration and Crime."

38. Josh Hammer, "Analysis: Homegrown Terrorism in the U.S. and UK," Foreign Policy Association, September 11, 2008, Accessed in 2008, *www.fpa.org/topics_info2414/topics_info_show.htm?doc_id=705094*.

39. Hammer, "Homegrown Terrorism."

40. Silber and Bhatt, *Radicalization in the West*.

41. Krishnadev Calamur, "Are Immigrants Prone to Crime and Terrorism?" *The Atlantic*, June 15, 2016, *www.theatlantic.com/news/archive/2016/06/immigrants-and-crime/486884/*.

42. Patrick Simon, "France and the Unknown Second Generation: Preliminary Results on Social Mobility," *International Migration Review* 37, 4 (March 2006): 1091–1119.

43. Cris Beauchemin et al., *Trajectoires Et Origines Enquête Sur La Diversité Des Populations En France*, French Institute for Demographic Studies (INED), 2016, *www.ined.fr/en/publications/grandes-enquetes/trajectoires-et-origines/#tabs-3*.

44. Venhaus, *Why Youth Join al-Qaeda*.

45. Souad Mekhennet, "What Are the Root Causes of Islamic Terrorism?" *Global Agenda*, World Economic Forum, January 18, 2016, accessed in 2017, *www.weforum.org/agenda/2016/01/what-are-the-root-causes-of-islamic-terrorism/*.

46. Souad Mekhennet, Excerpt from *I Was Told to Come Alone: My Journey Behind the Lines of Jihad* (New York: Henry Holt and Company, 2017), accessed on *http://americanempireproject.com/recommended-reading/i-was-told-to-come-alone/excerpt/*.

47. *Global Terrorism Index 2017* (Institute for Economics and Peace, November 2017), *visionofhumanity.org/app/uploads/2017/11/Global-Terrorism-Index-2017.pdf*.

48. "Four of the Five Terrorists in Europe Have North African Roots," *The International Massmedia Agency*, June 29, 2017, *intmassmedia.com/2017/06/29/four-of-the-five-terrorists-in-europe-have-north-african-roots/*.

49. Stephan Vopel and Yasemin El-Menouar, "Special Study of Islam, 2015: An Overview of the Most Important Findings," *Bertelsmann Stiftung Religion Monitor*, 2015, *www.bertelsmann-stiftung.de/fileadmin/files/Projekte/51_Religionsmonitor/Religionmonitor_Specialstudy_Islam_2014_Overview_20150108.pdf*.

50. Vopel and El-Menouar, "Special Study of Islam."

51. Zak Ebrahim, *The Terrorist's Son: A Story of Choice* (New York: TED Books, 2014). See also *www.ted.com/talks/zak_ebrahim_i_am_the_son_of_a_terrorist_here_s_how_i_chose_peace?language=en*.

52. Ebrahim, *The Terrorist's Son*.

53. Hamed El-Said and Richard Barrett. *Enhancing the Understanding of the Foreign Terrorist Fighters Phenomenon in Syria,* United Nations Office of Counter-Terrorism, 2017, *www.un.org/en/counterterrorism/assets/img/Report_Final_20170727.pdf.*

54. El-Said and Barrett, *Understanding Foreign Terrorist Fighters.*

55. El-Said and Barrett, *Understanding Foreign Terrorist Fighters.*

56. Bondokji, Wilkinson, and Aghabi, "Trapped Between Destructive Choices."

7. Mirror, Mirror

1. Barbara Ehrenreich, *Blood Rites: Origins and History of the Passions of War* (New York: Henry and Holt, 1997).

2. "Who Is Osama Bin Laden?" *BBC News,* December 6, 2009, *http://news.bbc.co.uk/2/hi/south_asia/1551100.stm.*

3. Abdel Bari Atwan, *The Secret History of Al Qaeda* (New York: University of California Press, 2008), 57.

4. Peter Bergen, *The Osama Bin Laden I Know: An Oral History of Al Qaeda's Leader* (New York: Free Press, 2006), 119.

5. Bergen, *The Osama Bin Laden I Know,* 338.

6. Bergen, *The Osama Bin Laden I Know,* 119.

7. Bergen, *The Osama Bin Laden I Know,* 119.

8. Bergen, *The Osama Bin Laden I Know,* 86.

9. Graham Vyse, "'Compassionate Conservatism' Won't Be Back Anytime Soon," *The New Republic,* March 30, 2018, *https://newrepublic.com/article/147694/compassionate-conservatism-wont-back-anytime-soon.*

10. Abu Bakr Naji, *The Management of Savagery: The Most Critical Phase the Umma Will Experience* (2004), 31, *https://www.cia.gov/library/abbottabad-compound/20/207DE0C1094BC68A7061C96629DD5C1A_adara_twahsh.pdf.*

11. Atwan, *Secret History of Al Qaeda,* 78–9.

12. Gilles Kepel, *Al Qaeda in Its Own Words,* ed. Jean-Pierre Milelli, trans. Pascale Ghazaleh (New York: Belknap Press, 2008), 72.

13. Kepel, *Al Qaeda in Its Own Words.*

14. Kepel, *Al Qaeda in Its Own Words,* 47.

15. Kepel, *Al Qaeda in Its Own Words,* 47.

16. Kepel, *Al Qaeda in Its Own Words,* 58.

17. Kepel, *Al Qaeda in Its Own Words,* 52.

18. Kepel, *Al Qaeda in Its Own Words,* 72.

19. Ora Coren and Nadan Feldman, "U.S. Aid to Israel Totals $233.7b Over Six Decades," *Haaretz*, March 20, 2013, *www.haaretz.com/israel-news/business/u-s -aid-to-israel-totals-233-7b-over-six-decades.premium-1.510592*.

20. Bergen, *The Osama Bin Laden I Know*, 347.

21. Haroon Janjua, "'Unspeakable Numbers': 10,000 Civilians Killed or Injured in Afghanistan in 2017," *The Guardian*, US edition, February 16, 2018, *www.theguardian.com/global-development/2018/feb/16/10000-civilians-killed -injured-afghanistan-2017-united-nations*.

22. Dan Vergano, "Half-Million Iraqis Died in the War, New Study Says," *National Geographic*, October 16, 2013, *news.nationalgeographic.com/news/2013/10/ 131015-iraq-war-deaths-survey-2013/*.

23. Kathryn Watson, "Fight against ISIS Has Shifted to 'Annihilation Tactics,' Mattis Says," CBS News, May 28, 2017, *www.cbsnews.com/news/ fight-against-isis-has-shifted-to-annihilation-tactics-mattis-says/*.

24. "Rising from the Rubble: Iraq's Mosul Takes Steps to Deal with War Debris," *UN Environment*, United Nations Environment Programme, March 26, 2018, *www.unenvironment.org/news-and-stories/story/rising-rubble-iraqs-mosul -takes-steps-deal-war-debris*.

25. Ben Brimelow, "A New Terrorist Group Is Popping Up in Syria and Capitalizing on ISIS' Defeat," *Business Insider UK*, April 19, 2018, *http://uk.businessinsider.com/ syria-terrorist-group-hayat-tahrir-al-sham-2018-4?r=US&IR=T*.

26. Samuel Oakford, "Counting the Dead in Mosul," *The Atlantic*, April 5, 2018, *www.theatlantic.com/international/archive/2018/04/counting-the-dead-in -mosul/556466/*.

27. Oakford, "Counting the Dead in Mosul."

28. Molly Hennessy-Fiske and Alexandra Zavis, "Civilian Victims of U.S. Coalition Airstrike in Iraq Dig Up Graves in Desperate Bid for Compensation," *Los Angeles Times*, December 18, 2017, *www.latimes.com/world/middleeast/la -fg-iraq-airstrike-compensation-20171218-story.html*.

29. Atwan, *Secret History of Al Qaeda*, 250.

30. Bergen, *The Osama Bin Laden I Know*, 321–22.

31. Atwan, *Secret History of Al Qaeda*, 275.

32. Emile Bruneau, "Understanding the Terrorist Mind," *Cerebrum*, (2016), *www .ncbi.nlm.nih.gov/pmc/articles/PMC5198759/*.

33. Bruneau, "Understanding the Terrorist Mind."

34. Sean Hannity, *Deliver Us from Evil: Defeating Terrorism, Despotism, and Liberalism* (New York: William Morrow, 2004).

35. Madeline Batt et al., *Extraordinary Rendition and Torture Victim Narratives*, UNC School of Law, December 2017, *www.law.unc.edu/documents/academics/ humanrights/extraordinaryrenditionandNC.pdf*.

36. Batt et al., *Extraordinary Rendition and Torture*, 550.

37. Batt et al., *Extraordinary Rendition and Torture*, 22–39.

38. Souad Mekhennet, "I Was Told to Come Alone," *The Huffington Post*, June 14, 2017, *www.huffingtonpost.com/entry/i-was-told-to-come-alone_us _59404ab0e4b04c03fa261631*.

39. Shannon E. French, "The Warrior's Code. International Society for Military Ethics," International Society for Military Ethics, 2001, *http://isme.tamu .edu/JSCOPE02/French02.html*.

40. French, "The Warrior's Code."

41. K. P. Mohanan, "Preventing Violent Extremism through Education," *The Blue Dot: Exploring New Ideas for a Shared Future*, Issue 4 (2016): 12, *www .gcedclearinghouse.org/sites/default/files/resources/180094eng.pdf*.

42. United Nations, Security Council, "Resolution 1377 (2001): Adopted by the Security Council at Its 4413th Meeting, on 12 November 2001," United Nations, November 12, 2001, *https://unispal.un.org/DPA/DPR/unispal.nsf/0/ B9410BA1CB3A802085256E7D00547807*.

43. Albert Bandura, "Selective Moral Disengagement in the Exercise of Moral Agency," *Journal of Moral Education* 31, 2 (2002): 102–119, *http://web.stanford .edu/~kcarmel/CC_BehavChange_Course/readings/Additional%20Resources/ Bandura/bandura_moraldisengagement.pdf*.

44. "8. Conclusion: A Kafkaesque Element," Stanford Prison Experiment, 1999, *www.prisonexp.org/conclusion*.

45. "A Class Divided," *Frontline*, Season 3, Episode 9, produced by William Peters, aired on March 26, 1985 on PBS, *www.pbs.org/wgbh/frontline/film/class -divided/*.

46. "A Class Divided," *Frontline*.

47. Nitin Nohria, "Practicing Moral Humility," TEDxNewEngland, November 1, 2011, *www.youtube.com/watch?v=NCHnK5ZK9iI*.

48. Stanley Milgram, *Obedience to Authority: An Experimental View* (New York: Harper and Row, 1974).

49. Peter Byrne, "Anatomy of Terror: What Makes Normal People Become Extremists?" *New Scientist* 3139, August 16, 2017, *www.newscientist.com/ article/mg23531390-700-anatomy-of-terror-what-makes-normal-people-become -extremists/*.

50. Chagdud Tulku Rinpoche, *Change of Heart: The Bodhisattva Peace Training of Chagdud Tulku*, ed. Lama Shenpen Drolma (Junction City, CA: Padma Publishing, 2003).

51. Rinpoche, *Change of Heart.*

8. Counterproductive

1. *Global Terrorism Index 2017* (Institute for Economics and Peace, November 2017), 77, *visionofhumanity.org/app/uploads/2017/11/Global-Terrorism-Index -2017.pdf.*

2. Seth G. Jones and Artin C. Libicki, *How Terrorist Groups End: Lessons for Countering Al Qa'Ida* (RAND Corporation, 2008), *www.rand.org/content/dam/rand/ pubs/monographs/2008/RAND_MG741-1.pdf.*

3. *Global Terrorism Index 2016* (Institute for Economics and Peace, November 2016), 2, *http://economicsandpeace.org/wp-content/uploads/2016/11/Global -Terrorism-Index-2016.2.pdf.*

4. Paul Steyn, "This Will Shatter Your View of Apex Predators: How Wolves Change Rivers—National Geographic Blog," *National Geographic,* February 16, 2014, *blog.nationalgeographic.org/2014/02/16/this-will-shatter-your-view-of -apex-predators-how-wolves-change-rivers/.*

5. Peter Byrne, "Anatomy of Terror: What Makes Normal People Become Extremists?" *New Scientist,* August 16, 2017, *www.newscientist.com/article/mg23531390 -700-anatomy-of-terror-what-makes-normal-people-become-extremists/.*

6. Byrne, "Anatomy of Terror."

7. Emile Bruneau, "Understanding the Terrorist Mind," *Cerebrum,* US National Library of Medicine, November 1, 2016, *www.ncbi.nlm.nih.gov/pmc/articles/ PMC5198759/.*

8. Byrne, "Anatomy of Terror."

9. Abu Rumman, Mohammad Suliman et al., *Methods of Preventing and Combatting Terrorism in the MENA Region and the West*, trans. by Banan Fathi Malkawi (Amman: Friedrich-Ebert-Stiftung, 2016), 39–49, *http://library.fes.de/pdf -files/bueros/amman/13089.pdf.*

10. Department of Defense, *Report of the Defense Science Board Task Force on Strategic Communication*, Defense Science Board (DSB), 2004, *fas.org/irp/agency/ dod/dsb/commun.pdf.*

11. Zuri Linetsky, "Jobs, Not Bombs, Will Win the War on Terror," *Foreign Policy,* March 14, 2017, *foreignpolicy.com/2017/03/13/this-poll-proves-that-trumps -counterterrorism-strategy-will-fail-africa-nigeria-boko-haram/.*

12. UNDP, *Journey to Extremism in Africa: Drivers, Incentives, and the Tipping Point for Recruitment* (United Nations Development Programme, Regional Bureau for Africa, 2017), *journey-to-extremism.undp.org/content/downloads/UNDP-JourneyToExtremism-report-2017-english.pdf*.

13. Jideofor Adibe, "Explaining the Emergence of Boko Haram," *Brookings*, May 6, 2014, *www.brookings.edu/blog/africa-in-focus/2014/05/06/explaining-the-emergence-of-boko-haram/*.

14. Rachelle Hampton, "How People Become Terrorists," *New America*, March 2, 2017, *www.newamerica.org/weekly/edition-155/how-people-become-terrorists/*.

15. UNDP, *Journey to Extremism in Africa*, 87.

16. K. P. Mohanan, "Preventing Violent Extremism through Education," *The Blue Dot: Exploring New Ideas for a Shared Future*, Issue 4 (2016): 5, *www.gcedclearinghouse.org/sites/default/files/resources/180094eng.pdf*.

17. David Gold, "Economics of Terrorism," CIAO: Columbia International Affairs Online. New School University, May 8, 2009, *www.files.ethz.ch/isn/10698/doc_10729_290_en.pdf*.

18. "Top 10 Findings: What do 200 Million Arab Youth Have to Say about Their Future?" ASDA'A Burson-Marsteller Arab Youth Survey Middle East, 2018, *www.arabyouthsurvey.com/findings.html*.

19. "Top 10 Findings," Arab Youth Survey.

20. Iain Boal, T.J. Clark, Joseph Matthews, and Michael Watts, *Afflicted Powers Capital and Spectacle in a New Age of War* (New York: Verso, 2005), 154.

21. Samia Nakhoul, "Saddam's Former Army Is Secret of Baghdadi's Success," *Reuters*, June 16, 2015, *www.reuters.com/article/us-mideast-crisis-baghdadi-insight-idUSKBN0OW1VN20150616*.

22. Department of Defense, *Report on Strategic Communication*, 41.

23. "From Hypocrisy to Apostasy: The Extinction of the Grayzone," *Dabiq*, Bayt Al Masadir, January 2015, *https://clarionproject.org/docs/islamic-state-dabiq-magazine-issue-7-from-hypocrisy-to-apostasy.pdf*.

24. William McCants and Christopher Meserole, "Radicalization, Laïcité, and the Islamic Veil," *Religional*, April 26, 2016, *religional.org/2016/04/25/french-connection-part-ii-radicalization-laicite-and-the-islamic-veil/*.

25. McCants and Meserole, "Radicalization, Laïcité, and Islamic Veil."

26. "The Extinction of the Grayzone," *Dabiq*.

27. CJ Werleman, "#LoveAMuslimDay: A Textbook Example of How to Defeat Terrorism," *Middle East Eye*, April 13, 2018, *www.middleeasteye.net/columns/loveamuslimday-textbook-example-how-defeat-terrorism-414721064*.

28. Sabeeha Rehman, "Not a Mosque, and Not at Ground Zero," *Salon,* September 23, 2017, *www. salon. com/2017/09/23/not-a-mosque-and-not-at-ground -zero/.*

PART III

9. Spiritual Counterterrorism

1. Steven Swinford, "It Is Lazy to Say Paris Terror Attacks Have Nothing to Do with Islam, Sajid Javid Says," *The Telegraph,* January 11, 2015, *www. telegraph . co. uk/news/religion/11338258/It-is-lazy-to-say-Paris-terror-attacks-have -nothing-to-do-with-Islam-Sajid-Javid-says. html.*

2. Steven Swinford, "David Cameron: Muslims Must Do More to Tackle Terrorism in Wake of Paris Shootings," *The Telegraph,* January 12, 2015, *www . telegraph. co. uk/news/religion/11340004/David-Cameron-Muslims-must-do -more-to-tackle-terrorism-in-wake-of-Paris-shootings. html.*

3. UNDP, *Journey to Extremism in Africa: Drivers, Incentives, and the Tipping Point for Recruitment* (United Nations Development Programme, Regional Bureau for Africa, 2017), *journey-to-extremism. undp. org/content/downloads/ UNDP-JourneyToExtremism-report-2017-english. pdf.*

4. Audu Bulama Bukarti, "Islam Is Both a Sword and a Shield to Violent Extremism," Institute for Global Change, September 13, 2017, *institute. global/insight/ co-existence/islam-both-sword-and-shield-violent-extremism.*

5. Melinda Holmes, "Preventing Violent Extremism through Peacebuilding: Current Perspectives from the Field." ICAN: International Civil Society Action Network, August, 11 2017, *www. icanpeacework. org/2017/08/09/preventing -violent-extremism-peacebuilding-current-perspectives-field/.*

6. Dr. Fatima Akilu, in discussion with the author via Skype, June 5, 2008.

7. "Peace Heroes: How Nigerian Psychologist Fatima Akilu Rehabilitates Extremist Societies," ICAN, June 7, 2018, *www. icanpeacework. org/2018/06/07/ peace-heroes-nigerian-psychologist-fatima-akilu-rehabilitates-extremist-societies/.*

8. Camille Schyns and Andreas Müllerleile, "How to Prevent Violent Extremism and Radicalisation?" European Institute of Peace, accessed on September 29, 2018, *www. eip. org/en/news-events/how-prevent-violent-extremism-and-radicalisation.*

9. Dominic Casciani, "Analysis: The Prevent Strategy and Its Problems - BBC News," BBC, August 26, 2014, *www. bbc. co. uk/news/uk-28939555.*

10. *Global Terrorism Index 2017* (Institute for Economics and Peace, 2017), *visionofhumanity. org/app/uploads/2017/11/Global-Terrorism-Index-2017. pdf* and *Global Terrorism Index 2016* (Institute for Economics and Peace, 2016), *http://economicsandpeace. org/wp-content/uploads/2016/11/Global-Terrorism -Index-2016.2.pdf.*

11. Coleman Barks, *Rumi: Bridge to the Soul: Journeys into the Music and Silence of the Heart* (New York: HarperOne, 2007), 1.

12. Sarah Feuer, *State Islam in the Battle against Extremism: Emerging Trends in Morocco and Tunisia* (Washington, DC: The Washington Institute for Near East Policy, Policy Focus 145, June 2016), *www.washingtoninstitute.org/uploads /Documents/pubs/PolicyFocus145_Feuer-4.pdf.*

13. Assia Bensalah Alaoui, "Morocco's Security Strategy: Preventing Terrorism and Countering Extremism," *European View* 16, 1 (June 2017): 103–120, *https://link.springer.com/article/10.1007/s12290-017-0449-3.*

14. Abu Bakr Naji, *The Management of Savagery: The Most Critical Phase the Umma Will Experience* (2004), *https://www.cia.gov/library/abbottabad-compound/20/ 207DE0C1094BC68A7061C96629DD5C1A_adara_twahsh.pdf.*

15. "Basit Jamal." Ashoka, September 29, 2018, *www.ashoka.org/en/fellow/basit -jamal.*

16. Basit Jamal, in discussion with author via Skype, June 9, 2018.

17. Jamal, in discussion with author.

18. Jamal, in discussion with author.

19. "What you cultivate during the next seven years, when the time of harvest comes, leave the grains in their spikes, except for what you eat." (Quran, 12:47–49), Ijaz Chaudry, *The Quran: The Latest and Most Modern Translation of the Quran* (Lulu Publishing, 2013.)

20. "Good and evil are not alike, repel evil with good and your enemy will become your dearest friend" (Quran, 41:34), trans. by author.

21. Niaz A. Shah, "The Use of Force under Islamic Law," *European Journal of International Law* 24, 1 (February 2013): 343–65, *https://doi.org/10.1093/ejil /cht013.*

22. Harriet Sherwood, "More Muslim Leaders Refuse Funeral Prayers for London Attackers," *The Guardian*, June 6, 2017, *www.theguardian.com/uk-news/2017/ jun/06/more-muslim-leaders-refuse-funeral-prayers-london-attackers.*

23. Caroline Mortimer, "Archbishop of Canterbury: It's Wrong to Say That Isis Attack Nothing to Do with Islam," *The Independent*, June 5, 2017, *www .independent.co.uk/news/uk/home-news/archbishop-canterbury-justin-welby -london-attack-islam-twisted-misused-muslim-faith-a7772916.html.*

10. Radicalizing Inclusion

1. Martin Luther King, *Strength to Love* (Minneapolis, MN: Fortress Press, 2010).

2. "Conflict-Sensitivity and Do No Harm," CDA: Practical Learning for International Action, September 29, 2018, *www.cdacollaborative.org/what-we-do/ conflict-sensitivity/.*

3. "Secretary-General's Remarks at the 16th Meeting of the United Nations Counter-Terrorism Centre Advisory Board [as Delivered]," United Nations Secretary-General, April 17, 2018, *www.un.org/sg/en/content/sg/statement/ 2018-04-17/secretary-generals-remarks-16th-meeting-united-nations -counter.*

4. United Nations, "Preventing Violent Extremism through Inclusive Development and the Promotion of Tolerance and Respect for Diversity," United Nations Development Programme, February 14, 2017, *www.undp.org/content/undp/en/home/librarypage/democratic-governance/conflict-prevention/ discussion-paper---preventing-violent-extremism-through-inclusiv.html.*

5. Robert Booth, "'With You, Whatever': Tony Blair's Letters to George W Bush," *The Guardian*, July 6, 2016, *www.theguardian.com/uk-news/2016/jul/06 /with-you-whatever-tony-blair-letters-george-w-bush-chilcot.*

6. Shannon N. Green and Keith Proctor, "Turning Point: A New Comprehensive Strategy for Countering Violent Extremism," *CSIS: Center for Strategic and International Studies*, November 2016, *csis-ilab.github.io/cve/report/Turning _Point.pdf.*

7. Seth G. Jones and Martin C. Libicki, "How Terrorist Groups End: Lessons for Countering Al Qa'ida." RAND Corporation, 2008, *www.rand.org/content/ dam/rand/pubs/monographs/2008/RAND_MG741-1.pdf.*

8. Benjamin Wormald, "The World's Muslims: Religion, Politics and Society," Pew Research Center: Religion and Public Life, April 30, 2013, *www.pewforum .org/2013/04/30/the-worlds-muslims-religion-politics-society-overview/.*

9. Uri Friedman, "How Indonesia Beat Back Terrorism—For Now," *The Atlantic*, September 25, 2016, *www.theatlantic.com/international/archive/2016/09 /indonesia-isis-islamic-terrorism/500951/.*

10. Agence France-Presse, "Scandal Hits Indonesia's Islamic Parties," *The National*, December 15, 2013, *www.thenational.ae/world/asia/scandal-hits-indonesia -s-islamic-parties-1.306918.*

11. "Indonesian MP Resigns after Porn Scandal," *The Telegraph*, April 11, 2011, *www.telegraph.co.uk/news/worldnews/asia/indonesia/8443411/Indonesian-MP -resigns-after-porn-scandal.html.*

12. Anthony Bubalo, Greg Fealy, and Whit Mason, "Zealous Democrats: Islamism and Democracy in Egypt, Indonesia and Turkey," Lowy Institute for International Policy, 2008, *www.files.ethz.ch/isn/93125/2008-10-22.pdf.*

13. Bubalo, Fealy, and Mason, "Zealous Democrats."

14. Bubalo, Fealy, and Mason, "Zealous Democrats."

15. Umar Juoro, "Why Populist Islam Is Gaining Ground in Indonesia," *The Huffington Post,* September 22, 2017, *www.huffingtonpost.com/entry/ indonesia-islamist-populism_us_59c0060ce4b06f9bf04873d1.*

16. "Opening Indonesia: A Conversation with Joko Widodo," *Foreign Affairs,* November/December 2014, *www.foreignaffairs.com/interviews/2014-10-20/ opening-indonesia.*

17. Keith Proctor, "Youth and Consequences: Unemployment, Injustice and Violence—Afghanistan, Colombia, Somalia." Mercy Corps, February 13, 2015, *www.mercycorps.org/research-resources/youth-consequences-unemployment -injustice-and-violence?source=WOW00088&utm_source=release&utm _medium=media%20relations&utm_campaign=youth%20conflict%20report.*

18. Proctor, "Youth and Consequences."

19. Ahmad Alhendawi, UN Youth Envoy (speech, *Session 549: Youth, Economics and Violence: Implications for Future Conflict Salzburg Global Seminar,* Schloss Leopoldskron, Salzburg, Austria, April 26–May 1, 2015).

20. IPI, "Inclusion an Essential First Step in Preventing Violent Extremism," IPI: International Peace Institute, September 27, 2016, *www.ipinst.org/2016/09 /violence-prevention-west-africa-sahel#7.*

21. "'The President' Reality Show Catches on among Palestinians," Search for Common Ground, June 1, 2016, *www.sfcg.org/the-president-nbc-news/.*

22. PCBS, "Main Statistical Indicators in the West Bank and Gaza Strip," PCBS: Palestinian Central Bureau for Statistics, September 29, 2018, *www.pcbs.gov .ps/Portals/_Rainbow/StatInd/StatisticalMainIndicators_E.htm.*

23. Nick Schifrin, "He's Not the Palestinian President, But He Played One On TV," NPR, August 16, 2016, *www.npr.org/sections/parallels/2016/08/16/490174054 /he-s-not-the-palestinian-president-but-he-played-one-on-tv.*

24. United Nations, "Launching Global Campaign Promoting the Right of Young People to Run for Public Office," United Nations, November 22, 2016, *www.un.org/youthenvoy/2016/11/launching-global-campaign-promoting-rights -young-people-run-public-office/.*

25. United Nations Security Council, "Adopting Resolution 2419 (2018), Security Council Calls for Increasing Role of Youth in Negotiating, Implementing Peace," United Nations: Meetings Coverage and Press Releases, June 6, 2018, *www.un.org/press/en/2018/sc13368.doc.htm.*

26. Christian Cito Cirhigiri, "DRC's Future: Youth Must Be Engaged in Non-Violent Movements," Peace News Network, December 6, 2017, *www .peacenews.com/single-post/2017/12/06/DRC%25E2%2580%2599s-future-Youth -must-be-engaged-in-non-violent-movements.*

27. Saji Prelis, Director of Children and Youth at Search, in discussion with the author via Skype, June 18, 2018.

28. Lauren Burrows, "Girl Power in Pakistan: Aware Girls," Atlas of the Future, June 12, 2017, *atlasofthefuture. org/project/aware-girls/*.

29. "Aware Girls Founders under Threat in Pakistan." IHEU: International Humanist and Ethical Union, June 18, 2014, *iheu. org/aware-girls-founders-under -threat-in-pakistan/*.

11. Can't We All Just Belong?

1. Keneshbek Sainazarov, Central Asia Program Director, Search for Common Ground, conversation with author via Skype, June 20, 2018.

2. "Youth as Agents of Peace and Stability in Kyrgyzstan," Search for Common Ground, May 15, 2018, *www. sfcg. org/youth-agents-of-peace-kyrgyzstan/*.

3. Susan Sim, "Countering Violent Extremism: Leveraging Terrorist Dropouts to Counter Violent Extremism in Southeast Asia," QIASS: Qatar International Academy for Security Studies, January 2013, *soufangroup. com/wp-content /uploads/2013/12/CVE-PHASE-II-VOL.-II-Final-Feb-13.pdf*.

4. "Fatima Al-Bahadly Single-Handedly Disarms Young Men in Iraq," ICAN: International Civil Society Action Network, March 2, 2017, *www. icanpeace- work. org/2017/03/02/fatima-al-bahadly-iraq/*.

5. Bruce Hoffman, "Gaza City—All You Need Is Love: How the Terrorists Stopped Terrorism," *The Atlantic*, December 2001, *www. theatlantic. com/past/docs /issues/2001/12/hoffman. htm*.

6. Hoffman, "All You Need Is Love."

7. Hoffman, "All You Need Is Love."

8. Arno Michaelis, conversation with author via Zoom, June 14, 2018.

9. Michaelis, conversation with author.

10. Michaelis, conversation with author.

11. Michaelis, conversation with author.

12. Michaelis, conversation with author.

13. Steve Hendrix, "In the Army and the Klan, He Hated Muslims. Now One Was Coming to His Home," *The Washington Post*, June 5, 2018, *www. washingtonpost . com/news/local/wp/2018/06/05/feature/in-the-army-and-the-klan-he-hated -muslims-now-one-was-coming-to-his-home/?noredirect=on&utm_term =.ea3e771c8f1a*.

14. Paul Glader, "Neo-Nazi Rehab: How Do You Change the Mind of an Extremist?" *Fast Company*, April 17, 2012, *www. fastcompany. com/1679670/ neo-nazi-rehab-how-do-you-change-the-mind-of-an-extremist*.

15. Glader, "Neo-Nazi Rehab."

16. Violence Prevention Network, "Talking to Extremists . . . ," Prevention Network, *www.violence-prevention-network.de/en.*

17. "Judy Korn," Ashoka, 2007, *www.ashoka.org/en/fellow/judy-korn.*

18. Julie Farrar, "Same Roots and Cures for Neo-Nazis and Jihadists," Worldcrunch, September 23, 2014, *www.worldcrunch.com/culture-society/same-roots -and-cures-for-neo-nazis-and-jihadists.*

19. Farrar, "Same Roots and Cures."

20. Peter Byrne, "Anatomy of Terror: What Makes Normal People Become Extremists?" *New Scientist,* August 2017, *www.newscientist.com/article/ mg23531390-700-anatomy-of-terror-what-makes-normal-people-become-extremists/.*

21. Bart Somers (Mayor of Mechelen, Belgium), discussion with author via telephone, June 20, 2018.

22. Somers, discussion with author.

23. Somers, discussion with author.

24. Somers, discussion with author.

25. Somers, discussion with author.

26. Preeta Bannerjee, "Mechelen: How a Flemish City Fought Off ISIS Recruiters," *The Smart Citizen,* February 28, 2017, *https://thesmartcitizen.org/citizen -engagement/mechelen-counter-radicalisation/.*

27. Somers, discussion with author.

28. Somers, discussion with author.

29. Bannerjee, "Mechelen."

30. Allison Peters and Jahanara Saeed, "Promoting Inclusive Policy Frameworks for Countering Violent Extremism," GIWPS, December 2017, *www .inclusivesecurity.org/wp-content/uploads/2017/12/Pakistan-CVE-Case-Study-1.pdf.*

31. Sanam Naraghi Anderlini, "The Best Weapon to De-Radicalise Isis Returnees? Our Own Humanity," *The Guardian,* US edition, September 15, 2017, *www .theguardian.com/commentisfree/2017/sep/15/de-radicalise-isis-reurnees-humanity -syria-bond-movie-bad-guy.*

32. ICAN, "Mossarat Qadeem and Tolana Mothers: Cutting off Extremists' Resources—One Thread at a Time." ICAN: International Civil Society Action Network, January 25, 2018, *www.icanpeacework.org/2018/01/25/mossarat -qadeem-tolana-mothers-cutting-off-extremists-resources-one-thread-time/.*

33. ICAN, "Pakistani Activist Mossarat Qadeem Responds to Donald Trump," ICAN: International Civil Society Action Network, October 31, 2017, *www.icanpeacework.org/2017/10/31/peace-heroes-pakistan-mossarat-qadeem -respnds-trump/.*

34. The Redman TV, "'I'll Be Muslim Too!'" YouTube, February 14, 2018, *www .youtube.com/watch?v=b-icmPutQDk.*

35. Ahmad Fadam and Alissa J. Rubin, "Iraq Finds Unity on the Global Soccer Field," *New York Times,* July 20, 2007, *www.nytimes.com/2007/07/20/world/ africa/20iht-baghdad.1.6750436.html.*

36. Amelia Johns, Michele Grossman, and Kevin McDonald, "'More Than a Game': The Impact of Sport-Based Youth Mentoring Schemes on Developing Resilience toward Violent Extremism," *Social Inclusion* 2, 2 (Aug. 2014): 57–70, *www.cogitatiopress.com/socialinclusion/article/view/167/110.*

12. Show Me the Money

1. Muhammad Yunus, "Muhammad Yunus – Nobel Lecture" (Lecture, Oslo, Sweden, December 10, 2006), *www.nobelprize.org/nobel_prizes/peace/ laureates/2006/yunus-lecture-en.html.*

2. Maher Chmaytelli and Ahmed Hagagy, "Allies Promise Iraq $30 Billion, Falling Short of Baghdad's Appeal," *Reuters,* February 14, 2018, *www.reuters .com/article/us-mideast-crisis-iraq-reconstruction-ku/allies-promise-iraq-30-billion -falling-short-of-baghdads-appeal-idUSKCN1FY0TX.*

3. Yunus, "Nobel Lecture."

4. The following are the websites from which the information in this graphic was acquired.

"Islamic State of Iraq and the Levant," Wikipedia, September 30, 2018, *https://en.wikipedia.org/wiki/Islamic_State_of_Iraq_and_the_Levant.*

"One Way to Fight ISIS? Target the Group's Wallet," *All Things Considered,* NPR, April 3, 2016, *www.npr.org/2016/04/03/472890941/ one-way-to-fight-isis-target-the-groups-wallet.*

Sarah Begley, "Report: ISIS Makes $80 Million a Month in Revenue," *Time,* December 7, 2015, *http://time.com/4139562/isis-80-million-monthly-revenue/.*

Tim Meko, "Now That the Islamic State Has Fallen in Iraq and Syria, Where Are All Its Fighters Going?" *The Washington Post,* February 22, 2018, *www .washingtonpost.com/graphics/2018/world/isis-returning-fighters/?noredirect=on &utm_term=.37f6d5e51304 https://rctom.hbs.org/submission/the-islamic-state/.*

Jason Abbruzzese, "Here's How ISIS Makes—and Spends—Its Money," Mashable: Business, December 8, 2015, *http://mashable.com/2015/12/08/ isis-makes-its-money-like/#Jp9Q5UpFXEqJ.*

Orlando Crowcroft, "ISIS: Inside the Struggling Islamic State Economy in Iraq and Syria," *International Business Times:* Politics, April 11, 2015, *www .ibtimes. co. uk/isis-inside-struggling-islamic-state-economy-iraq-syria-1495726.*

Johnlee Varghese, "Forbes Israel: ISIS Is World's Richest Terrorist Organization in History," *International Business Times:* Home/Society, November 12, 2014,*www.ibtimes.co.in/forbes-israel-isis-worlds-richest-terrorist-organisation -history-613806.*

Anja Kaspersen, "3 Ways to Defeat ISIS," World Economic Forum: Global Governance,November 20,2015,*www.weforum. org/agenda/2015/11/3-ways-to -defeat-isis/.*

Saikat Pyne,"Economics of Terror – Financial Model of ISIS,"*Business Insider: India,* September 4, 2015, *www.businessinsider.in/Economicsof-Terror-Financial -model-of-ISIS/articleshow/48811725.cms.*

"The Business Model Canvas," Strategyzer, October 1, 2018, *https:// strategyzer.com/canvas/business-model-canvas.*

5. "Q&A: Awakening Councils," BBC News: World, Middle East, July 18, 2010, *http://news.bbc.co.uk/2/hi/middle_east/7644448.stm.*

6. Aryn Baker, "Why Iraq's Awakening Councils Can't Save the Country from al-Qaeda This Time," *Time:* World, Iraq, June 18, 2014, *time.com/2894757 /iraq-al-qaeda-awakening-council/.*

7. Derek Harvey and Michael Pregent,"Opinion: Who's to Blame for Iraq Crisis," CNN, June 12, 2014, *edition.cnn.com/2014/06/12/opinion/pregent-harvey -northern-iraq-collapse/.*

8. Kim Cragin and Peter Chalk, *Terrorism and Development: Using Social and Economic Development to Inhibit a Resurgence of Terrorism* (RAND, 2003), 34, *www.rand.org/pubs/monograph_reports/2005/MR1630.pdf.*

9. Cragin and Chalk, *Terrorism and Development,* 4.

10. Cragin and Chalk, *Terrorism and Development,* x.

11. Cragin and Chalk, *Terrorism and Development,* xiii.

12. Cragin and Chalk, *Terrorism and Development,* xii.

13. Cragin and Chalk, *Terrorism and Development,* xii.

14. Cragin and Chalk, *Terrorism and Development,* xi.

15. Cragin and Chalk, *Terrorism and Development,* x.

16. Cragin and Chalk, *Terrorism and Development,* xi.

17. Cragin and Chalk, *Terrorism and Development,* xii.

18. Nina Strochlic, "Could Farmers Bring Peace to Nigeria?" *National Geographic*, November 5, 2017, *www.nationalgeographic.com.au/people/could-farmers-bring-peace-to-nigeria.aspx*.

19. Kola Masha, conversation with author via Skype, June 20, 2018.

20. "Babban Gona: BMGF Grant Annual Report," *Babban Gona: Reports*, October 1, 2018, *www.babbangona.com/2015-reports/*.

21. Kola Masha, conversation with author via Skype, June 20, 2018.

22. "The Creative Skills for Peace Inter Prison Essay Competition," Local Youth Corner Cameroon, August 14, 2018, *www.loyocameroon.org/the-creative-skills-for-peace-inter-prison-essay-competition-2/*.

23. "Creative Skills for Peace," Local Youth Corner Cameroon.

24. Steven R Koltai, "Entrepreneurship Needs to Be a Bigger Part of US Foreign Aid," *Harvard Business Review*, August 15, 2016, *https://hbr.org/2016/08/entrepreneurship-needs-to-be-a-bigger-part-of-us-foreign-aid*.

25. Koltai, "Entrepreneurship Needs to Be Bigger Part."

26. Zuri Linetsky, "Jobs, Not Bombs, Will Win the War on Terror," *Foreign Policy*, March 13, 2017, *https://foreignpolicy.com/2017/03/13/this-poll-proves-that-trumps-counterterrorism-strategy-will-fail-africa-nigeria-boko-haram/*.

27. *Global Terrorism Index 2016* (Institute for Economics and Peace, November 2016), *economicsandpeace.org/wp-content/uploads/2016/11/Global-Terrorism-Index-2016.2.pdf*.

28. Alisa Helbitz, "World's 1st Social Impact Bond Shown to Cut Reoffending and to Make Impact Investors a Return," *Social Finance*, July 27, 2017, *www.socialfinance.org.uk/sites/default/files/news/final-press-release-pb-july-2017.pdf*.

13. Peace Pays and Morality Trumps

1. Institute for Economics and Peace, *Global Peace Index 2018: Measuring Peace in a Complex World* (Sydney: Institute for Economics and Peace, June 2018), *http://visionofhumanity.org/reports*.

2. Institute for Economics and Peace, *Measuring Peacebuilding Effectiveness* (New York: Institute for Economics and Peace, 2017), 2–5, *visionofhumanity.org/app/uploads/2017/03/Measuring-Peacebuilding_WEB.pdf*.

3. Institute for Economics and Peace. *Global Peace Index 2018*.

4. Institute for Economics and Peace. *Global Peace Index 2018*.

5. Abdel Bari Atwan, *The Secret History of Al Qaeda* (New York: University of California Press, 2008), 284.

6. US Department of the Treasury, Bureau of the Fiscal Service, "April 2018," Treasury Direct, May 3, 2018, *www.treasurydirect.gov/govt/reports/pd/mspd/ 2018/2018_apr.htm.*

7. Alice Slater, "The US Has Military Bases in 80 Countries. All of Them Must Close," *The Nation,* US Wars and Military Action, January 24, 2018, *www .thenation.com/article/the-us-has-military-bases-in-172-countries-all-of-them- must-close/.*

8. Jeff Janaro, "The Danger of Imperial Overstretch." *Foreign Policy Journal:* News and Analysis, US, July 15, 2014, *www.foreignpolicyjournal.com/2014/07/15 /the-danger-of-imperial-overstretch/.*

9. United Nations Development Programme, *Arab Human Development Report 2016: Youth and the Prospects for Human Development in a Changing Reality* (Beruit: UNDP: Regional Bureau for Arab States [RBAS], 2016), 174, *www .arab-hdr.org/reports/2016/english/AHDR2016En.pdf.*

10. Institute of Economics and Peace, *Measuring Peacebuilding Effectiveness.*

11. Stephanie Blenckner and Alexandra Manolache, "Global Military Spending Remains High at $1.7 Trillion," Stockholm International Peace Research Institute (SIPRI), May 2, 2018, *www.sipri.org/media/press-release/2018/global -military-spending-remains-high-17-trillion.*

12. Institute for Economics and Peace, *Global Peace Index 2016* (New York: Institute for Economics and Peace, 2016) *http://visionofhumanity.org/app /uploads/2017/02/GPI-2016-Report_2.pdf.*

13. Tom H. Hastings, *Nonviolent Response to Terrorism* (Boston: McFarland and Company, Inc., 2004), 137.

14. Philip H. Gordon, *Winning the Right War: The Path to Security for America and the World* (New York: Times Books, 2007), 86.

15. Foundation Center and Peace and Security Funders Group, "Peace and Security Funding Index: An Analysis of Global Foundation Grantmaking," Foundation Center, October 2, 2018, *http://peaceandsecurityindex.org/reports/.*

16. Foundation Center, "Advancing Human Rights: The State of Global Foundation Grantmaking, 2015," Foundation Center and Human Rights Funders Network, 2015, October 2, 2018, *humanrightsfunding.org/overview/year/2015/.*

17. United Nations, Security Council, "Young People Powerful Agents for Resolving, Preventing Conflict, Speakers Tell Security Council Open Debate amid Calls to Change Negative Stereotypes," United Nations: Meetings Coverage, April 23, 2018, *www.un.org/press/en/2018/sc13312.doc.htm.*

18. Blenckner and Manolache, "Global Military Spending Remains High."

19. Lena Slachmuijlder, Search's Vice President of Programs, conversation with author via Skype, June 24, 2018.

20. Jillian J. Foster, *Plateau Will Arise! Phase II (PWA II): Consolidating an Architecture for Peace, Tolerance and Reconciliation—Final Evaluation Report*, Search for Common Ground, October 2, 2018, *www.sfcg.org/wp-content/uploads/2017/12 /NGR505-Final-Evaluation-report-FINAL.pdf*.

21. Foster, *Plateau Will Arise!*

22. Foster, *Plateau Will Arise!*

23. Foster, *Plateau Will Arise!*

24. Seth G. Jones and Artin C. Libicki, *How Terrorist Groups End: Lessons for Countering Al Qa'Ida* (Santa Monica, CA: RAND Corporation, 2008), *www.rand.org/ content/dam/rand/pubs/monographs/2008/RAND_MG741-1.pdf*.

25. Hamed El-Said and Richard Barrett, *Enhancing the Understanding of the Foreign Terrorist Fighters Phenomenon in Syria*, United Nations Office of Counter-Terrorism, 2017, *www.un.org/en/counterterrorism/assets/img/Report_Final_20170727.pdf*.

26. K. P. Mohanan, "Preventing Violent Extremism through Education," *Blue Dot* (United Nations Educational, Scientific, and Cultural Organization | Mahatama Gandhi Institute of Education for Peace and Sustainable Development, 2016), 12, *https://gcedclearinghouse.org/sites/default/files/resources/180094eng.pdf*.

27. Buckminster Fuller Institute, "GreenWave," Accessed on October 21, 2018, *www.bfi.org/ideaindex/projects/2015/greenwave*.

28. Foundation Center and Peace and Security Funders Group, "Peace and Security Funding Index."

29. European Venture Philanthropy Association, "What Is Venture Philanthropy?" EVPA, October 2, 2018, *https://evpa.eu.com/about-us/what-is-venture -philanthropy*.

30. CDA, "Conflict-Sensitivity and Do No Harm," CDA, Practical Learning for International Action, October 2, 2018, *www.cdacollaborative.org/what-we-do /conflict-sensitivity/*.

31. Linda Booth Sweeney, "Systems Resource Room," October 2, 2018, *www .lindaboothsweeney.net/resources*.

32. John Kania and Mark Kramer, "Collective Impact," *Stanford Social Innovation Review: Informing and Inspiring Leaders of Social Change*, 2011, *ssir.org/articles/ entry/collective_impact*.

33. CDA, "Do No Harm."

34. Daniel W. Drezner, "Why Neoconservatives Should Love West Point Even More Than They Do Now," *The Washington Post*, November 19, 2014, *www .washingtonpost.com/posteverything/wp/2014/11/19/why-neoconservatives-should -love-west-point-even-more-than-they-do-now/?utm_term=.567e5d4caed4*.

INDEX

—ACKNOWLEDGMENTS—

MY GRATITUDE GOES to the collaborative team at Berrett-Koehler—I couldn't have found a more perfect and values-aligned publisher for this book! My brother, cofounder, and companion in social change, Tariq Al Olaimy, I am indebted to you for carrying our various social ventures—3BL Associates, Public-Planet Partnerships, and Diversity On Board—during my intense and total isolation writing absences. My family, friends, colleagues, and all those who backed my Publishizer crowd-publishing campaign: this book would not exist without your support. Thank you for your faith, patience, and investments in peace. To everyone who provided input on content, book titles, designs, sources, and other details—and in particular Luma Shihabeldin and my global family at the THNK School of Creative Leadership—thank you!

And in no small part, my deep gratitude and appreciation goes to all the peace-builders, social entrepreneurs, and disruptors whose work has, in some way, influenced and contributed to shaping my thinking and informed the theories of change in this book. A special thanks goes to those who took the time to engage in lengthy discussions with me: Lena Slachmuijlder, Saji Prelis, and the amazing team at Search for Common Ground, Mayor Bart Somers, Arno Michaelis, Kola Masha, Dr. Fatima Akilu, Basit Jamal, Robert Örell, and the many others who have provided their contributions to this work.

—ABOUT THE AUTHOR—

 LEENA AL OLAIMY is a leading social innovator in the Arab world. In 2010, she cofounded 3BL Associates (3BL), a people+planet strategy consultancy working on interconnected sustainable development issues like peace, environment, innovation, and equitable economic growth. Through 3BL's consultancy arm, she advises companies, governments, multilaterals, and international NGOs on designing inclusive and financially sustainable models to advance social and environmental progress. Through 3BL's think-do-tank, Olaimy cofounded award-winning ventures like Public-Planet Partnerships, Nonviolent Resilience, and Diversity On Board.

Olaimy serves on the Chatham House steering committee for the Future Dynamics in the Gulf project. She previously served on the advisory board of His Royal Highness Prince El Hassan Bin Talal of Jordan's West Asia-North Africa Forum and on the Board of Trustees for the Bahrain Foundation for Dialogue. Post-Arab Awakening, she was invited to meet with leaders representing both sides of "The Troubles" in Northern Ireland and with the African National Congress and former de Klerk administration government leaders from South Africa's Apartheid era to learn from their experiences in reconciliation.

Olaimy also serves as an impact advisor to the London-based impact investment firm Future Planet Capital. She is a cofounding board member of Global Entrepreneurship Network-Bahrain, and she has served as a judge and mentor for numerous entrepreneurship competitions, like His Royal Highness the Duke of York's Pitch@Palace, MIT's Arab Enterprise Forum, and MIT's Innovate for Refugees.

Olaimy is a Dalai Lama Fellow, a Fulbright Scholar, a *Wall Street Journal* "Woman of Note," a Salzburg Global Fellow, and a Soliya Conflict Resolution Fellow, and she is listed among Bahrain's most influential women. She has given over 150 talks globally and has written on politics, entrepreneurship, and sustainability for the World Economic Forum's *Global Agenda* blog, *openDemocracy, Stanford Social Innovation Review,* the *Huffington Post,* and *Wamda.*

Of Bahraini origin, Olaimy began her career as a communications consultant in 1998 advising Fortune 500s, and later she worked at the Bahrain Ministry of Foreign Affairs on key regional security forums convening Middle Eastern heads of state, G8 foreign secretaries, and other dignitaries. She holds a BS in Culture and Interpersonal Communications from New York University and an MA in Globalization Studies from Dartmouth College, and is an alumna of both the THNK School for Creative Leadership in Amsterdam and Singularity University. She is a lover of jazz, lions, and nature.

Berrett–Koehler
BK Publishers

Berrett-Koehler is an independent publisher dedicated to an ambitious mission: *Connecting people and ideas to create a world that works for all.*

Our publications span many formats, including print, digital, audio, and video. We also offer online resources, training, and gatherings. And we will continue expanding our products and services to advance our mission.

We believe that the solutions to the world's problems will come from all of us, working at all levels: in our society, in our organizations, and in our own lives. Our publications and resources offer pathways to creating a more just, equitable, and sustainable society. They help people make their organizations more humane, democratic, diverse, and effective (and we don't think there's any contradiction there). And they guide people in creating positive change in their own lives and aligning their personal practices with their aspirations for a better world.

And we strive to practice what we preach through what we call "The BK Way." At the core of this approach is *stewardship,* a deep sense of responsibility to administer the company for the benefit of all our stakeholder groups, including authors, customers, employees, investors, service providers, sales partners, and the communities and environment around us. Everything we do is built around stewardship and our other core values of *quality, partnership, inclusion,* and *sustainability.*

This is why Berrett-Koehler is the first book publishing company to be both a B Corporation (a rigorous certification) and a benefit corporation (a for-profit legal status), which together require us to adhere to the highest standards for corporate, social, and environmental performance. And it is why we have instituted many pioneering practices (which you can learn about at www.bkconnection.com), including the Berrett-Koehler Constitution, the Bill of Rights and Responsibilities for BK Authors, and our unique Author Days.

We are grateful to our readers, authors, and other friends who are supporting our mission. We ask you to share with us examples of how BK publications and resources are making a difference in your lives, organizations, and communities at www.bkconnection.com/impact.